Growing leaders in the church

Growing leaders
in the church

A leadership development resource

Gareth Crossley

EVANGELICAL PRESS

EVANGELICAL PRESS
Faverdale North, Darlington, DL3 0PH, England

e-mail: sales@evangelicalpress.org

Evangelical Press USA
P. O. Box 825, Webster, New York 14580, USA

e-mail: usa.sales@evangelicalpress.org

web: http://www.evangelicalpress.org

First published 2008

British Library Cataloguing in Publication Data available

ISBN 13 978 0 85234 553 5   ISBN 0 85234 553 4

Printed and bound in the USA

Contents

Prologue

This book is intended for the training of elders, whether serving in a supported or honorary capacity. It is not designed as a self-help manual for the individual. The format depends upon close interaction between trainer(s) and trainee(s). The experience and expertise of the trainer are crucial.

The manual is intended for use in training church leaders of many Christian persuasions. No attempt has been made in this volume to argue the relative merits of one view as over against another (e.g. believer's baptism versus paedo-baptism), since all church leaders should be capable of handling different perspectives and know the biblical arguments supporting the teachings and practices of their church. Consequently the recommended reading often presents arguments from diametrically opposed viewpoints.

Some of the people quoted are considered controversial. They are included as a means of encouraging church leaders to think, and thus be trained to handle differing viewpoints.

Most theological colleges provide residential and non-residential training courses for ministers of the gospel. This manual is not a substitute for such training, but is intended to complement it, since this book deals with practical issues of church life in a living church setting on which it is rarely possible for theological colleges to provide specific guidance. It is likely, however, to be especially useful for spiritually mature men, well grounded in Christian doctrine, who have not attended a theological college, yet to whom the pastoral oversight of a local body of believers has been committed.

The most helpful method of using this manual may be for the trainer to supply a copy of this handbook to each trainee. He may also be able to suggest further reading, especially in cases where some of the titles listed may prove difficult to obtain. In advance of meeting together trainees would be required to study the relevant chapter and to read as widely as possible on the subject, and thus prepare for thorough discussion and debate.

Introduction

Introduction

Is church leadership necessary?

Every group of two or more persons has some form of leadership. The group as a whole may function democratically, deciding its course of action by majority approval; or a number from the group may be appointed to lead by consensus; or one or more individuals may emerge who lead by design or default. Every church has a leader or leaders, whether official or unofficial, publicly acknowledged or unacknowledged – someone is leading, for good or ill.

Effective leadership is vital for the health and welfare of the church of Jesus Christ. A local assembly of believers cannot function in a God-honouring manner unless it has a godly and caring leadership. When church leaders do their work well, the church will be well. The health of a congregation depends upon its leaders. 'A biblically patterned, spiritually qualified, pastorally involved, working eldership is essential to the well-being of the Church.'[1]

> 'A biblically patterned, spiritually qualified, pastorally involved, working eldership is essential to the well-being of the Church' (J. D. MacMillan).

Who were the New Testament church leaders?

At his ascension the Lord Jesus Christ gave gifts to his New Testament church: '... some to be apostles, some prophets, some evangelists, and some pastors and teachers' (Eph. 4:11). The *apostles* and *prophets* served the Lord Jesus Christ by laying down a solid foundation (Eph. 2:20). Once the foundations were laid, there was no further need of these offices in the church. The New Testament Scriptures are an abiding record of 'the apostles' doctrine' in which the early

> And he [Christ] himself gave some to be apostles, some prophets, some evangelists, and some pastors and teachers, for the equipping of the saints for the work of ministry, for the edifying of the body of Christ, till we all come to the unity of the faith and the knowledge of the Son of God, to a perfect man, to the measure of the stature of the fulness of Christ (Eph. 4:11-13).

Christian converts 'continued steadfastly' (Acts 2:42). *Evangelists* are those who travel from place to place preaching the gospel, drawing new converts together and establishing new Christian churches. The leaders who remain in the local church are the *pastors* and *teachers*. Differences of opinion exist between Christians as to whether these two terms, 'pastors' and 'teachers', refer to a single office – i.e., men who pastor and teach the people of God – or whether there are two offices, the one of pastors who are teachers, and the other of teachers who are not pastors. Our concern in this manual is with church leaders as pastors who are 'able to teach' (1 Tim. 3:2).

In the Scriptures an 'elder' is also a 'bishop,' a 'pastor' and a 'shepherd' at one and the same time. These terms were used in the synagogue and so were well known among the Jews. 'Elder' ('old man' – at least in spiritual maturity and wisdom, if not in age) designates the office; 'bishop' and 'pastor' indicate the two functions of an elder: namely, overseeing and shepherding the flock. Both Peter and Paul instruct the elders to minister faithfully as bishops and shepherds (Acts 20:28; 1 Peter 5:2-3).

The New Testament elders are frequently described in terms of what they did: pastoring, teaching, equipping, edifying, shepherding, overseeing, leading, ruling and giving example (Eph. 4:11; 1 Tim. 5:17: Heb. 13:7; 1 Peter 5:1-4). 'These very designations begin to indicate their importance to a healthy, flourishing, witnessing church...'[2]

'The message is beautifully simple, the position crystal clear. The function of the elder is a pastoral one; it involves caring for, looking after, being concerned about, the welfare of the people of God – the "flock" – that God has called him to superintend, care for, nourish, cherish and feed. Those officers clearly had the oversight ... of the flock that was entrusted to their care. They had to provide for it, govern it, and protect it, as the very household of God.'[3]

> Take heed to yourselves and to all the flock, among which the Holy Spirit has made you overseers, to shepherd the church of God which he purchased with his blood (Acts 20:28).

Is training of church leaders necessary?

Training is a fundamental part of Christian life and experience. Implicit in evangelism is the command to train converts: 'make disciples', said Jesus in the Great Commission (Matt. 28:19-20). The grace of God has appeared to train people how to live for the glory of God (Titus 2:11-13) and will not be completed until the Saviour presents his people 'to himself ... not having spot or wrinkle' (Eph. 5:27). Children need training for life (Eph. 6:2; Deut. 6:4-7; Prov. 22:6); and Christians need training for their individual ministries (Eph. 4:11-13).

> For the grace of God that brings salvation has appeared to all men, teaching us that, denying ungodliness and worldly lusts, we should live soberly, righteously, and godly in the present age, looking for the blessed hope and glorious appearing of our great God and Saviour Jesus Christ, who gave himself for us, that he might redeem us from every lawless deed and purify for himself his own special people, zealous for good works (Titus 2:11-14).

Church leaders ('ministers') who devote their working lives to labouring 'in the word and doctrine' (1 Tim. 5:17) usually undertake some form of residential training. Church leaders not financially supported by the church tend to struggle along with skills derived from personal experience, secular employment and private reflection. Sadly, formal ministerial training tends to major (sometimes exclusively) upon academic skills and doctrinal understanding, with the result that an entire eldership may be devoid of practical skills training.

This course is designed to meet two objectives: to provide ideas and structure for the training of potential church leaders; and also to stimulate 'in-house' or 'in-service' training of existing elders.

Since one of the essential duties of pastors or church leaders is to equip 'the saints for the work of ministry' (Eph. 4:12), this involves, of necessity, the training and equipping of future church leaders (2 Tim. 2:2). This course is designed to 'train the trainers' — that is, to equip present and future church leaders for their God-given task.

> *The single most important task that is laid upon the shoulders of existing church leaders is to seek out and train those men from whom the church will select future church leaders.*

The best form of leadership training (in fact the New Testament model) is first hand with a mentor (a wise and trusted adviser or guide). Jesus took twelve men 'to be with him'. He trained them by example, through discussion and by formal teaching sessions. This pattern was continued by the apostle Paul, and expressly commended to the future church by the clear instructions given in Scripture (2 Tim. 2:2).

Ideally this course will be used by experienced church leaders to stimulate or facilitate their training of other men. Those considering the course should take every possible step to obtain the support and help of an experienced pastor/ elder. This training course is designed for present or potential church leaders — elders, pastors and ministers of the gospel. It was originally prepared for nine men in a church of 160 believers.

There is little doubt that churches, and their leaders, are suffering through an untrained or ill-trained leadership.

Why this method of training?

The Lord Jesus spent three years carefully preparing his twelve apostles for the work that lay before them. Their training was meticulously undertaken — it was intensive and extensive.

> And the things that you have heard from me among many witnesses, commit these to faithful men who will be able to teach others also (2 Tim. 2:2).

The apostle Paul trained Timothy and Titus. These two men were evidently serving an apprenticeship as they travelled with, or on behalf of, Paul. Even though they were deriving benefit from their immediate contact with the apostle, he still considered it necessary to send them letters that amounted to manuals for church leadership.

In the Old Testament leaders like Moses, Joshua, Samuel and David were subject to lengthy and varied periods of training (see Acts 7:20-23; Exod. 17:9; 24:13; 32:17; 1 Sam. 2:11,18-21; 16:21).

While the qualifications for becoming church leaders are largely those of Christian character (1 Tim. 3:2-7; Titus 1:6-9), nevertheless skill and competence in pastoral oversight and leadership do not come naturally. Understanding and applying the doctrines of Scripture in public and private takes study, consideration and training. Practical skills are best developed by following the example and guidance of competent and godly church leaders.

Pastoral care does not come easily. Training is needed for pastoral visitation, teaching and preaching, preparation for marriage, and conducting weddings and funerals, as well as for more serious pastoral problems, such as marital breakdown, helping the dying and the bereaved and counselling the depressed and suicidal.

The New Testament training method

The training method adopted by the Lord Jesus is clear: for about three years the apostles accompanied him on his extensive preaching and healing tours. He called the Twelve to 'be with him' so that they, when properly trained, might be 'like' him (Mark 3:14; Luke 6:40). This likeness was not just that they might think like him because they had attended his lectures, but that they might be disciples who had been carefully trained so as to resemble him in other ways too — attitudes, skills of everyday living and handling relationships with others.

Judging from the record of the New Testament, Tutor and students, Master and disciples, were constantly engaged in conversation. As events took place, as they met and interacted with many different people, as issues came to their minds — so the group discussed them openly and freely.

When the disciples saw a man who they knew had been blind from birth, they raised the question with Jesus: 'Rabbi, who sinned, this man or his parents, that he was born blind?' (John 9:2). Sometimes the Lord himself raised a topic for discussion, as when the apostolic band came into the region of Caesarea Philippi. Here Jesus raised the question: 'Who do men say that I, the Son of Man, am?' (Matt. 16:13). This provoked a clear declaration by the apostle Peter: 'You are the Christ, the Son of the living God.' This was followed by wonderful teaching from the Lord: 'Blessed are you, Simon Bar-Jonah, for flesh and blood has not revealed this to you, but my Father who is in heaven' (Matt. 16:16,17).

> Now when they saw the boldness of Peter and John, and perceived that they were uneducated and untrained men, they marvelled. And they realized that they had been with Jesus (Acts 4:13).

> Then he came to Capernaum. And when he was in the house he asked them, 'What was it you disputed among yourselves on the road?' But they kept silent, for on the road they had disputed among themselves who would be the greatest. And he sat down, called the twelve, and said to them, 'If anyone desires to be first, he shall be last of all and servant of all.' Then he took a little child and set him in the midst of them. And when he had taken him in his arms, he said to them, 'Whoever receives one of these little children in my name receives me; and whoever receives me, receives not me but him who sent me' (Mark 9:33-37).

> Then the apostles gathered to Jesus and told him all things, both what they had done and what they had taught (Mark 6:30).

On another occasion, while they were walking along the road together, conversation about crops in the fields was used by the Lord to bring home truths about spiritual sowing and reaping (John 4:35-38). When the disciples were arguing on the road about who was the greatest among them, Jesus took a little child in his arms and taught that true greatness is gentle, compassionate service to the weakest (Mark 9:33-37). The hunger of the crowds became an opportunity for the miraculous feeding of the five thousand, which in turn became an occasion for preaching the great sermon on 'the bread of life', and driving home a challenge to the Twelve (John 6:1-67).

Galilee, Judea and Samaria formed the university precincts; roads, seaside and homes were the lecture theatres; life events provided the curriculum. The key to this training was the quality and capacity of the Mentor to utilize experiences and events, coupled with the enthusiasm of the disciples to learn from him. He drew from a reserve of knowledge coupled with perception and insights. They learned in an environment where everything was made relevant.

A didactic or a dialectic approach

The 'didactic' method of teaching refers to instruction received by a student in a largely passive recipient role. The Sermon on the Mount is an example of this method (Matt. 5:1 – 7:29). By contrast, the 'dialectic' method keeps a constant eye on the goal — that of the disciple gaining the ability, or improving the capability, to think and discuss in a reasoned and orderly manner (as in the Lord's dealings with the Twelve in the examples cited above).

Communication skills through the spoken word are essential in a church leader. If he is to be competent in teaching the truth *and* correcting error (2 Tim. 4:2-5), he must have not only a sound grasp of doctrine and a perception of where others are in error, but an ability to express the truth so that they are persuaded. This only comes by learning to think and discuss in a reasoned and orderly way. Writing of the education received by Puritan Thomas Hooker, Frank Shuffelton notes: 'Learning was a dialectic process between reader and writer, teacher and student, knowledge and ignorance, and the young scholar was implicitly encouraged to conceive of his studies as a training in the art of communicating truth to men.'[4] Ideally this church-leadership training course should be undertaken by a student with a mentor with whom he can engage in regular discussion.

Learning by example

There is great power in a godly example, as the apostle Paul said to Timothy: '... you have carefully followed my doctrine, manner of life, purpose, faith, long-suffering, love, perseverance, persecutions, afflictions...' (2 Tim. 3:10-11).

'Hold fast the pattern of sound words which you have heard from me, in faith and love which are in Christ Jesus' (2 Tim. 1:13; cf. 2:2; 3:14).

Critics will challenge this method of training as 'cloning' in that it produces too close a resemblance to the mentor. In defence it may be noted:

1. This is *the* method used in the New Testament church. While it may reasonably be argued that the approach of the Lord Jesus Christ is not a procedure others *could* adopt, the apostle Paul also followed this method. No other system of training is presented in the New Testament.

> Imitate me, just as I also imitate Christ
> (I Cor. 11:1).
>
> The things which you learned and received and heard and saw in me, these do, and the God of peace will be with you (Phil. 4:9).

2. Training conducted by the total leadership in a church will minimize the passing on of one person's idiosyncrasies.

3. Having a number of men engaged in training together should increase the development of individual gifts and potential, with mutual respect.

With an emphasis upon the dialectic method of training, the team of trainers and trainees will learn together: '... iron sharpens iron' (Prov. 27:17).

Theological education

From the contents of the course it will be evident that many of the regular subjects taught in college — Systematic Theology, Greek, Hebrew, Old Testament Survey, New Testament Introduction, Church History, Hermeneutics — are not included. Many admirable institutions provide these basic courses. This church-leadership training programme is seeking to meet a deficiency by being church-based, practical and relevant to a variety of church settings.

> All Scripture is given by inspiration of God, and is profitable for doctrine, for reproof, for correction, for instruction in righteousness, that the man of God may be complete, thoroughly equipped for every good work (2 Tim. 3:16-17).

Many churches long for 'thoroughly equipped' men of God, well grounded in Scripture, to lead them in a God-honouring direction. Perhaps what has been missing from much traditional training is the nurturing of the biblical leadership skills that so often make all the difference to the well-being of a local church. Many men are academically well prepared, but it soon becomes evident in their early days of ministry that they have not been trained for week-by-week ministry of God's Word, nor educated in the skills needed to lead a church through the multifarious difficulties of modern church life.

> ... holding fast the faithful word as he has been taught, that he may be able, by sound doctrine, both to exhort and convict those who contradict (Titus 1:9).

An effective course of training requires the re-examination of previous convictions within a biblical context and the development of clear-cut ideas about the many issues that face Christians in the churches and in society. 'If teaching elders and pastors do not have definite convictions about contentious issues both doctrinal and practical then they cannot expect that the rest of the church membership will develop them either.'[5] 'The elder must be watchful that he be first among the learners in order that he may be best among the teachers.'[6]

Knowledge and understanding are quite distinct. A man may know much and understand little: 'Knowing is the fruit of diligence in study, while understanding is the fruit of using knowledge in life.'[7]

Pastoral care of God's people requires church leaders to love them, lead them, feed them, protect them, rescue them, restore them and carry them spiritually, even when exercising the legitimate authority inherent in the elders' right to rule.

Church leadership is a gift from God; to exercise this gift requires appropriate grace from God (Rom. 12:6,8). While men may possess this gift, it needs to be nurtured and developed through increased knowledge and the enhancement or acquisition of appropriate skills.

> The training of the mind to think carefully and systematically about contemporary theological issues is a major task facing church leaders.

1.
The training method

The training method

The method and means of training future church leaders are receiving considerable attention at the present time. Churches are often dissatisfied with the men trained in theological institutions. Many men are not coping with the ministry and consequently leave within the first two or three years following graduation. An unrealistic view of ministry, the demands of modern church life, the pressures imposed by society and increased stresses and expectations in the family combine to place an unbearable strain on young and middle-aged shoulders.

Serious questions have arisen about the training of church leaders. The 'academic model' ('Send them away to theological seminary or Bible college') has dominated the churches for many years. Evangelicals have been slow to return to their roots and ask the fundamental question: 'What does Scripture say?'

The teaching of Scripture is clear:

1. Men are chosen for training who have distinct qualities of character, spiritual maturity and some evidence of leadership/teaching ability (1 Tim. 3:2-7; Titus 1:6-9).

2. Training for church leadership is carried out by existing church leaders (2 Tim. 2:2).

3. Training is conducted in the context of a local church.

4. The trainer provides himself as a 'role model' and together they build a relationship in which their characters can be observed, their convictions can be examined, their actions can be questioned and their thinking can be clarified. In other words, this is the approach to training that was used by the Lord Jesus Christ in preparing his apostles, and continued by the apostle Paul in training Timothy and Titus. It is the method of training now known as 'mentoring'.

Different kinds of mentoring

The term 'mentoring' derives from a wise counsellor called 'Mentor' who in-structed Telemachus, son of Odysseus. A mentor is 'a wise or trusted adviser or guide'. A relationship is formed between two individuals, the mentor and the trainee, or 'mentoree'. In practice there are many different ways in which this relationship may be exercised in the context of church leadership training.

The 'apprenticeship' model

Richard Coekin urges the practice of a pre-theological college apprenticeship: 'Residential theological education can't provide the necessary practical experi-ence of ministry. Of course, most pastors go from theological college to an assistant-pastorship or curacy to learn how to apply their education, but they commonly discover that their time at theological college has been poorly used, because the student had little experience of what real ministry would be like... Apprenticeships are a familiar model for a close relationship in which a trainee can observe, learn, discuss, practice and be assessed in the skills and attitudes of ministry. Sharing with a pastor in trying to apply Scripture to real pastoral issues and questions of church strategy, an apprentice will begin to realize the link be-tween theology and practical ministry. The huge advantage of an apprenticeship before college is that trainees have faced genuine issues and problems which they are then keen to explore at their chosen seminary.'[1]

The 'supervision' model

This is the approach favoured by counselling tutors and counselling agencies. Each counsellor is committed to spending time with another, more experienced counsellor in a supervisory role. Difficult cases are discussed, without breaking confidentiality, and the counsellor is encouraged to share and explore his/her own thoughts and feelings in response to the client and the problem. In the pastoral context there is the added dimension of relating theology to pastoral care: 'Central to pastoral supervision is the need to enable the person who is offering care under supervision to integrate theological understanding with pas-toral practice.'[2]

    Foskett and Lyall call this approach to mentoring 'Learning from experience'. They divide it into four phases:

Phase 1:   Experience of what actually happened.
Phase 2:   Reflection and observation of the experience and its effect.
Phase 3:   Understanding the experience and its effect, and discovering something of its meaning.
Phase 4:   Experiment in preparation for future experiences.[3]

The 'assistant' model

This is the more familiar approach. Following institutional theological training, a man joins an experienced pastor. Sadly, this arrangement may involve nothing more than taking youth meetings, conducting pastoral visits, preaching when the minister is absent and generally being used by the diaconate and the church. With careful thought it could be a very valuable learning experience, but this will require the experienced pastor to allocate considerable time and effort to individual and personal interaction.

The 'veteran/junior' model

Charles Boyd urges an experienced pastor in one church to keep an eye on a younger pastor in another church: 'Every veteran pastor would do well to find a younger preacher who's eager for direction, and offer him ongoing encouragement and advice. Then see how both of you grow.'[4]

The 'discipling' model

Steve Timmis opened his heart and his home in this form of mentoring: 'Integral to the whole process was *relationship*, and for this reason no more than two people were taken on at the same time... They worked alongside me, and witnessed first-hand, not only how I conducted myself in public, but also how I related to my family. They saw the kind of husband I was, and observed my attempts at being a father to four growing children. It was, of necessity, a life-to-life thing, and as such, it was close, intimate and demanding.'[5]

The key feature in mentoring

While all these approaches to training may fit the definition of a mentoring relationship, the key feature of the distinct approach advocated in this manual is the intimate and prolonged relationship between the trainer and the trainee. For this book to be of real benefit it should be used by a mentor concerned to guide, instruct, challenge and nurture a trainee in the art of church leadership. As Jay E. Adams points out, 'Discipleship is the proper method for training ... because it is the biblical method. I have set it over against the academic method (which we adopted from the Greek academy) as fuller, different, biblical and (therefore) the more effective method.'[6]

The discipleship method is the 'with him' model. When Jesus chose his disciples, it does not say that he chose them to attend his lectures (though at times they did just that) but, rather, 'that they might be with him' (Mark 3:14). This indicates that the disciples were to spend time with Jesus. This is the Lord's philosophy of education. He says that a student 'who is perfectly trained will be like his teacher' (Luke 6:40).[7] For a church leader, or potential church leader, in secular employment this may mean at least three or four hours per week. For a full-time trainee this will obviously be much more.

A clear testimony to the effectiveness of this kind of training comes from a surprising source. The members of the Sanhedrin, the ruling council of the Jews, were astonished at the powerful reasoning of two of the Lord's apostles: 'Now when they saw the boldness of Peter and John, and perceived that they were uneducated and untrained men, they marvelled. And they realized that they had been with Jesus' (Acts 4:13). Those whom Jesus chose to be with him, that they might become like him, were so changed by this method that at length they were recognized by others as having 'been with Jesus'.

The basic ingredients in mentoring

Church leaders train church leaders

In laying the groundwork for a biblical concept of mentoring, Ray Evans has identified a number of elements of church leadership training displayed in Scripture:[8]

1. Formal teaching with questions from the mentor.
2. Life circumstances.
3. Questions from the trainees.
4. Problem-solving.
5. Fieldwork (and seminars).

Mentoring as partnership

Central to the biblical concept of mentoring for leadership is the establishment of an intentional, intensive, voluntary relationship between an existing church leader and a potential church leader. The fundamental thesis is that 'While knowledge can be transmitted in a variety of forms and media, learning occurs in interactive relationships.'[9]

Thus mentoring in the context of church leadership is 'an interactive learning relationship mutually recognized and defined by both leader and follower with the purpose of increasing the follower's maturity in leadership'.[10]

'It is within a partnership that knowledge is imparted, experience compared, skills perfected, practice assessed and insight nurtured. Furthermore there is another kind of relationship involved, that between the participants and their task: the apprentice/master and the craft, the novice/expert and the skills, the pupil/teacher and the knowledge, and the client/counsellor and the insight.'[11]

Mentoring as a shared learning experience

Mentoring is a powerful form of leadership. It is a very effective way of influencing and of being influenced, of teaching and of learning. The trainee completes assignments, such as conducting a pastoral visit, preaching a sermon, leading a discussion group, or preparing a couple for marriage. The mentor helps the mentoree to 'reflect critically upon that action when they meet together. Reflection of course involves both the intelligence and the imagination.'[12]

'Jesus did not call without detailed follow-up. The call is followed by careful instruction, personal guidance, interpersonal dialogue, and the gradual clarification of the divine purpose.'[13]

Mentors meet with trainees to talk through any impediments or problems that may be hindering their personal spiritual growth or leadership function. Mentorees 'are encouraged to speak up about any obstacles and explore potential remedial action with the mentor, facilitating constructive reflection'.[14]

'Pastoral leadership consists principally in learning how to empower, enable, and enrich the leadership of others. It often seems simpler for the pastor to do the job alone according to self-defined criteria.'[15]

Qualities required in a mentor

Those who train others biblically must themselves be biblically qualified. Too many tutors in academic institutions, who are charged with the responsibility of training pastors, would fail in the real world of a local church. Their knowledge is largely theoretical and their understanding 'second-hand'. There are, of course, exceptions.

The foremost qualification for a mentor in church leadership is that he should be an active practising church leader fulfilling the criteria of 1 Timothy 3:2-7 and Titus 1:6-9, with years of experience in church life and leadership and a 'track record' to verify his competence *and grace* in office. As a mentor he is a 'role model'. 'He becomes a model not merely of someone *talking* about his subject, but of someone vitally engaged in pursuing it.'[16] He must so live and labour that he can sincerely say, 'Imitate me, just as I also imitate Christ' (1 Cor. 11:1) and, 'The things which you learned and received and heard and saw in me, these do' (Phil. 4:9).

Though Alliott is speaking in the context of medical practice, his words translate well into the framework of church leadership training: 'Mentors ... need such attributes as an understanding, caring nature, enthusiasm, and an ability to encourage reflection and constructive action. Experience both of success and failure is also important, as are up-to-date knowledge and clinical skills.'[17]

The mentor should be knowledgeable in the subject. He should not counsel in matters in which he is not expert, or pass judgement on subjects that are beyond his limitations. There is to be no embarrassment in saying, 'I do not know,' or 'I have no experience of that.'

A mentor is a guide to accompany his colleague. He makes no decisions on behalf of the trainee. Counselling should be non-directional, considering various options rather than suggesting a specific route. Mentors need compassion, so they can demonstrate care for mentorees in their predicament; tact, in order that they do not make the situation worse; and honesty, so that trust can develop. Counselling skills such as listening, eye contact, feedback, use of open questions and appreciation of non-verbal cues are essential to establish and maintain the relationship. Mentors need to have a degree of self-awareness, of their own strengths, weaknesses and personal characteristics, and to guard against imposing their own attitudes and agenda upon those whom they are training.[18] The mentor needs the experience and originality to develop options rather than to make decisions. If he gives advice, then he is taking over responsibility for decision-making. Furthermore, 'How a decision is carried out is as important as the decision, and the mentor can't control the carrying out.'[19]

Practical steps in mentoring

Choice

Care must be taken over the choice of those recruited, because the nature of this approach to training requires a certain maturity: 'People have to be self-motivated, and to be able to see the long-term benefits, more than any short-term gains.'[20]

An individual undergoing this kind of training should be willing:

1. To admit his ignorance, since a wise person is always more aware of his ignorance than his knowledge.

2. To think hard — to analyse, to learn, to understand, and to discern.

3. To work hard at all assignments.

4. To keep careful notes of questions and issues to raise with his mentor — something that will save both of them from wasting valuable time.

5. Not to 'use' his mentor as a means of achieving status among other Christians or to gain access to other Christian leaders. Private conversations with a mentor should be kept private. As he profits from the training he should grow 'in the grace and knowledge of our Lord and Saviour Jesus Christ' (2 Peter 3:18). Growth, development and increased maturity — these are the 'pay' he gives his mentor.

Conviction

The mentor and the person he is mentoring must share a compatible philosophy. Christian wisdom is the knowledge and application of scriptural principles. Without a clearly stated foundation the relationship will inevitably flounder. Objectives, expectations and boundaries need to be clearly established. A good mentor helps define the vision, the goal and the plan. Is the goal realistic, considering the trainee's talent, opportunities and facilities?

Confidence

Both parties must have confidence in each other. Mentoring necessitates the development of a caring and trusting relationship. Mentoring happens only when mentorees 'trust, feel accepted by, and view their mentors as role models'.[21] At the same time the mentor must genuinely believe in the trainee's potential. There may be times when the learner loses confidence in himself, particularly after a failure, and he will need the mentor to restore his confidence. When trust and confidence develop there is freedom to express fears, doubts and temptations in a 'safe' environment. Both are able to open their hearts and be vulnerable to each other. Acceptance without conditions communicates the fact that concern comes without strings attached.

Confidence demands confidentiality. A friendly manner, observing all the social graces and a respectful attitude towards each other all help the process of mentoring. Serious problems may be revealed at mentoring sessions, and a mentor should be careful not to leave the trainee disturbed or without a safety net. Addressing problems is challenging and sometimes ways forward can be unsettling. The trainee needs to know where he can turn in a crisis. It is better to help to prevent stress than to treat it when it has gained a hold.

Commitment

The mentor must be able to commit to a person and to a situation. Nothing that a church leader does for God is more important than nurturing the next generation of leaders. In the local church context the 80/20 rule applies (giving 80% of their time to 20% of the people); church leaders should give more time to the next generation of leaders (2 Tim. 2:2; cf. Eph. 4:11-16). Time devoted to being with these men will be disproportionate to the time spent with other church members. A mentor should assume that he is the giver in the relationship. Regular contact is the responsibility of the mentor. Consistent contact demonstrates dependability and builds trust.

Communication

Clear communication is based on understanding, not on agreement. Complete honesty is essential. It is 'speaking the truth in love' which enables growth in Christ (Eph. 4:15). Trust and respect are the foundations on which mentoring relationships are built. Good communications depend upon the establishment and maintenance of a good relationship. While 'much information can be imparted, certain techniques can be learned, particular skills can be acquired ... without the relational dimension, it will always fall short of what can be done'.[22] Whether a mentor should commit his whole family, as Steve Timmis recommends and practises, is open to question. There are no biblical guidelines for this kind of family exposure to scrutiny. Such involvement may impose unhelpful pressures on growing children, and indeed on a wife and mother.

Character

The qualifications for church leadership major almost exclusively upon the quality of character and life (1 Tim. 3:2-7; Titus 1:6-9). Spiritual gifts without spiritual graces confuse the church, hinder the spread of the gospel and, most importantly of all, dishonour the Lord. Church leaders and potential church leaders require to be 'full of the Holy Spirit and wisdom' (Acts 6:3; cf. Eph. 5:18). The fruit of the indwelling Holy Spirit should be abundantly evident (Gal. 5:22-23). Care in the smallest details maintains consistency. Keep alert for the 'dead flies' in the perfume (Eccles. 10:1).

Counselling

The mentor is a counsellor, not a boss. Mentoring, at its best, is a modest intervention. The most caring and effective mentor is still only one of many influences in the life of the trainee. Don't do for him what he can do for himself. Your greatest gift is to help him discover his own solutions to problems. Don't expect to have all the answers. Sometimes just listening attentively is all that is needed. Avoid being overwhelmed by his problems. Remain calm and dispassionate to help him solve problems. Mentoring helps a mentoree to understand his true thoughts and feelings. Mentoring encourages constructive reflection before exploring alternative courses of action. For the relationship to work effectively the mentoree must recognize this aspect of the relationship; it will help keep him from becoming resentful, or quietly rebellious, or hostile.

Counting the cost

Mentoring is costly on both sides: in time, energy and commitment. The responsibility of the mentor is to be open, honest and genuine, so that the trainee receives a clear, consistent signal. The responsibility of the mentoree is to observe correctly and to absorb effectively: 'You know,' says the apostle Paul, 'from the first day that I came to Asia, in what manner I always lived among you, serving the Lord with all humility, with many tears and trials' (Acts 20:18-19).

Mentors make themselves vulnerable. The trainee may ask questions about what he sees, as well as about what he hears. 'It's impossible to be aloof and detached, and as relationships form, tensions arise and disappointment can set in. In effect you're giving people free rein to scrutinize your life and to question whatever they see and hear.'[23] But sharing yourself usually teaches you something about yourself in the process. It is a good learning experience.

Mentors will come under attack from unsympathetic fellow-ministers who may criticize them of 'cloning' or 'brainwashing'. Christian modesty makes a church leader recoil from such accusations and he will be tempted to give up on this form of training. But this is God's method!

Conclusion

It is difficult to expect church leaders to function properly if they have no role models and have to face disturbing personal problems and difficult church situations. Mentoring provides a framework not simply for the initial training of a new generation of church leaders, but for the establishment of a network where all church leaders have mentors, whose judgement they respect and to whom they can turn, for the whole of their life. Those of us who have served in church leadership for many years still depend upon our mentors – the men who love us, listen to us, share our hopes and our fears, who are there for us, especially when we need them most.

2.
Pastoral oversight

Shepherds love all the flock
Shepherds are responsible for the flock
Shepherds lead the flock
Shepherds feed the flock
Shepherds tend the lambs
Shepherds guard the flock

Pastoral oversight

What are the most important duties of church leaders?

....

....

....

....

How do church leaders win the love and support of the church?

....

....

....

....

List the Scripture references you already know which relate to church leadership

....

....

....

What time will you commit each week to pray and study God's Word in preparation for leadership?

....

....

Recommended reading

The papers listed below are written from differing, and initially convincing, viewpoints and therefore will stretch and train thinking and ability in handling Scripture.

Alexander, E. J. 'A Biblical View of the Eldership', *Rutherford Journal of Church and Ministry*, vol. 3, no.1, Spring 1996, pp.4-6.

Berghoef, G. and De Koster, L. 'Sects and Cults', *The Elder's Handbook: a practical guide for church leaders* (Grand Rapids, Michigan: Christian's Library Press, 1979, pp.249-58).

MacMillan, J. D. 'Eldership Today', *Monthly Record*, February 1988, pp.28-31.

Shakespeare, J. 'The Functions of Pastors/Elders/Bishops', *Pastors, Elders and Bishops: a study in N.T. church order* (Walsall: Midland Road Strict and Particular Baptist Church, 1983), pp.7-8.

Pastoral oversight

The Lord is the church leader's example: 'I am among you as the one who serves,' said the Saviour (Luke 22:27). The Lord Jesus is the Good Shepherd who knows his sheep, loves his sheep, leads his sheep, protects his sheep and lays down his life for his sheep (John 10:11,27-28).

Church leaders care for *all* the flock: 'Take heed ... to all the flock' (Acts 20:28). As J. Oswald Sanders says, 'A shepherd's work cannot be done effectively without a shepherd's heart.'[1] The 'flock' refers to those who are children of God, born of the Holy Spirit, testifying to repentance towards God and faith in our Lord Jesus Christ.

A major problem facing spiritual shepherds is what to do about wandering sheep. The Lord has severe words of criticism towards Israel's shepherds who failed to retrieve the sheep that had wandered away from the flock (Ezek. 34:6). It is a common feature of church life that Christian 'sheep' move freely, at will, from one flock to another. They may be attracted by the other shepherd, or by one or more of his sheep; they may be reacting to their own shepherd, wanting to be free of his oversight; or they may just be wanting a change. So sheep come and go. They will take their food with the new flock and yet may not become an 'official' part (member) of that flock. So who is their shepherd? Who has responsibility? Christians must be made aware that they cannot flit from church to church at will (Heb. 13:17).

When students move away from their home church for prolonged periods of study, or for a period of short-term employment in order to gain experience of the workplace, pastors must agree as to whose responsibility it is to watch over them.

He will feed his flock like a shepherd;
He will gather the lambs with his arm,
And carry them in his bosom,
And gently lead those who are with young
(Isa. 40:11).

Thus says the Lord GOD to the shepherds: 'Woe to the shepherds of Israel who feed themselves! Should not the shepherds feed the flocks? You eat the fat and clothe yourselves with the wool; you slaughter the fatlings, but you do not feed the flock. The weak you have not strengthened, nor have you healed those who were sick, nor bound up the broken, nor brought back what was driven away, nor sought what was lost; but with force and cruelty you have ruled them'
(Ezek. 34:2-4).

Otherwise shepherds will fail the sheep over whom the Holy Spirit has made them overseers (Acts 20:28).

Shepherds love all the flock

> Who is weak, and I am not weak? Who is made to stumble, and I do not burn with indignation? (2 Cor. 11:29).
>
> For these things I weep; My eye, my eye overflows with water; Because the comforter, who should restore my life, Is far from me. My children are desolate Because the enemy prevailed (Lam. 1:16).

Shepherds follow the example of the Chief Shepherd and love all his sheep (John 10:11-15). In Acts 20:28 Paul binds every sheep upon the hearts of the elders. They are to 'take heed ... to all' — not merely the elder's friends, nor a faction that he has allowed to form and that clings to him, nor the well-to-do, neglecting the poor and the unassuming. The true shepherd knows no dividing line, no factions; he loves every sheep, especially the weak and the needy. He loves the lambs as well as the sheep. As R. C. H. Lenski puts it, 'If your heart is not big enough to embrace "all the flock", it is not big enough to shepherd any of the flock.' [2]

Pastors suffer hurt when the church is wounded.

Shepherds are responsible for the flock

Shepherds are answerable to God for the spiritual well-being of the flock entrusted to them by the Holy Spirit (Acts 20:28). In the treatment of the flock they will gather, not scatter; heal, not wound; feed, not fleece; bind up, not break (Ezek. 34:1-16; Jer. 23:1-4). As spiritually-minded men, sound in faith and blameless in life, they require special gifts of the Holy Spirit (patterned on the example of Christ, Isa. 11:2; 42:3) to preside in the gatherings of the church and to see that all

> Take heed to yourselves [addressing the elders of verse 17] and to all the flock, among which the Holy Spirit has made you overseers, to shepherd the church of God which he purchased with his own blood (Acts 20:28).

goes well with the flock of God. They are to ensure that everything is conducted 'decently and in order' (1 Cor. 14:40), which means that it is to be in accordance with the revealed will of God in the Scriptures. They must not allow a weak believer, when given a task, to engage in 'complaining and disputing' (Phil. 2:14).

Shepherds lead the flock

Shepherds rule the church of God (1 Tim. 3:5; 5:17). The word 'rule' (literally, 'to stand before') here carries no connotations of 'ruling over', but means being out in front in the sense that they have gone further, know where they are going and are showing the direction because they are following Christ (cf. 1 Cor. 11:1). Peter specifically instructs elders to 'shepherd the flock of God ... serving as overseers, not by compulsion but willingly ... nor as being lords over [cf. Acts 19:16, where the same word is translated 'overpowered'] those entrusted' to them (1 Peter 5:2-3). Being 'overseers' does not mean an abuse of power, merely the exercise of a certain type of power. Peter is following the principles established by the Lord Jesus Christ.

What the Saviour teaches about leadership in the church is radical and revolutionary. He contrasts the behaviour of leaders in the world with

> The LORD is my shepherd;
> I shall not want.
> He makes me to lie down in green pastures;
> He leads me beside the still waters.
> He restores my soul;
> He leads me in the paths of righteousness
> For his name's sake
> (Ps. 23:1-3).
>
> Whoever desires to become great among you, let him be your servant. And whoever desires to be first among you, let him be your slave — just as the Son of Man did not come to be served, but to serve, and to give his life a ransom for many (Matt. 20:26-28).

the functioning of leaders in his church. The Lord Jesus Christ identifies the legitimate *and the illegitimate* exercise of authority, power and government when he says, 'You know that the rulers of the Gentiles lord it over them, and those who are great exercise authority over them' (Matt. 20:25). He then draws the contrast with his own teaching with the startling words: 'Yet it shall not be so among you; but whoever desires to become great among you, let him be your servant. And whoever desires to be first among you, let him be your slave' (Matt. 20:26).

The Acts of the Apostles testify to the fact that a concept of leadership devoid of hierarchical authority (either in relation to the church or between themselves) was clearly practised in the early church. The sin of Diotrephes was that he loved 'to have the pre-eminence [philoproteuo, to love being first] among them' (3 John 9).

Shepherds function in a manner that is totally different from other forms of leadership! Their leadership is service — that is, ministry. It is leadership by godly example, biblical teaching, spiritual counsel and gracious humility. They do not 'lord it' over the church of God, nor over one another.

> Obey those who rule over you, and be submissive, for they watch out for your souls, as those who must give account. Let them do so with joy and not with grief, for that would be unprofitable for you (Heb. 13:17).
>
> And he [i.e. Christ] himself gave some to be apostles, some prophets, some evangelists, and some pastors [shepherds] and teachers, for the equipping of the saints for the work of ministry, for the edifying of the body of Christ, till we all come to the unity of the faith and of the knowledge of the Son of God, to a perfect man, to the measure of the stature of the fulness of Christ; that we should no longer be children, tossed to and fro and carried about with every wind of doctrine, by the trickery of men, in the cunning craftiness of deceitful plotting (Eph. 4:11-14).
>
> And the things that you have heard from me among many witnesses, commit these to faithful men who will be able to teach others also (2 Tim. 2:2).
>
> Let the elders who rule well be counted worthy of double honour, especially those who labour in the word and doctrine. For the Scripture says, 'You shall not muzzle an ox while it treads out the grain,' and, 'The labourer is worthy of his wages' (1 Tim. 5:17-18).

Shepherds lead the flock regularly in prayer. They lead by example (1 Peter 5:3) by their godliness, by their behaviour to others (including the way they treat their wives and children), by showing respect and esteem for colleagues, and in their concern for evangelism at home and abroad (1 Cor. 10:33 – 11:1).

Shepherds are to be followed and respected by the whole church. In Hebrews 13:17 the word 'obey' translates *peitho*, which means 'be persuaded or convinced by argument', so, where appropriate, church leaders are to give reasons for their decisions or actions. The principle should be that elders are obeyed *unless* good biblical argument can be presented for disobedience. Their influence is to be dependent upon their godliness, entirely spiritual and derived exclusively from their handling of the Word of God. They are to be esteemed 'very highly in love for their work's sake' (1 Thess. 5:13).

Shepherds are responsible 'for the equipping of the saints for the work of ministry' so that the church may be built up (Eph. 4:12). The teaching and example of Christ define leadership as the *empowering of* others rather than *power over* others. Shepherds recognize the diversities of spiritual gifts from the Holy Spirit, the differences of ministries from the Lord Jesus Christ and the diversities of activities promoted by God, given 'to each one for the profit of all' (1 Cor. 12:4-7). All the flock should be given opportunity to exercise their God-given gifts.

Shepherds, together with evangelists like Timothy, are on the watch for other men whom they will train as teachers (2 Tim. 2:2). This is particularly important from one generation to another. Leaders train leaders.

Shepherds 'labour in the word and doctrine' (1 Tim. 5:17). John Shakespeare comments: 'It would be foolish, wrong and disobedient to God for a church to fail to give appropriate weight to the opinions of its elders in matters of teaching, especially if those elders were labourers in word and doctrine, in which case they should be accorded double honour.'[3]

Shepherds feed the flock

'Feeding' means imparting knowledge and understanding from God's Word (Jer. 3:15; cf. Ps. 119:103; 1 Cor. 3:2; Heb. 5:12-14; 1 Peter 2:2).

Shepherds are responsible for all teaching given throughout the church, whether in the context of worship, evangelism, children's work, informal contact, or any other sphere. While others may be recognized as gifted to teach in all these areas, the shepherds are nevertheless answerable to God for the maintenance of sound doctrine (1 Tim. 1:3-4).

> As newborn babes, desire the pure milk of the word, that you may grow thereby (1 Peter 2:2).
>
> Be diligent to present yourself approved to God, a worker who does not need to be ashamed, rightly dividing the word of truth (2 Tim. 2:15).

Shepherds spend much time studying the Scriptures in order to feed the flock with the best of spiritual food, the pure word, 'sound doctrine' (Titus 1:9; 1 Tim. 4:16; 2 Tim. 2:15). As those 'able to teach', they will be clear and accurate in communicating and applying that doctrine in order to feed the sheep (John 21:15-17; Acts 20:28; 1 Peter 5:2).

Shepherds tend the lambs

> Feed my lambs...
> Tend my sheep...
> Feed my sheep...
> (John 21:15,16,17).
>
> Receive one who is weak in the faith, but not to disputes over doubtful things (Rom. 14:1).
>
> We then who are strong ought to bear with the scruples of the weak, and not to please ourselves. Let each of us please his neighbour for his good, leading to edification (Rom. 15:1-2).

Shepherds care for 'lambs', which may be understood as those who are young in the faith or those who are young in age.

Shepherds ensure that new converts are properly cared for: visited, instructed, baptized and integrated into the full life of the church.

Shepherds keep watch over the young and vulnerable within the church community. The Lord Jesus has a special regard for them: 'Let the little children come to me, and do not forbid them; for of such is the kingdom of God' (Luke 18:16). He gave a serious warning against causing them to stumble: 'It is impossible that no offences [*skandalon* — a scandal, trap, stumbling block] should come, but woe to him through whom they do come! It would be better for him if a millstone were hung around his neck, and he were thrown into the sea, than that he should offend one of these little ones' (Luke 17:1-2).

Shepherds guard the flock

Preach the word! Be ready in season and out of season. Convince, rebuke, exhort, with all long-suffering and teaching. For the time will come when they will not endure sound doctrine, but according to their own desires, because they have itching ears, they will heap up for themselves teachers; and they will turn their ears away from the truth, and be turned aside to fables (2 Tim. 4:2-4).

But avoid foolish and ignorant disputes, knowing that they generate strife. And a servant of the Lord must not quarrel but be gentle to all, able to teach, patient, in humility correcting those who are in opposition, if God perhaps will grant them repentance, so that they may know the truth... (2 Tim. 2:23-25).

For I [Paul] know this, that after my departure savage wolves will come in among you, not sparing the flock. Also from among yourselves men will rise up, speaking perverse things, to draw away the disciples after themselves. Therefore watch, and remember that for three years I did not cease to warn everyone night and day with tears (Acts 20:29-31).

Shepherds instruct the flock so that the people of God are not 'tossed to and fro and carried about with every wind of doctrine, by the trickery of men, in the cunning craftiness of deceitful plotting' (Eph. 4:14).

Shepherds seek to convince those in error, by teaching from Scripture — giving reproof, correction and instruction in righteousness (2 Tim. 3:16), 'in humility correcting those who are in opposition, if God perhaps will grant them repentance, so that they may know the truth' (2 Tim. 2:24-26).

Shepherds guard the flock against 'savage wolves' and deceitful teachers from outside (Acts 20:29; Eph. 4:14), and divisive leaders from within (Acts 20:30; Rom. 16:17; 3 John 9-10). To quote Neil Summerton, 'Both Christ and Paul stress the need to be alert for, to be able to discern, and to neutralize, those who will disrupt the local congregation, particularly through false teaching (John 10:7-13; Acts 20:29-31).'[4]

Shepherds need 'the Spirit of wisdom and understanding' (Isa. 11:2), to perceive error in its early stages. Such wisdom, 'the wisdom that is from above' (James 3:17), comes only through prayer (James 1:5) and the careful study of God's Word (2 Tim. 2:15), individually and collectively.

Conclusion

Serving the Lord Jesus Christ as under-shepherds is no easy task. The office carries heavy responsibilities; nevertheless those pastors/shepherds who function well will receive a special reward from the Chief Shepherd himself — 'the crown of glory that does not fade away' (1 Peter 5:4).

> For you were like sheep going astray, but have now returned to the Shepherd [the same word as in Ephesians 4:11, where it is translated 'pastors'] and Overseer of your souls (1 Peter 2:25).

3.
Team spirit

Team spirit

Suggest ways in which church leaders may develop friendship with each other.

....

....

....

Is plurality of elders a matter of cultural setting, expediency, or biblical authority? (Cite Scripture.)

....

....

....

What do you understand to be the role of a 'minister'?

....

....

....

If elders are unable to agree among themselves on a vital matter, what can they do?

....

....

....

Recommended reading

The papers listed below are written from differing, and initially convincing, viewpoints and therefore will stretch and train thinking and ability in handling Scripture.

Alexander, C. D. *The Great Eldership Fallacy* (Liverpool: Bible Exposition Fellowship, no date).

Hulse, E. 'The Eldership and Protocol', R. O. Beardmore (ed.), *Shepherding God's Flock: essays on leadership in the local church* (Harrisonburg, Virginia: Sprinkle, 1988), pp.35-62.

Jensen, P. D. and Payne, T. 'Effective Decision Making', *Fellow Workers: Discussion Papers for the church committee* (London: St Matthias Press, 1989), pp.17-22.

MacMillan, J. D. 'Eldership Today', *Monthly Record*, March 1988, pp.53-5.

Shakespeare, J. 'The Wisdom of Plural Elders', *Pastors, Elders and Bishops: a study in New Testament church order* (Walsall: Midland Road Strict & Particular Baptist Church, 1983). pp.8-9.

Summerton, N. 'The Effectiveness of the Eldership Group', *A Noble Task: eldership and ministry in the local church* (Carlisle: Paternoster Press, 1987), pp.83-92.

Watts, M. H. 'The Gospel Ministry', *Evangelical Times*, November 1993, p.15.

Zens, J. '"Paul Summoned the Elders of the Assembly": problems with the "pastor" separate doctrine', *Searching Together*, no date, pp.1-7.

Team spirit

C. D. Alexander warns against diverting attention 'from the all-important priority of the preaching of Christ and Him Crucified, to the dangerous irrelevancies of how the sheep of the flock are to be governed... It is so easy to lose sight of the fact that the most important people in the Church are not the porters and shepherds, but the sheep of Christ's pasture.'[1]

If Alexander is equating governing the flock with church leadership then we must disagree with him on two counts: church leadership does not involve governing and, secondly, it must not be ignored. The Word of God contains much teaching on this vital subject. The sheep will safely graze only when the shepherds are diligently attending to their duties.

'Take heed to yourselves,' says Paul, since before caring for the flock there must be careful attention given by the shepherds to themselves and to each other. 'In some parts,' says William Arnot, 'they paint garden walls black, that they may absorb more of the sun's heat and so impart more warmth to the fruit-trees that lean on them. Those who in any sphere care for souls, stand in the position of the garden wall. The more that the teacher absorbs for himself of Christ's love, the more benefit will others obtain from him.'[2]

> Take heed to yourselves and to all the flock, among which the Holy Spirit has made you overseers, to shepherd the church of God which he purchased with his own blood (Acts 20:28).
>
> Take heed to yourself and to the doctrine. Continue in them, for in doing this you will save both yourself and those who hear you (1 Tim. 4:16).

Single or plural eldership

Single eldership

Those who oppose a plurality of elders in each church explain the universal use in Scripture of the plural form by arguing that in each geographic area there were several congregations, each of which was presided over by a single elder. Alexander argues that 'No doubt the church became so numerous that there would have to be some separation into communities to solve the problem of numbers and distance. Hence there would be a plurality of elders ordained to take care of the separate communities making up so vast a "church".'[3] For a given area there would therefore be a number of churches, each with a single elder.

> From Miletus he [Paul] sent to Ephesus and called for the elders of the church (Acts 20:17).
>
> Paul and Timothy, bondservants of Jesus Christ, to all the saints in Christ Jesus who are in Philippi, with the bishops and deacons... (Phil. 1:1).
>
> The elders who are among you I exhort, I whom am a fellow elder and a witness of the sufferings of Christ... (1 Peter 5:1).

On this basis 'the elders of the church' at Ephesus (Acts 20:17) are viewed as a collection of individual pastors from the various 'churches' in the area; in other words, 'the elders *of the churches* at Ephesus' collectively constituted 'the elders *of the church* at Ephesus'. This form of argument can be applied to many of the biblical references to elders (Acts 11:30; 21:18; Phil. 1:1; Titus 1:5; 1 Peter 5:1).

A further argument in favour of a single elder in each church is that in the qualifications for bishops and deacons in 1 Timothy 3:2-13 everything referring to a 'bishop' is in the singular (e.g. 'husband ... *one* who rules *his* own *house* ... the church [not 'the churches] *a novice* ... *he* must have a good testimony ... lest *he* fall...', emphasis added). By contrast, everything referring to deacons is in the plural (e.g., 'let *these* ... be tested ... let *them* serve ... husbands ... *their* own *houses* ... *those* who have served well ... obtain for *themselves*...').

Plural eldership

The evidence for plurality in eldership is seen in the appointment of 'elders [plural] in every church [singular]' in the region of Galatia (Acts 14:23). A very convincing argument for plurality in a local church is seen in the advice of

James: 'Is anyone among you sick? Let him call for the elders of the church, and let them pray over him...' (James 5:14). Furthermore, in 1 Timothy 5:17, if there were only one elder there could be no 'especially', as every elder would by definition have to 'labour in the word and doctrine'.

As there are clear examples in the New Testament of plural eldership, all the earlier arguments in favour of single eldership evaporate.

> Let the elders who rule well be counted worthy of double honour, especially those who labour in the word and doctrine (1 Tim. 5:17).
>
> Where there is no counsel, the people fall; but in the multitude of counsellors there is safety (Prov. 11:14).

Single eldership is often referred to as 'one-man ministry'. As John Shakespeare points out, the disadvantages of such a system are that it is likely to promote the minister's personal idiosyncrasies; it provides no checks on heresy or error; it stifles the teaching gifts of others in the church; it results in too much work for one man to accomplish; it creates problems in the event of his prolonged illness, departure or death; it fosters an unhealthy division between clergy and laity and opens temptation to popery; it means that he is not 'fed' by his brethren and it necessitates his standing alone when dealing with problems.[4]

Plural but unequal eldership

A popular approach is to favour plurality of elders but with a hierarchical structure. This means that one man, usually 'the minister' (paid or honorary), is described as *primus inter pares* (first among equals), 'chief elder', or 'an elder among elders'. Malcolm Watts argues for this view from:

1. The use of the singular word 'angel' (or 'messenger') in Revelation 2:1,8,12,18; 3:1,7,14.

2. The clear pattern of single leadership in church and state throughout Scripture, such as Moses, Joshua, David, Nehemiah, James and Paul.

3. The success granted by God to those churches which practise this form of leadership.

4. The fact that the word translated 'bishop' in 1 Timothy 3:2 is in the singular and has a definite article — i.e. 'the bishop' — whereas the word translated 'deacons' in 1 Timothy 3:8 is in the plural and without the definite article.[5]

Erroll Hulse displays a similar kind of thinking in favour of unequal eldership when he writes, 'There is a difference between a man who has been called to leave his profession of medicine, accounting, or other expertise to devote all his time and talents to the vineyard of Christ and those who remain in their professions.'[6]

Plurality of eldership with parity

'Parity' means 'equally shared authority' and is preferable to the word 'equality', since where there is a parity of position or responsibility among the elders, there is not equality in the sense of all having the same gifts and abilities.[7] There should be parity in authority coupled with diversity in function. J. D. MacMillan writes, 'The New Testament does not know anything of one elder being higher in rank than another. All are on the same footing, the same platform, with equal status and equal responsibility for the flock.'[8] The sin of Diotrephes was that he loved 'to have the pre-eminence [*philoproteuo*, to love being first] among them' (3 John 9).

Objections to plurality and parity in eldership are probably based upon the inability of elders to function effectively together. In many cases they are a response to the frustration experienced by ministers of the gospel due to the 'overlording', diverting and restricting influence of fellow elders who are unable to perform the task themselves.[9] But the same criticism may be addressed to a minister who 'lords it over', or disregards, his colleagues.

Financially supported elders

Do the principles of plurality and parity militate against the financial support of one or more of the elders in a local church?

John Shakespeare is emphatic in his assertion that no elder should be financially supported. In a tripartite syllogism he reasons:

1. There should always be more than one elder in a church.
2. It is impractical or impossible to provide financial support for more than one elder.
3. Therefore the financial support of a minister 'must be out of the question, whatever biblical arguments may be advanced in its support'.[10]

There are evident weaknesses in this form of reasoning since it is based upon deductions made from a singe premise which is not proven. Furthermore, there are biblical references *which do indicate* the support of elders. According to the apostle Paul, they may be financially supported to 'labour in the word and doctrine', for 'the labourer is worthy of his wages' (1 Tim. 5:17-18). Those who are taught the word are urged to share their material good things with those who teach (Gal. 6:6). 'The Lord has commanded that those who preach the gospel should live from the gospel' (1 Cor. 9:14).

John Zens goes further when he argues:

> Let the elders who rule well be counted worthy of double honour, especially those who labour in the word and doctrine. For the Scripture says, 'You shall not muzzle an ox while it treads out the grain,' and, 'The labourer is worthy of his wages' (1 Tim. 5:17-18).
>
> Who ever goes to war at his own expense? Who plants a vineyard and does not eat of its fruit? Or who tends a flock and does not drink of the milk of the flock? Do I say these things as a mere man? Or does not the law say the same also? For it is written in the law of Moses, 'You shall not muzzle an ox while it treads out the grain.' Is it oxen God is concerned about? Or does he say it altogether for our sakes? For our sakes, no doubt, this is written, that he who ploughs should plough in hope, and he who threshes in hope should be partaker of his hope. If we have sown spiritual things for you, is it a great thing if we reap your material things? (1 Cor. 9:7-11).

> First, 1 Timothy 5:17 clearly assumes a *body* of elders... Those who work hard in the Word and teaching are part of a body of overseers. No distinction is made in this sense. The distinction in the text is one of *function*, not 'office'. All elders must be 'apt to teach', but not all will be in the 'especially' category.
>
> Secondly, the text says that it is totally appropriate to support [i.e., pay] elders who do *not* labour in the Word. The text says 'especially those', not '*only* those' or '*solely* those'...
>
> Thirdly, the 'teaching-ruling/ruling elder' distinction is not to be found in 1 Timothy 5:17. According to the qualifications of 1 Timothy 3, all bishops must be both 'apt to teach' and involved in 'ruling' the church of God (vv. 2,4-5). All elders teach and rule. Not in the same way, or degree, of course, but they are all involved in these areas. How elders function as a body is a matter of varying *gifts*, not of different 'offices'. [11]

Financially supporting one or more elders while not financially supporting *all* the elders does mean there is a potential risk of discrimination, but this is not inevitable, or otherwise Paul would not have indicated it.

Elders who are financially supported by a local church face specific dangers:

1. Being influenced, not by spiritual motives and faithfulness to the Word of God, but by financial considerations (1 Peter 5:2).

2. Being regarded as 'employees' and therefore under the control of the church members or their fellow elders.

3. Being 'used', as a convenient labour force, to carry out numerous tasks which are outside the sphere of pastoral oversight, thus diverting them from their true work.

4. Being the means of hindering the functioning of the whole church by assuming a false professionalism, taking upon themselves duties and responsibilities that others are gifted by the Holy Spirit to perform.

Elders are intended to be facilitators (Eph. 4:12). When an elder is financially supported by the church in order that he might 'labour in the word and doctrine' (1 Tim. 5:17), this means 'that such freedom from other pastoral duties as is required for preaching must be guaranteed from within the oversight [or eldership] of any church or congregation'. Furthermore, 'No preacher will minister the word in power if his eldership does not support him with prayer, pastoral concern and personal encouragement. He should know that he is not fighting the battle entirely on his own.'[12]

Praying together

Prayer is an indispensable duty of church leaders, whether in the conducting of public prayer in the assembly (Acts 2:42; 1 Tim. 2:1-2), pastoral care in homes (James 5:14), or in the secret place (Matt. 6:5-13).

> ... but we will give ourselves continually to prayer and to the ministry of the word (Acts 6:4).
>
> As they ministered to the Lord and fasted, the Holy Spirit said, 'Now separate to me Barnabas and Saul for the work to which I have called them.' Then, having fasted and prayed, and laid hands on them, they sent them away (Acts 13:2-3).

Church leaders pray together (and sometimes fast) before making major decisions or taking crucial steps (Acts 13:3; cf. Luke 6:12-13), in seeking blessing upon God's work committed to their charge (Ps. 90:16-17), for children (Matt. 19:13) and for healing (Matt. 17:21).

We cannot read, study, meditate upon and pray over God's Word too much (Ps. 119:97,103).

Handling differences

In any church there are numerous issues that arise sooner or later to cause sharp differences of opinion among the membership. A major problem which often faces church leaders is the lack of unanimity within their own ranks too. Even where there is total agreement upon fundamental doctrine, there may be a hundred and one matters which are potentially divisive: pastoral discipline, church policy, approaches to evangelism, inter-church relationships, and so on.

> But avoid foolish and ignorant disputes, knowing that they generate strife (2 Tim. 2:23).
>
> Also from among yourselves men will rise up, speaking perverse things, to draw away the disciples after themselves. Therefore watch, and remember that for three years I did not cease to warn everyone night and day with tears (Acts 20:30-31).

Differences of view causing disagreement may lead to division. Disagreement is inevitable; division is not. While Paul anticipated division coming even from within the body of elders, he nevertheless urged them to 'take heed to' themselves.

Elders should be so opposed to leading division or promoting division that they seek by all means to prevent and heal division, 'that there should be no schism in the body' (1 Cor. 12:25). Church leaders are to give a worthy example, as those who are, 'with all lowliness and gentleness, with long-suffering, bearing with one another in love, endeavouring to keep the unity of the Spirit in the bond of peace' (Eph. 4:2-3).

Difficulties, differences and disagreements must be resolved amicably. The glory and honour of God and the good name of the Lord Jesus Christ demand it. Problems are to be worked through with patience and perseverance.

As Erroll Hulse says, 'When Paul says that we should all be of one mind, we take that to mean that we should be at peace with one another, not that we must agree exactly on every issue.'[13]

Group cohesion

The ideal is for the eldership to be composed of men with a variety of temperaments, social backgrounds, political convictions and life experiences, as is illustrated in the twelve chosen by the Lord Jesus. Their common goal is to be of one mind and heart (Phil. 1:27; 2:1-4; 3:16; 4:2; 1 Peter 3:8-9). Where this cannot be achieved, respect and esteem for others will control their actions and temper their decisions. The quality of fellowship in a church rarely rises above the example given by its leaders in their relationship together: 'Like people, like priest' (Hosea 4:9).

Neil Summerton comments: 'However spiritual, competent and diligent elders may be as individuals, it is essential that any group holding and teaching plural eldership should function as a *coherent entity*, and be seen by the rest of the congregation to do so.'[14]

The very nature of eldership forbids unilateral action in the rule and pastoral care of the church. Shepherds are to act in unison and not merely as individuals. Each man may have individual responsibilities based upon personal gifts and experience, but at the same time they are part of a team and so their responsibilities are basically corporate rather than individual.[15]

For elders to become an effective group, strong and steady relationships are required, founded upon:

> 1. Accurate self-knowledge and self-assessment (including insight from fellow-elders and others who may have a clearer understanding of their characteristics and performance than they have themselves).
> 2. A sympathetic knowledge, understanding and appreciation of each other.
> 3. An objective assessment and mutual recognition of each other's spiritual gifts and roles in the church, and mutual encouragement in them.
> 4. Mutual trust, including the willingness to accept and stand behind the actions of colleagues even when those actions are not carried out precisely as they personally would have done them.[16]

Eldership is a 'team ministry' in which a number of godly and mature men work together for the glory of God and the common good of the church under their oversight. The New Testament recognizes what Jethro pointed out to Moses — that one man cannot do everything. Together they function in a manner which is totally different from all other forms of leadership. Their leadership is service (ministry) — leadership by godly example, biblical teaching, spiritual counsel and gracious humility. They do not 'lord it' over the church of God, nor over one another!

Plurality in eldership brings many benefits: a pool of resources from which to minister to the people of God; shared obligation, with a practical division of labour; different perspectives to be brought to discussion, ensuring more adequate treatment of particular issues. These benefits may only be achieved where there is solidarity between elders, even when there are differences of emphasis or approach between them. Not admitting any charge against an elder without two or three witnesses (1 Tim. 5:19) is designed to maintain individual integrity *and* team cohesion.

Church leaders are brothers in Christ, and brothers are to love each other (1 John 3:14). Next to the relationship between Christ and his church, nothing is more important in the local church than the relationship between the elders. Jesus taught the apostles to love one another (John 13:34-35; 15:12-13). Like all brothers, they are to forgive one another (Matt. 18:21-22).

> Do not receive an accusation against an elder except from two or three witnesses. Those who are sinning rebuke in the presence of all, that the rest also may fear. I charge you before God and the Lord Jesus Christ and the elect angels that you observe these things without prejudice, doing nothing with partiality (1 Tim. 5:19-21).

Friendship and fellowship between elders is vital:

1. To avoid the sense of acute loneliness and isolation which may result from their pastoral responsibilities.

2. To shepherd each other in love.

3. To provide a worthy example of what the whole church should be like.[17]

Effective decision-making

Three decision-making models[18]

1. The single leader

In situations where it is more important that the job is done than that everybody has the opportunity to express their opinion, the single-leader model works well. To ask one of our brothers in eldership to take a decision on our behalf is a great expression of confidence in that person, and an indication of our basic unity in the gospel. It is also a challenge to our godliness to submit to the decision of someone else.

2. Majority rule

This is an effective way of resolving tensions within a group, provided that the individual members are committed to accepting the majority verdict. There are drawbacks in a democracy: justice is determined by the will of the majority, not by what is right and true. And democracy tends to be divisive, since majority rule often creates a dissatisfied minority.

3. Consensus

Here the aim is to get everybody to agree, either by persuasion or by willingness to accept a compromise. 'Consensus decision-making is also more likely to produce original and creative solutions to a problem.'

Consensus on major issues is essential, although there may be agreement to differ on minor ones. In the words of Neil Summerton, 'It is not practicable to suppose that upon major matters affecting the life and work of the congregation an eldership could proceed other than on the principle of substantial agreement, if not unanimity. Persistent disagreement in such matters would be bound to be debilitating to the elders and to threaten the credibility of their leadership.'[19]

There will be times when one elder will need to make a decision without being able to consult with his brethren. At other times only a minority may be able to confer on a pressing issue. It is difficult to communicate with all elders when some are out at work. It is also time-consuming to consult each one individually. In such situations the mutual respect and mutual confidence within the eldership will be of paramount importance. As with Christians in general, so with elders in particular: 'love never fails', but rather 'bears all things, believes all things, hopes all things, endures all things' (1 Cor. 13:8,7).

4.
Pastoral leadership

A friendly church
Organization
Planning strategy
Communication
Church government
Church membership
Church discipline

Pastoral leadership

How can church members be made more caring towards each other?

....

....

....

Does the leadership of your church allow too much individual enterprise or too little?

....

....

....

What is the purpose of your church?

....

....

....

What are the marks of a friendly church?

....

....

....

Recommended reading

The papers listed below are written from differing, and initially convincing, viewpoints and therefore will stretch and train thinking and ability in handling Scripture.

Berghoef, G. and De Koster, L. 'The Elder as Leader', *The Elder's Handbook: a practical guide for church leaders* (Grand Rapids, Michigan: Christian's Library Press, 1979), pp.67-75.

Honeysett, M. *Training and Sustaining Biblical Leaders for Tomorrow.* Discussion document for leadership forum FIEC, 1 November 2006, www.fiec.org.uk

James, J. A. 'Democracy Comes to Church', *Sword and Trowel,* July / August, 1982, pp.29-31.

Jensen, P. D. and Payne, T. 'The User-friendly Church', *Fellow Workers: Discussion Papers for the church committee* (London: St Matthias Press, 1989, pp.51-9.

Mack, W. A. and Swavely, D. 'Committing Ourselves to Church Membership', *Life in the Father's House: a member's guide to the local church* (Phillipsburg, New Jersey: P &R,) 1996, pp.18-31.

Payne, Tony. 'Genetically Modified Churches: making training part of your church's DNA,' *The Briefing,* July/August 2007, pp.24-5

Spurgeon, J. A. 'The System of Church Government at the Metropolitan Tabernacle', *Sword and Trowel,* July / August, 1982, pp.31-2.

Warren, R. 'The Foundation for a Healthy Church', *The Purpose Driven Church: growth without compromising your message and mission* (Grand Rapids, Michigan: Zondervan, 1995), pp.85-94,119, 125.

Pastoral leadership

'If you are preaching the positive, life-changing Good News of Christ, if your members are excited by what God is doing in your church, if you are providing a service where they can bring unsaved friends without embarrassment, and if you have a plan to build, train, and send out those you win to Christ, attendance will be the least of your problems,' claims Rick Warren.[1]

A friendly church

'There is an increasing awareness that churches need to present a "user-friendly interface" to the world,' write Jensen and Payne. 'We can no longer afford to shroud our activities in complex language and incomprehensible practices.'[2]

The New Testament teaches concern for the outsiders who come into our meetings. Technical jargon can be just as difficult for them to understand as New Testament 'tongues'. Jensen and Payne continue: 'This is the mark of the friendly church: when a complete stranger with little or no knowledge of Christianity comes to one of its meetings, he feels welcomed and included. He can understand what is going on, and feels encouraged to come again. Before long he feels like this is his church.'[3]

While we can agree with some of the sentiments that these two writers express, there is a danger of going to the other extreme in thinking that the only reason for the church's existence is for the benefit of those outside the church. The unbeliever and uninformed should indeed comprehend the language we use (1 Cor. 14:23-24). They should feel welcome and encouraged to return. But whether an unbeliever should soon 'feel like this is his

> Therefore if the whole church comes together in one place, and all speak with tongues, and there come in those who are uninformed or unbelievers, will they not say that you are out of your mind? But if all prophesy, and an unbeliever or an uninformed person comes in, he is convinced by all, he is convicted by all. And thus the secrets of his heart are revealed; and so, falling down on his face, he will worship God and report that God is truly among you (1 Cor. 14:23-25).

church' is questionable. This is quite different from the response predicted by Paul in the New Testament, where there is conviction and an acknowledgement that God is present in the worship meeting (1 Cor. 14:25).

Being friendly is possible without compromise of belief, or removal of the distinction between 'in the church' and 'out of the church', or 'in Christ' and 'out of Christ'. The Lord Jesus earned the reputation of being 'a friend of tax collectors and sinners' (Matt. 11:19), without compromise or confusion.

> For we ourselves were also once foolish, disobedient, deceived, serving various lusts and pleasures, living in malice and envy, hateful and hating one another. But when the kindness and the love of God our Saviour toward man appeared, not by works of righteousness which we have done, but according to his mercy he saved us (Titus 3:3-5).
>
> 'You shall love the LORD your God with all your heart, with all your soul, and with all your mind'... And ... 'You shall love your neighbour as yourself' (Matt. 22:37,39).

At the heart of Christianity is a God who cares enough to establish friendship with sinners. Abraham 'was called the friend of God' (James 2:23; 2 Chr. 20:7; cf. John 15:13-14). Paul refers to the Lord God as having love for human beings (Titus 3:4). The Saviour teaches his disciples to love one another, to love their neighbours and to love their enemies (John 13:34; Matt. 22:39; 5:44). A friendly disposition towards the stranger, the seeking unbeliever and the uninformed is the minimal expression of love required of us.

Maybe many Christians do not really want sinners to be saved — at least not in *their* local congregation, because church growth threatens our established relationships and ways of doing things.

In the words of Rick Warren, 'The church should be *seeker sensitive*, but it must not be *seeker driven*.'[4]

There are questions to be faced:

- How many people in your city or town know of the existence of your church?
- How many know what are your distinguishing features — i.e. your beliefs and practices?
- Does the outward appearance of the building look inviting?
- Is there a board outside the church displaying information about the times of services and whom to contact?
- Is the building floodlit at night?
- Is there ease of access?
- Are the door stewards welcoming?
- Are strangers shown to a seat by a steward, welcomed by believers sitting nearby and spoken to after the service?

- Is there an unobtrusive method for obtaining their names and addresses?
- Is a follow-up letter sent?
- Is a follow-up visit carried out? If so, does the person conducting the visit meet the stranger and sit with him on his next visit to worship?
- Is he introduced to committed believers and, if a believer himself, integrated into an existing home group, or into a newly formed 'newcomers' group'? If the person is an unbeliever, is he quickly linked up to your study group for the unconverted?
- Would occasional weekends away for newcomers and selected members of the church be beneficial?
- Do you do enough to help the unbelieving seeker find answers about God at your church?

> *'There is no method, programme, or technology that can make up for a lack of love for unbelievers'* (Rick Warren).

'There is no method, programme, or technology that can make up for a lack of love for unbelievers,' warns Rick Warren.[5]

Just as you are engaging in a training programme for church leaders, should your church provide a more structured training programme for your deacons, stewards and the leaders of your various groups — children and young people, home groups, parents and toddlers, etc?

> And Jesus came and spoke to them, saying, 'All authority has been given to me in heaven and on earth. Go therefore and make disciples of all the nations, baptizing them in the name of the Father and of the Son and of the Holy Spirit, teaching them to observe all things that I have commanded you; and lo, I am with you always, even to the end of the age.' Amen (Matt. 28:18-20).

The church provides people with things they cannot find anywhere else in the world: the *gospel* for the forgiveness of sin; *worship* to bring them to God; *teaching* to build them up as disciples of Christ; *fellowship* to help them face life's problems; *service* to find and use their talents; and *evangelism* that they may fulfil their mission in the world. It is our responsibility to make these blessings readily available 'to all who are afar off, as many as the Lord our God will call' (Acts 2:39).

Organization

Organization fits people and activities together in the best ways to get work done. Being *efficient* is not the same as being *effective*: 'Efficiency is *doing things right*. Effectiveness is *doing the right things*.'[6]

Churches may be efficient in that they are well organized and maintain a full range of groups and activities. But while they generate a lot of *activity*, there is often little *productivity*. Energy is often wasted on inconsequential projects.

Church leaders, as overseers and facilitators, are ultimately responsible for *all* church activities. They are specifically accountable for the content and conducting of worship (including baptisms, the Lord's Supper, prayer meetings, marriages and funerals), the ministry of the Word of God throughout the church (from children's meetings to the gathered assembly) and the appointment of suitable persons to each office.

> And he [Christ] himself gave some to be apostles, some prophets, some evangelists, and some pastors and teachers, for the equipping of the saints for the work of ministry, for the edifying of the body of Christ (Eph. 4:11-12).
>
> ....according to the effective working by which every part does its share, causes growth of the body for the edifying of itself in love (Eph. 4:16).

Job description

It may be helpful to introduce the notion of a 'job description' or 'job profile' into the life of the church. All positions within the church could be clearly defined:

1. Description: what the goals are
                   what the means are
                   how the results are evaluated
2. Relationships: what you are responsible for
                   whom you are responsible to
                   who is responsible to you
                   what authority you have

Planning strategy

Leadership is 'the art of successfully achieving desired results through and with the energies of others'. 'Planning is programming to achieve clearly stated results.' Planning sets goals, considers alternative strategies, establishes the steps to be taken, anticipates problems and difficulties and prepares responses. Planning is crucial to the life of a church leader: plan your sermon preparation, your evaluation of church groups and activities, your co-ordination of others, your pastoral visits, your approach to problems, the answers you could give to likely questions and the Scripture passages you could use. Pastoral leadership involves motivating, delegating, supervising and evaluating the work of those you are called to lead.[7]

Planning strategy to achieve goals in church leadership
(see diagram on page 66)

Stage I: Goal

1. *State objective.* A clear goal needs to be established. The goal should be written down in a few, short sentences. What do you want to achieve?

2. *Gather information* from as many sources as possible, i.e. books, articles in journals, discussion with others. What has been done before? Who was involved? What was the outcome? What has been done in other churches?

3. *Analyse information.* Assess the relevance of the information to the particular goal.

4. *Revise objective.* New information may cause an abandonment, adjustment, or clarification of the original goal.

Stage II: Evaluation

1. *Restate the objective* determined at the conclusion of stage I.

2. *Anticipate problems,* such as how to maintain a united front, the pressures felt by any elders who dissent, or difficulties in implementing decisions.

3. *Foresee implications.* What are the likely reactions from the church, from specific families, from individuals? Think through: if this happens — then what? Ultimately this will save time and trouble.

4. *Review alternatives.* Reflect on all the different ways of achieving the goal. Weigh the alternatives. Choose the best, but remain open to change if it becomes desirable.

Planning strategy to achieve goals in church leadership

2
Gather information

I
Goal

3
Analyse information

1
State objective

4
Revise objective

2
Anticipate problems

II
Evaluation

3
Foresee implications

1
Restate objective

4
Review alternatives

2
Decide when

III
Strategy

3
Decide who

1
Decide action

4
Inform the church

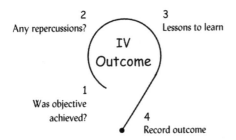

2
Any repercussions?

IV
Outcome

3
Lessons to learn

1
Was objective
achieved?

4
Record outcome

Stage III: Strategy

1. *Decide action to be taken.* Will this achieve the agreed goal?
2. *Decide when* that action should be taken.
3. *Decide who* is most appropriate to take the action.
4. *Inform the church* where necessary or desirable.

Stage IV: Outcome

1. *Was the objective achieved?*
2. *Any repercussions* — for individuals, the church or the eldership?
3. *Lessons to learn* for the eldership.
4. *Record outcome* — i.e. the agreed goal, reactions and results.

Communication

Communication within the leadership

Communication between church leaders is crucial. Discussion is a vital activity of the eldership. Good communication requires lucid explanation of thoughts and convictions, together with effective listening.

Whether you understand what your colleague is really saying, or whether you *just think* you understand, can be resolved through questions intended to clarify his meaning, and even by attempting to restate what your colleague has said. Understanding involves far more than merely hearing the words that are spoken. Some Christians have great difficulty in expressing what they want to say.

> The first one to plead his cause seems right,
> Until his neighbour comes and examines him
> (Prov. 18:17).
>
> The heart of the prudent acquires knowledge,
> and the ear of the wise seeks knowledge
> (Prov. 18:15).

> *I know you believe you understand what you think I said, but I am not sure you realize that what you heard is not what I meant.*

Elders should also listen carefully to themselves — noting their reactions to their colleagues when they differ from them. Be aware of what is going on in your own head and heart so that you respond in a truly Christian spirit. Is there a real difference of view, or is it just a matter of using different words to describe the same thing?

Communication with members collectively

> There shall come forth a Rod from the stem of Jesse,
> And a Branch shall grow out of his roots.
> The Spirit of the LORD shall rest upon him,
> The Spirit of wisdom and understanding,
> The Spirit of counsel and might,
> The Spirit of knowledge and of the fear of the LORD
> (Isa. 11:1-2).

Where appropriate, plans, and especially decisions, made by the eldership should be explained to the church as soon and as clearly as possible. A free flow of information is to be encouraged from the eldership to the church and from the members to the eldership. The analogy of sheep should not be pressed too far at this point. Unlike the four-legged variety, these 'sheep' *have the right to know* what their 'shepherds' are planning and the direction in which they are being led.

Assume that, if something is capable of being misunderstood, then it most certainly will be! Communicate clearly by the spoken *and* written word wherever possible.

Communication with members individually

When a member shares a concern with you, it is good to check that you understand the issue. This may be done quite simply by retelling the concern in your own words to the satisfaction of the member. Merely repeating the person's words verbatim indicates a good memory, not a clear understanding.

Church government

As J. Angell James says, 'The government of a Christian church is perfectly unique, it is a Christocracy, in which He is the supreme and only legislator; the New Testament is His code of laws; the pastor is His minister to explain and enforce by authoritative persuasion His laws upon the people; while they are to carry the law so explained and enforced, into effect, unless they can bring forward scriptural proof, that it is not a law of Christ.'[8]

Many evangelical churches emulate the political sphere of the Western world by adopting the democratic form of government. This means that all matters affecting the life of the church and its various departments are determined by majority vote at a regular meeting of church members. In practice there are serious problems with such a procedure. In the first place, a new convert has the same voting power as a mature and experienced believer. Secondly, a powerful personality can sway the meeting to vote in his particular way. Thirdly, relationships are often strained. Fourthly, hours are spent debating trivial issues. Finally, and most seriously, the eldership loses its biblical authority (Heb. 13:17; 1 Tim. 3:5; 5:17).

In spite of such difficulties of democracy there is another extreme to be avoided also: dictatorship. As democracy undermines biblical leadership, so dictatorship demoralizes and disheartens the people of God.

A third model, a combination of elders and gathered church, is explained by J. Angell James. He claims that the Lord Jesus Christ as 'the great Head of the church has provided a sufficient guard against democratic insubordination on the one hand, and priestly domination on the other'. Pastors rule by explaining the meaning of the laws of Christ, and showing their bearing on any specific case before the church. The flock are bound to the execution of the law thus expounded unless they can show scriptural grounds for another way of proceeding than the one recommended. 'They must, indeed, judge whether he has given a right exposition of the law. Still, they are not called specifically and officially to sit in judgement, but to give their consent to the execution of the law of Christ.'[9]

A careful combination has to be achieved between the eldership texts (Heb. 13:17; 1 Tim. 3:4-5; 5:17) and the texts which speak of the gathered church (Matt. 18:17; Acts 6:2-3; 15:22; 1 Cor. 5:4-5). We must take seriously the *ruling* verbs used in connection with elders, and avoid the democratic church-meeting pattern. Under the guidance of the elders, the gathered church appoints officers, receives and removes members, hears disputes, chooses practical workers, endorses major plans and initiatives, authorizes gifts and approves the annual accounts.

The elders who are among you I exhort, I who am a fellow elder and a witness of the sufferings of Christ, and also a partaker of the glory that will be revealed: Shepherd the flock of God which is among you, serving as overseers, not by compulsion but willingly, not for dishonest gain but eagerly; nor as being lords over those entrusted to you, but being examples to the flock; and when the Chief Shepherd appears, you will receive the crown of glory that does not fade away (1 Peter 5:1-4).

Obey those who rule over you, and be submissive, for they watch out for your souls, as those who must give account. Let them do so with joy and not with grief, for that would be unprofitable for you (Heb. 13:17).

You know that the rulers of the Gentiles lord it over them, and those who are great exercise authority over them. Yet it shall not be so among you; but whoever desires to become great among you, let him be your servant. And whoever desires to be first among you, let him be your slave — just as the Son of Man did not come to be served, but to serve, and to give his life a ransom for many (Matt. 20:25-28).

Whatever principles and procedures are adopted, whatever form of government is enacted, there must be confidence between the members in respect of each other's intentions and integrity. Behaviour between members must always be governed by spiritual considerations. Church meetings are notorious for the absence of the fruit of the Holy Spirit (Gal. 5:22-23). As C. H. Spurgeon's brother noted in 1869, without confidence between elders, deacons and members, 'No rules, human or divine, can make them work harmoniously.'[10]

Church membership

Some churches resist a formal church membership by reasoning that, firstly, the Scriptures are highlighted as the governing standard rather than a church constitution; secondly, arguments as to the interpretation of procedures are avoided; thirdly, new Christians are not required to assent to 'Articles of Faith' which they are unlikely to understand; and, fourthly, membership of the church is a living reality (those actually attending and participating), rather than a formality of names on paper.

There are decided disadvantages in this position:

1. How do new Christians understand what is required of them in their commitment to the church?

2. How do Christians arriving from churches in other towns register their acceptance of responsibility towards their new church community?

3. Issues of pastoral care and discipline are difficult to practise: the shepherd has responsibilities to the flock, and the flock responsibilities towards the shepherd. Both shepherd and flock need to be clearly identified in the local setting.

To quote Rick Warren, 'As Christians we're called to *belong*, not just to *believe*. We are not meant to live lone-ranger lives; instead, we are to belong to Christ's family and be members of his body.'[11]

An increasing number of believers are only loosely connected to a local church. The notion is growing of a 'floating church population' where Christian individuals and families exercise total flexibility as to where, when and how they worship and serve God. Allegiance to one body of believers is thought to be neither desirable nor obligatory. They attend where they want, when they want. Such people ignore the leadership role of pastors, though they still expect visits and support. Their commitment is to the universal church, not to a particular local church. This is contrary to the activity of the early believers (Acts 2:42).

The Bible teaches that Christians are to be committed to one local church. Consequently some form of official qualification and recognition of membership of that local church is essential.

In the New Testament the church (*ekklesia*) is a group of people who love, worship and serve the living God through his Son Jesus Christ. The word 'church' refers sometimes to the universal church (seventeen times, e.g. Matt. 16:18; Eph. 5:23-27) and at all other times to a local gathering of believers (ninety times, e.g. Matt. 18:17; Acts 13:1; 14:23) who worship, work and witness together.

The people of God are likened to a flock of sheep (John 10:14-16), a temple of living stones (Eph. 2:21; 1 Peter 2:5), members of a physical body (1 Cor. 12:12,27), a household or family (Gal. 6:10; Eph. 2:19; 1 Tim. 3:15), a bride (Rev. 19:7-8), a royal priesthood (1 Peter 2:9) and branches united to a vine (John 15:5).

> Then those who gladly received his word were baptized; and that day about three thousand souls were added to them. And they continued steadfastly in the apostles' doctrine and fellowship, in the breaking of bread, and in prayers... And the Lord added to the church daily those who were being saved (Acts 2:41-42,47).
>
> And they were all with one accord in Solomon's Porch. Yet none of the rest dared join them, but the people esteemed them highly. And believers were increasingly added to the Lord, multitudes of both men and women (Acts 5:12-14).

Peter Masters argues that some of these metaphors are general and include the entire, universal church of God, but three are used specifically to describe an individual, local church: the images of a temple, a body and a family. These '... are descriptions of local churches [and] prove beyond all possible doubt that believers have an obligation to seek church membership. These metaphors or illustrations also show very clearly that such church membership involves a *pledge* or *commitment* to the local church. It involves a humble acceptance of the *doctrines, discipline and service* of the local church.'[12]

> A bride
> A temple
> A flock of sheep
> Branches of a vine
> A royal priesthood
> Parts of a body
> A family

Does the context of the three metaphors justify this conclusion?

A more convincing reason is presented by Wayne Mack and David Swavely when they assert that 'The New Testament does not contain even a hint of someone who was truly saved but not a part of the local church.'[13] They base this conviction upon command, obligation and privilege.

The command for commitment

'If the church is the household of God, the pillar and support of the truth, the body for whom Christ died, and the current form of His kingdom and His people, then every person who claims to belong to Him must belong to the local church.'[14]

> And let us consider one another in order to stir up love and good works, not forsaking the assembling of ourselves together, as is the manner of some, but exhorting one another ... and so much the more as you see the Day approaching (Heb. 10:24-25).

All of the many instructions to the gathered church are meaningless if individual Christians are not committed to one local church. It should be instinctive to one who is united to Christ to endeavour to be united with a local company of Christ's people. Acts 5:12-14 suggests a distinction between a congregation, composed of believers and unbelievers, and a church, composed of believers who had joined the membership.

The obligation of obedience

Church membership makes it easier for the leaders of the church to shepherd the flock because:

1. Membership clarifies the difference between believers and unbelievers.
2. Membership causes the visible church to be a better reflection of the invisible church.
3. Membership is essential to an orderly administration of the church.
4. Membership provides an opportunity to educate people about the nature and distinctives of the church.

> And we urge you, brethren, to recognize those who labour among you, and are over you in the Lord and admonish you, and to esteem them very highly in love for their work's sake. Be at peace among yourselves (1 Thess. 5:12-13).

Erroll Hulse comments: 'It is obvious that we cannot obey elders unless they are specified, nor can elders rule unless there are specific people for whom they are responsible.'[15]

The privileges of partnership

Commitment to a local church provides opportunities for ministry, helpful service and loving accountability (1 Cor. 5).

'Leadership, teaching, evangelism, handling of funds, music, ushering, and even such seemingly mundane tasks as nursery care and grounds-keeping should be performed by those who love Christ and are committed to the church. That is because the members of the body are gifted by the Spirit for the purpose of accomplishing the work of the ministry (1 Cor. 12; Eph. 4:11-16). One way to make sure that takes place is by making membership a requirement for such service.'[16]

The body can only develop in a manner pleasing to God when it is 'joined and knit together by what every joint supplies, according to the effective working by which every part does its share, causes growth of the body for the edifying of itself in love' (Eph. 4:16).

Being filled with the Holy Spirit is in evidence when believers are 'submitting to one another in the fear of God' (Eph. 5:21). Hence the local church is a community, and one which takes precedence over the individual.

> And when they had come and gathered the church together, they reported all that God had done with them, and that he had opened the door of faith to the Gentiles (Acts 14:27).

Church membership is implied when the church at Corinth is urged to exercise discipline of a wayward brother (1 Cor. 5:4-5). Peter Masters says this passage 'is of very great relevance for it describes how a special meeting of believers had the power to exclude from their company and privileges someone guilty of serious sin'.[17] The necessity for a proper membership structure in local churches is seen also in Matthew 18, where the Lord Jesus Christ gives the general principle for dealing with offences among believers.

> In the name of our Lord Jesus Christ, when you are gathered together, along with my spirit, with the power of our Lord Jesus Christ, deliver such a one to Satan for the destruction of the flesh, that his spirit may be saved in the day of the Lord Jesus (1 Cor. 5:4-5).

To quote Peter Masters once more, 'The Lord Jesus Christ has put into the hands of local churches an authority and responsibility which proves beyond all doubt that the local church must be a stable, properly defined, constituted, orderly community — not some kind of amoeba-like form, with no specific membership.'[18]

The following guidelines are those laid down by the Grace Baptist Assembly:

Recognition of a local church[19]

A local church is the company of Christian believers gathered together in one particular place by the work of God. It is properly distinguished by a membership which

   i. is committed to a clear affirmation of sound biblical doctrine (Acts 2:42; 1 Timothy 4:6-7,13,16; 6:20; 2 Timothy 1:13);

  ii. consists of those who have confessed, by believer's baptism, their faith in Jesus Christ as their own Lord and Saviour and are living a godly life (Acts 2:38; 10:47-48; Galatians 3:27; Acts 18:8; cf. 1 Corinthians 1:2);

 iii. is given, each to the other, in fellowship, prayer, worship, mutual service and evangelism (2 Corinthians 8:5; 1 Thessalonians 1:2,3,7-9; Acts 2:42);

 iv. is provided, under God, with an eldership to regulate and maintain the ministry of the Word, the regular observance of the ordinances, and the exercise of a biblical discipline (1 Timothy 3:1-7,15; 5:17; Titus 1:5-9).

Without these distinguishing marks, a group of believers does not form a properly constituted church.

The guide quoted above raises a number of questions:

1. Would the absence of an eldership mean that a group of believers could not be 'a properly constituted church'?

2. What would happen where churches were temporarily without elders?

3. Is there no place for paedobaptist believers? Must they establish another church in the town?

4. Is it true that the Scriptures require an elder to officiate at 'the regular observance of the ordinances'?

Church discipline

Elders are responsible to ensure that discipline is exercised according to the Scriptures. Their pastoral care includes the private application of the Scriptures in correcting those who are in doctrinal error (Titus 1:9), and confronting those who are living inconsistently with their Christian profession (1 Thess. 5:12). 'To admonish' or 'to train' at times requires reproof, correction and instruction in righteousness (2 Tim. 3:16). The church, not the elders, is the final disciplinary body (cf. Matt. 18:17; 1 Cor. 5:4-5).

Elders share responsibility with all other church members for the correcting of sinful behaviour, according to the principles laid down by our Lord (Matt.18:15-17). There is no suggestion that the 'one or two more' of verse 16 refers to elders. In fact it would seem wiser for these witnesses not to be elders. Perhaps the eldership should only be involved if and when the third stage is reached, and should not receive complaints from Christians about a third party without insisting that the first two stages of the procedures of Matthew 18:15-16 have been faithfully enacted.

> Moreover if your brother sins against you, go and tell him his fault between you and him alone. If he hears you, you have gained your brother. But if he will not hear, take with you one or two more, that 'by the mouth of two or three witnesses every word may be established'. And if he refuses to hear them, tell it to the church. But if he refuses even to hear the church, let him be to you like a heathen and a tax collector (Matt. 18:15-17).

> Brethren, if a man is overtaken in any trespass, you who are spiritual restore such a one in a spirit of gentleness, considering yourself lest you also be tempted (Gal. 6:1).

The goal of discipline is always to 'restore' the offender 'in a spirit of gentleness' (Gal. 6:1). 'The restoration of a fallen brother is not to be undertaken in a distant or haughty spirit, or in a hard, dictatorial, or censorious style, which dwells bitterly on the sin, or brings its aggravations into undue relief, or condemns in self-complacent severity the weakness which led to the fall.'[20]

The spirit of gentleness is full of compassion, though it must hold accountable; it seeks to bring relief even as it reasons in correction; it is faithful though full of sympathy (Prov. 27:6), true to the example of Christ, of whom it is said, 'A bruised reed he will not break, and smoking flax he will not quench' (Matt. 12:20).

Those restoring an erring brother must take due care lest they themselves fall under temptation (Gal. 6:1). This means being tempted in one of the following ways:

1. To arrogance and pride because they have not sinned in that particular way.
2. To harshness which exceeds the appropriate level.
3. To a similar sin. All are vulnerable (1 Cor. 10:12-13), for it is only by the grace of God that we are kept 'from stumbling' (Jude 24).

Christians are forbidden to go to civil law against each other. Where their differences cannot be resolved before the church they ought to accept the wrong and suffer the loss of their goods, so that the name of Christ is not dishonoured before the world (1 Cor. 6:1-8).

Conclusion

The well-being of the church lies very largely in the hands of its leadership. Leading by example, giving teaching and motivation, they are responsible to ensure that all things are done 'decently and in order' (1 Cor. 14:40). At the same time it can be a real delight for the people of God to worship, live and serve the Lord together (Ps. 16:2-3; 133:1). Like Peter on the Mount of Transfiguration, each believer can then say, 'Lord, it is good for us to be here' (Matt. 17:4). The reputation of such a spiritually healthy and happy church may well spread in the community and we might find our sleeves grasped by those who say, 'Let us go with you, for we have heard that God is with you' (Zech. 8:23).

5.
Pastoral visiting

Pastoral visiting

Please answer these questions before reading the articles, chapters and notes that follow.

What is pastoral visiting?

....

....

....

Is pastoral visiting taught in Scripture? (Cite Scripture in support of your answer.)

....

....

....

What hinders pastoral visiting?

....

....

....

What steps must be taken to prepare for this work?

....

....

....

Recommended reading

The papers listed below are written from differing, and initially convincing, viewpoints and therefore will stretch and train thinking and ability in handling Scripture.

Adams, J. E. 'The Shepherd Visits', *Shepherding God's Flock: a preacher's handbook on pastoral ministry, counseling, and leadership* (Phillipsburg, New Jersey: Presbyterian and Reformed, 1980), pp.75-84.

Adams, J. E. 'House Calling', *Shepherding God's Flock*, pp.85-97.

Baxter, R. 'The Manner of this Oversight', *The Reformed Pastor* (Edinburgh: Banner of Truth Trust, 1966), pp.111-24.

Oden, T. C. 'Pastoral Visitation', *Pastoral Counsel* (New York: Crossroad, 1989), pp.169-85.

Shedd, W. G. T. *Homiletics and Pastoral Theology* (London: Banner of Truth Trust, 1965), pp.340-55.

Pastoral visiting

No other trade or profession experiences the opportunity that is given to a pastor. He does not need to wait for an invitation to visit a family or an individual within the community of the church. Most will consider it a privilege for a pastor to call. Thomas Oden writes, 'Members of the congregation by tradition have implicitly issued an unwritten standing invitation to their minister to come on behalf of their spiritual welfare whenever it is felt to be in their interest.'[1]

Is pastoral visiting taught in Scripture?

The word translated 'care for' in Zechariah 11:16 (AV, 'visit') and 'attended to' in Jeremiah 23:2 (AV, 'visited') is *paqad* (rendered in Greek as *episkopeo*) and has two complementary shades of meaning: firstly, to examine by testing; and, secondly, to see that all is in order. A pastoral visit is conducted to see that faith is active and growing, and as an on-site review to check on present developments.[2] At its core 'visitation', in both Old and New Testaments, is *oversight that shows concern*.[3] It is caring enough to visit.

The Lord Jesus made frequent home visits (Luke 5:29; 7:36; 10:38; 14:1; Matt. 26:6). He was not restricted to visiting believers. He addressed a whole variety of people where they were — where they lived, worked or congregated (Matt. 9:9-10; Mark 4:1; 10:46; John 4:6-7).

> And the LORD said to me, 'Next, take for yourself the implements of a foolish shepherd. For indeed I will raise up a shepherd in the land who will not care for those who are cut off, nor seek the young, nor heal those that are broken, nor feed those that still stand. But he will eat the flesh of the fat and tear their hooves in pieces.
> 'Woe to the worthless shepherd, Who leaves the flock!'
> (Zech. 11:15-17).

> Therefore thus says the LORD God of Israel against the shepherds who feed my people: 'You have scattered my flock, driven them away, and not attended to them. Behold, I will attend to you for the evil of your doings,' says the LORD (Jer. 23:2).

> You know, from the first day that I came to Asia, in what manner I always lived among you, serving the Lord with all humility, with many tears and trials which happened to me by the plotting of the Jews; how I kept back nothing that was helpful, but proclaimed it to you, and taught you publicly and from house to house, testifying to Jews, and also to Greeks, repentance toward God and faith toward our Lord Jesus Christ (Acts 20:18-21).

The apostle Paul also made frequent home visits. John Calvin, commenting on Acts 20:20, says that Paul 'taught, not only all in the assembly, but individuals in their homes, as each man's need demanded. For Christ did not ordain pastors on the principle that they only teach the Church in a general way on the public platform, but that they also care for the individual sheep, bring back the wandering and scattered to the fold, bind up those broken and crippled ... heal the sick, support the frail and weak (Ezekiel 34:2,4).'[4]

Why is pastoral visiting necessary?

Only by visitation do pastors obtain an insight into the lives of the members of their congregation. Here people will open their hearts as they open their homes. They will share thoughts, feelings, hopes, fears, uncertainties and problems. Such visits may not only provide solutions, or point in the direction of solutions to these perplexities; they will also provide pastors with the means to pray with more relevance for the person concerned, and to preach with more usefulness and application.

> And daily in the temple, and in every house, they did not cease teaching and preaching Jesus as the Christ (Acts 5:42).

What hinders pastoral visiting?

> Woe to the shepherds of Israel who feed themselves! Should not the shepherds feed the flocks? ... The weak you have not strengthened, nor have you healed those who were sick, nor bound up the broken, nor brought back what was driven away, nor sought what was lost; but with force and cruelty you have ruled them (Ezek. 34:2,4).

The reluctance of some pastors to visit their flock in their homes may be due to a number of factors:

1. The *unreasonable demands* of some of the flock. We must learn to say 'no' to the incessant thoughtless requests of some members to make unnecessary home visits, giving veracity to the saying: 'The squeaky wheels gain all the oil.'

2. The difficulty of *apportioning time* to preparation, preaching, meetings, family, relaxation and being sufficiently flexible to be able to respond to needs faced by individuals or families within the church. The larger the church, the more frequent the demands.

3. The *restricted availability* of a large section of the community. With so many people out at work, fewer are at home during the day. Visiting wives in the absence of their husbands presents a danger of misunderstanding. Confining most pastoral visits to evenings results in considerable pressure upon other evening commitments and responsibilities.

Shepherds visit systematically

'What the church most needs today', says Jay Adams, 'is wise shepherding — shepherding that senses the true nature of the longings, the fears, the troubles and the acute needs of the flock. Creative shepherding will lead to guiding the flock into greener pastures and beside still waters.'[5]

In order to fulfil the duties identified by God through prophets like Zechariah and Ezekiel, it is necessary for pastors to set priorities, by visiting new converts, the broken-hearted, the unmotivated, those weak in faith, those struggling, backsliders, the offended and believing refugees. Primary concern for the spiritual welfare of the people of God must always be kept in mind. Other members of the church may be encouraged or directed to visit regularly and systematically those who are lonely, ill, housebound or infirm.

> Is anyone among you sick? Let him call for the elders of the church, and let them pray over him, anointing him with oil in the name of the Lord. And the prayer of faith will save the sick, and the Lord will raise him up. And if he has committed sins, he will be forgiven (James 5:14-15).

It may be far too idealistic to hope that time would permit the spiritual shepherds to cover the whole congregation on a regular basis.

Shepherds visit prayerfully

Pray before the visit

The pastoral visit begins in the study in prayer. Prayer is a vital part of the work. Richard Baxter warns that 'If we prevail not with God to give them faith and repentance, we shall never prevail with them to believe and repent. When our own hearts are so far out of order, and theirs so far out of order, if we prevail not with God to mind and help them, we are like to make but unsuccessful work.'[6]

Pray during the visit

Like Nehemiah in the presence of the king, listen, pray, speak (Neh. 2:4-5). Learn to seek the Holy Spirit's assistance even as you listen to the individual.

Pray afterwards

We pray for those we have visited with greater understanding of their needs and concerns. We seek to reflect upon our approach so that the Lord can teach us where we were unhelpful and in what ways we might improve.

Shepherds visit pastorally

> Therefore take heed to yourselves and to all the flock, among which the Holy Spirit has made you overseers, to shepherd the church of God which he purchased with his own blood (Acts 20:28).

We visit as shepherds of the flock. We are about the most important business in the world – the King's business. Therefore we 'go into a house upon a purely and wholly religious errand'.[7] 'Pastoral visitation of persons is one way of reflecting the glory of God's own visitation of humanity in Christ, seeking the lost, redeeming sin, mending pain.'[8]

With courtesy

Wait to be invited to sit down. Sit where directed. When visiting someone in hospital, always gain permission from the nursing staff to visit a patient. Never sit on the bed!

With diligence

'We are seeking to uphold the world, to save it from the curse of God, to perfect the creation, to attain the ends of Christ's death, to save ourselves and others from damnation, to overcome the devil, and demolish his kingdom, to set up the kingdom of Christ, and to attain and help others to the kingdom of glory. And are these works to be done with a careless mind, or a lazy hand?'[9]

Respecting confidentiality

Pastors are not to pry into the private lives of the people. Avoid giving the impression that you are conducting an inquisition. When personal information is shared, pastoral confidentiality must be scrupulously maintained within the eldership.

Do not listen to criticism about a third party. Point people to Matthew 18:15-17 and insist that they speak directly and exclusively with the person concerned.

> Moreover if your brother sins against you, go and tell him his fault between you and him alone. If he hears you, you have gained your brother. But if he will not hear, take with you one or two more, that 'by the mouth of two or three witnesses every word may be established'. And if he refuses to hear them, tell it to the church (Matt. 18:15-17).

To the point

Initial chitchat must be restricted. As William Shedd says, The pastor 'courteously concedes a few words to ordinary interests; but when this concession is made, he proceeds to the proper business of the occasion. This method brings the subject of the soul and its needs before the mind of a parishioner with a formal authority, that causes him to realize that it is no merely passing and secondary topic.'[10]

Christ-centred

Concentrate always upon the great central and fundamental truths of Christ. It is a spiritual work carried out purely for God and the salvation of souls. It is the major truths that save sinners and build up saints. Avoid interesting but unhelpful diversions (2 Tim. 2:16; 1 Tim. 4:6-7).

With tender love

> You know that the rulers of the Gentiles lord it over them, and those who are great exercise authority over them. Yet it shall not be so among you; but whoever desires to become great among you, let him be your servant. And whoever desires to be first among you, let him be your slave — just as the Son of Man did not come to be served, but to serve, and to give his life a ransom for many (Matt. 20:25-28).

Pastoral visiting is often painful. The general rule of body membership applies equally, if not more so, to pastors: 'And if one member suffers, all the members suffer with it' (1 Cor. 12:26). Pastors 'weep with those who weep' (Rom. 12:15). Backsliders need restoring 'in a spirit of gentleness' (Gal. 6:1). Those in error need correction and it is painful: 'My little children, for whom I labour in birth again until Christ is formed in you' (Gal. 4:19). There is a love bond between pastors and people where we are 'well pleased to impart ... not only the gospel of God, but also our own lives, because [they have] become dear to us' (1 Thess. 2:8).

With flexibility of approach

Adjust to different ages, experiences, intellects, cultures and levels of understanding. 'The pure milk of the word' is for 'newborn babes' (1 Peter 2:2), but 'solid food belongs to those who are of full age [i.e. mature]' (Heb. 5:14; cf. 1 Cor. 14:20). Shepherds follow the example of the Chief Shepherd in dealing with each person as an individual: e.g. Nicodemus (John 3:1-21), the woman of Samaria (John 4:1-42), little children (Mark 10:13-16), an adulteress (John 8:2-11), a lawyer (Matt. 8:19-20) and the Syro-Phoenician woman (Matt. 15:21-28).

With plain speech

All our conversation should be as plain and simple as possible. We want our hearers to understand what we say and what we mean. Paul declared, 'And I, brethren, when I came to you, did not come with excellence of speech or of wisdom declaring to you the testimony of God' (1 Cor. 2:1).

> And a servant of the Lord must not quarrel but be gentle to all, able to teach, patient, in humility correcting those who are in opposition, if God perhaps will grant them repentance, so that they may know the truth, and that they may come to their senses and escape the snare of the devil, having been taken captive by him to do his will (2 Tim. 2:24-26).

Direct where necessary

There will be times when it is appropriate to cut right through all pleasantries. As William Shedd says, the 'only true way for the pastor, when the proper time for it has come, and the pastoral visit is made, is to look him in the eye, and speak directly and affectionately upon the most momentous of all subjects'.[11]

> … holding fast the faithful word as he has been taught, that he may be able, by sound doctrine, both to exhort and convict those who contradict (Titus 1:9).

Representing the Saviour

> The elders who are among you I exhort, I who am a fellow elder and a witness of the sufferings of Christ, and also a partaker of the glory that will be revealed: Shepherd the flock of God which is among you, serving as overseers, not by compulsion but willingly, not for dishonest gain but eagerly; nor as being lords over those entrusted to you, but being examples to the flock; and when the Chief Shepherd appears, you will receive the crown of glory that does not fade away (1 Peter 5:1-4).

Visit 'in the name of Christ', working as an under-shepherd of 'that great Shepherd of the sheep' (Heb. 13:20), who is 'the Chief Shepherd' (1 Peter 5:4) and 'the good shepherd' who has given his life for these sheep (John 10:11). Consequently the pastor should always be conscious of representing Christ. Throughout the visit frequent references should be made to the Great Shepherd: to his will, his Word, his presence, his help and his counsel. We do not visit in our own name. This is not to be used as an opportunity to further our own reputation, but *his*!

As a good listener

A pastor needs to be aware of three persons intimately associated with all pastoral conversations: the one being visited, the Lord and the pastor himself. The pastor needs also to be self-aware and to recognize that his reactions and response may be coloured by his own experiences, past or present.

Willing to learn as well as to teach

A pastoral visit is often a blessing to the pastor as well as to the person visited (Rom. 1:11-12).

With great humility

There is no place for arrogance or conceit: 'Do not be wise in your own opinion' (Rom. 12:16). 'We must bear with many abuses and injuries from those to whom we seek to do good.'[12]

Depending on the Holy Spirit

Our whole work must be carried out under a deep sense of our own insufficiency, and of our entire dependence upon Christ.

Pastoral wisdom demands careful and accurate listening, coupled with:

The Spirit of wisdom and understanding,
The Spirit of counsel and might,
The Spirit of knowledge and of the fear of the LORD

(Isa. 11:2).

'If any of you lacks wisdom, let him ask of God, who gives to all liberally and without reproach, and it will be given to him' (James 1:5).

Grounded in Scripture

> All Scripture is given by inspiration of God, and is profitable for doctrine, for reproof, for correction, for instruction in righteousness, that the man of God may be complete, thoroughly equipped for every good work (2 Tim. 3:16-17).

The Scriptures should be read at the conclusion. Jay Adams advises that 'It is always good form to use the householder's Bible whenever it is readily available. The pastor then may insert a tract or pamphlet at the place from which he read so that the member may reread for himself at his leisure... Sometimes it is also necessary — when the Bible is not at hand — to jot down the Bible reference on a card or tract and leave that instead.'[13]

The shepherd will have a growing list of passages appropriate to various situations that he uses frequently with profit.

Conclusion

> Take heed to yourself and to the doctrine. Continue in them, for in doing this you will save both yourself and those who hear you (1 Tim. 4:16).

Pastoral visiting often raises issues that require further study in the Scriptures. Effective pastoral work will depend upon the constant interweaving of scriptural knowledge, theological reasoning, discussion with colleagues, sensitivity, perception and discernment.

As it is God's prescribed method for the growth and well-being of his people, we have confidence that good will come of our labours (1 Cor. 15:58).

In the words of Richard Baxter, 'If you would prosper in your work, be sure to keep up earnest desires and expectations of success.'[14]

6.
Leadership qualifications

Names describing church leaders
Biblical criteria
Christian character
A good husband
A good father
A good home manager
Able to teach
Boldness and courage

Leadership qualifications

Please answer these questions before reading the articles, chapters and notes that follow.

How can a church get to know a man and his family before extending an invitation to become an elder?

....

....

....

If a man is bitter about not being appointed an elder, how will you minister to him?

....

....

....

Where the wife is the dominant partner in the marriage of a leader, how can scriptural principles be honoured, and the wife not be frustrated?

....

....

....

Read 1 Timothy 3:2-7 and Titus 1:6-9. What do you need to rectify in your life, at home or at work?

....

....

....

Recommended reading

The papers listed below are written from differing, and initially convincing,
viewpoints and therefore will stretch and train thinking and ability in handling
Scripture.

Adams, J. E. 'The Pastor and his Family', *Reformation Today*, no. 81, 1984, pp.29-30.

Davies, J. K. 'A Man whose Children "Believe"?' *Reformation Today*, no. 63, 1981, pp.31-2.

Pond, C. C. 'The Character and Qualifications of an Elder', *Only Servants: a view of the place, responsibilities and ministries of elders in local churches* (London: Grace Publications Trust, 1991), pp.69-74.

Prime, D. *A Christian Guide to Leadership for the Whole Church* (Darlington: Evangelical Press, 2005), pp.23-45.

Summerton, N. *A Noble Task: eldership and ministry in the local church* (Carlisle: Paternoster Press, 1987, pp.24-5).

Sanders, J. O. *Spiritual Leadership* (Basingstoke, Marshall Morgan and Scott, 1967).

Whitworth, C. 'Elders,' *Reformation Today*, no. 72, 1983, pp.10-16.

Leadership qualifications

'Good pastors need a combination of qualities, not only an ability to listen: understanding, warmth, kindness, and so on. The implications for training are that good pastors, like good teachers, need to be identified at selection: the pastorally inept and insensitive are not going to improve significantly in training.'[1]

Names describing church leaders

Elders (*presbuteros*)

Associated with age, the name signifies maturity, especially moral and spiritual (1 Peter 5:1).

Overseers (*episkopos*)

They are to keep watch over the spiritual well-being of the sheep (Acts 20:28) 'as those who must give account' (Heb. 13:17).

Shepherds (*poimen*)

The emphasis falls upon 'feeding sheep' (Acts 20:28; cf. John 21:15-17) by causing them 'to lie down in green pastures ... beside the still waters', restoring their souls, and leading them 'in the paths of righteousness for his name's sake' (Ps. 23:1-3).

From Miletus he sent to Ephesus and called for the elders of the church... 'Therefore take heed to yourselves and to all the flock, among which the Holy Spirit has made you overseers, to shepherd the church of God which he purchased with his own blood' (Acts 20:17,28).

The elders who are among you I exhort, I who am a fellow elder and a witness of the sufferings of Christ, and also a partaker of the glory that will be revealed: Shepherd the flock of God which is among you, serving as overseers, not by compulsion but willingly, not for dishonest gain but eagerly; nor as being lords over those entrusted to you, but being examples to the flock; and when the Chief Shepherd appears, you will receive the crown of glory that does not fade away (1 Peter 5:1-4).

Teachers (*didaskolos*)

They give instruction by rightly handling 'the word of truth' (2 Tim. 2:15), declaring 'the whole counsel of God' (Acts 20:27) and preaching the word 'in season and out of season', so as to 'convince, rebuke, exhort, with all long-suffering and teaching' (2 Tim. 4:2).

Leaders (*proistemi*)

This comes from a word which means 'to stand before'. Shepherds lead the church of God. The word 'rule' (1 Tim. 3:5; 5:17) carries no connotations of 'ruling over', but means being out in front, in the sense that they have gone further, know where they are going and are showing the direction because they are following Christ (cf. 1 Cor. 11:1).

Stewards (*oikonomos*)

They are 'slaves' entrusted with the management of the household, responsible to the Master of the house (Titus 1:7; cf. Heb. 3:5-6).

> Preach the word! Be ready in season and out of season. Convince, rebuke, exhort, with all long-suffering and teaching (2 Tim. 4:2).
>
> Let the elders who rule well be counted worthy of double honour, especially those who labour in the word and doctrine (1 Tim. 5:17).
>
> Let a man so consider us, as servants of Christ and stewards of the mysteries of God. Moreover it is required in stewards that one be found faithful (1 Cor. 4:1-2).

All the terms are interchangeable to emphasize a variety of functions performed by the same group of men (Acts 20:17,28; Titus 1:5,7; 1 Peter 5:1-4).

Biblical criteria

(The numbers indicate the order in which the characteristics occur in the passage)

1 Timothy 3:1-7
1. Blameless
2. Husband of one wife
3. Temperate
4. Sober-minded
5. Of good behaviour

Titus 1:6-9
1. Blameless
2. Husband of one wife
6. Not quick-tempered
12. Sober-minded

> This is a faithful saying: if a man desires the position of a bishop [overseer], he desires a good work. A bishop then must be blameless, the husband of one wife, temperate, sober-minded, of good behaviour, hospitable, able to teach;

6. Hospitable
7. Able to teach
8. Not given to wine
9. Not violent
10. Not greedy for money
11. Gentle
12. Not quarrelsome
13. Not covetous
14. Good home manager
15. With submissive children
16. Mature – not a novice
17. Of good testimony outside

10. Hospitable
7. Not given to wine
8. Not violent
9. Not greedy for money
15. Self-controlled
3. With faithful children
4. A steward of God
5. Not self-willed
11. Lover of what is Good
13. Just
14. Holy
16. Of sound doctrine
17. Able to correct error

> not given to wine, not violent, not greedy for money, but gentle, not quarrelsome, not covetous; one who rules his own house well, having his children in submission with all reverence (for if a man does not know how to rule his own house, how will he take care of the church of God?); not a novice, lest being puffed up with pride he fall into the same condemnation as the devil. Moreover he must have a good testimony among those who are outside, lest he should fall into reproach and the snare of the devil (1 Tim. 3:1-7).
>
> … if a man is blameless, the husband of one wife, having faithful children not accused of dissipation or insubordination. For a bishop [overseer] must be blameless, as a steward of God, not self-willed, not quick-tempered, not given to wine, not violent, not greedy for money, but hospitable, a lover of what is good, sober-minded, just, holy, self-controlled, holding fast the faithful word as he has been taught, that he may be able, by sound doctrine, both to exhort and convict those who contradict (Titus 1:6-9).

J. O. Sanders comments: 'It should be observed that it is not the *office of overseer* but the *function of overseeing* that Paul asserts is honourable and noble. This is the most privileged work in the world, and its glorious character should be an incentive to covet it since, when sought from highest motives, it yields both present and eternal dividends. In Paul's times, only deep love for Christ and genuine concern for His church would provide men with a sufficiently powerful motive to aspire to this office. But in most lands today Christian leadership confers prestige and privilege; and unworthy ambition may easily induce self-seeking and unspiritual men to covet office.'[2]

The emphasis falls upon character (cf. Gal. 5:22-23; Eph. 4:1-3).

Christian character

You shall love the LORD your God with all your heart, with all your soul, and with all your mind (Matt. 22:37).

Since you have purified your souls in obeying the truth through the Spirit in sincere love of the brethren, love one another fervently with a pure heart… (1 Peter 1:22).

But the fruit of the Spirit is love, joy, peace, long-suffering, kindness, goodness, faithfulness, gentleness, self-control (Gal. 5:22-23).

But those who desire to be rich fall into temptation and a snare, and into many foolish and harmful lusts which drown men in destruction and perdition. For the love of money is a root of all kinds of evil, for which some have strayed from the faith in their greediness, and pierced themselves through with many sorrows (1 Tim. 6:9-10).

Give no offence, either to the Jews or to the Greeks or to the church of God, just as I also please all men in all things, not seeking my own profit, but the profit of many, that they may be saved. Imitate me, just as I also imitate Christ (1 Cor. 10:32 – 11:1).

Faith in God is demonstrated in many different ways: 'For as the body without the spirit is dead, so faith without works is dead also' (James 2:26; cf. Matt. 7:20). Church leaders lead first and foremost by example (2 Thess. 3:9). It is what they are that governs what they do; and what they are and do enables them to function effectively, or otherwise, in their church role.

Paul can write to Christians, 'The things which you learned and received and heard and saw in me, these do, and the God of peace will be with you' (Phil. 4:9). 'For though you might have ten thousand instructors in Christ, yet you do not have many fathers; for in Christ Jesus I have begotten you through the gospel. Therefore I urge you, imitate me' (1 Cor. 4:15-16). 'You know what kind of men we were among you for your sake. And you became followers of us and of the Lord' (1 Thess. 1:5-6).

Church leadership involves 'being examples to the flock' (1 Peter 5:3) in evident devotion to God the Father and the Lord Jesus Christ. This requires spiritual maturity, emotional stability, personal discipline, practical benevolence and generosity, coupled with social ease. As Paul comments elsewhere, in an entirely different context, 'And who is sufficient for these things?' (2 Cor. 2:16).

An elder must practise what he preaches. He is to be emulated only in so far as he is like Christ.

A good husband

'The husband of one wife' (1 Tim. 3:2; Titus 1:6)

'The emphasis is on *one* wife's husband, and the sense is that he have nothing to do with any other woman ... a man who is not strictly faithful to his one wife is debarred.'[3]

'The husband of one wife' cannot mean that he 'must be a married man', since both the Lord Jesus Christ and the apostle Paul suggest that singleness can be an advantage in Christian service (Matt. 19:12; 1 Cor. 7:7-8,25-27,32). Nor does it preclude a second marriage after the death of the first wife, since no discredit is ever associated with this in Scripture. Summerton supposes only the exclusion of 'the divorced and the sexually immoral'.[4] Clifford Pond says the restriction 'is primarily directed against polygamy', since the early converts were from paganism, in which it was not uncommon for a man to have multiple wives.[5]

> Husbands, likewise, dwell with them with understanding, giving honour to the wife, as to the weaker vessel, and as being heirs together of the grace of life, that your prayers may not be hindered (1 Peter 3:7).
>
> Husbands, love your wives, just as Christ also loved the church and gave himself for her (Eph. 5:25).
>
> Therefore let him who thinks he stands take heed lest he fall. No temptation has overtaken you except such as is common to man; but God is faithful, who will not allow you to be tempted beyond what you are able, but with the temptation will also make the way of escape, that you may be able to bear it (1 Cor. 10:12-13).

Since pastoral work involves contact with women, it is obviously important that the church leader should be above reproach in relationships. He must be living with consideration with his own wife, since the best safeguard from temptation is devotion to Christ *and* a happy marriage.

A good father

'Having faithful children' (Titus 1:6)

There is contention over the meaning of the word translated 'faithful'. The adjective *'pistos'* can be taken in two ways, active or passive:[6] as 'believing' — 'one who trusts' ('whose children believe', NIV); or as 'faithful' — 'one who can be trusted' ('having faithful children', NKJV, AV). John MacArthur argues strongly

> And you, fathers, do not provoke your children to wrath, but bring them up in the training and admonition of the Lord (Eph. 6:4).

that an elder's children are required to be 'in submission with all reverence' (1 Tim. 3:4) while young, and converted by the time they reach adulthood. He concludes that 'It is best to see Titus 1:6 as a reference to believing children, not faithful children.'[7]

There are teachers who would make exceptions. Clifford Pond writes, 'A distinction has to be made between unruliness and the immaturity and exuberance of youth. But we have to recognize that some children are naturally rebellious and difficult to handle despite belonging to the most godly family. The question then becomes, to what extent the parents have sought to teach and train their children. The end product can often be better than they deserve; it can also be much worse. This is the kind of mature evaluation that must be made when a man is suitable in every other respect.'[8]

Is this legitimate reasoning?

A good home manager

'One who rules his own house well' (1 Tim. 3:4)

The Greek word translated 'rule' is *proisthmi*, meaning management that involves 'planning, organization, enlistment, training and deployment of personnel, administration and discipline'. Only by adopting and firmly adhering to the biblical priorities can the pastor develop the sort of disciplined life necessary to carry on his roles as husband, father and pastor.[9]

> ... one who rules his own house well, having his children in submission with all reverence (for if a man does not know how to rule his own house, how will he take care of the church of God?)...
> (1 Tim. 3:4-5).

The pastor's failure in family responsibilities may lead to great suffering for his wife and children, and often for his church: '... responsibility in the congregation requires a subtle blend of love, guidance, counsel and authority, and these are the qualities required to lead an extended household.'[10]

Management skills are necessary to ensure a careful balance of responsibilities as husband, father, worker, worshipper, student, friend, pastor and teacher. No timetable can be constructed that will suit every elder in every family, in every year of his life. Careful adjustment and flexibility will be necessary and close consultation with his wife, since they are 'heirs together of the grace of life' (1 Peter 3:7).

If a man cannot manage his own family he will not be able to manage the family of God for the following reasons:

1. The principles and skills of management are the same wherever they are applied.

2. How can he succeed with the many in the church if he has failed with the few in the home?

3. Failure at home will create intolerable pressures against fulfilling his church responsibilities.

> He who is faithful in what is least is faithful also in much; and he who is unjust in what is least is unjust also in much (Luke 16:10).
>
> ... given to hospitality (Rom. 12:13).

4. Failure at home means he cannot be a worthy example for church families (cf. 1 Tim. 4:12).

5. Disregarding God's priorities here undermines the application of Scripture in other areas.

When his home is well managed he can readily extend hospitality to strangers (Heb. 13:2) and to church members (1 Peter 4:9), showing both kindness and a godly example of family life (1 Tim. 3:2; Titus 1:8).

Able to teach

> And he [Christ] himself gave some to be apostles, some prophets, some evangelists, and some pastors and teachers, for the equipping of the saints for the work of ministry, for the edifying of the body of Christ, till we all come to the unity of the faith and of the knowledge of the Son of God, to a perfect man, to the measure of the stature of the fulness of Christ; that we should no longer be children, tossed to and fro and carried about with every wind of doctrine, by the trickery of men, in the cunning craftiness of deceitful plotting ... (Eph. 4:11-14).

A balanced doctrinal grasp comes as a result of sound teaching (Titus 1:9), and, through their own prayerful study of the Scriptures pastors continue the process of being 'thoroughly equipped for every good work' (2 Tim. 3:17). Diligent and prolonged study will enable them to handle the word of truth with confidence and competence (2 Tim. 2:15). Through public preaching and private counsel from the Scriptures, the people of God will be 'rooted and built up in [Christ] and established in the faith' (Col. 2:7); and will no longer be 'children, tossed to and fro and carried about with every wind of doctrine' (Eph. 4:14). When error emerges the elders will be able to correct those who oppose the truth (Titus 1:9), for they are

> There shall come forth a Rod from the stem of Jesse,
> And a Branch shall grow out of his roots.
> The Spirit of the LORD shall rest upon him,
> The Spirit of wisdom and understanding,
> The Spirit of counsel and might,
> The Spirit of knowledge and of the fear of the LORD
> (Isa. 11:1-2).
>
> If you instruct the brethren in these things, you will be a good minister of Jesus Christ, nourished in the words of faith and of the good doctrine which you have carefully followed
> (1 Tim. 4:6).

'those who by reason of use have their senses exercised to discern both good and evil' (Heb. 5:14).

'Do not confuse knowledge with understanding. One may know much, yet understand little. Knowing is the fruit of diligence in study, while understanding is the fruit of using knowledge in life.'[11]

Being 'able to teach' (1 Tim. 3:2) — didaktikos = 'having the teaching gift', or being 'skilled in teaching' — is, significantly, the only qualification listed in either 1 Timothy 3 or Titus 1 which directly bears upon the pastor's function. In Titus it is more fully expressed: 'that he may be able, by sound doctrine, both to exhort and convict those who contradict' (Titus 1:9).

The question arises whether this stipulation that they must be 'able to teach' means that all elders should teach and preach in the worshipping assembly. If public preaching is not intended, then the teaching envisaged would be in personal counselling, leading small groups or teaching a Bible Class. Peter Masters seems to be of this opinion: 'In a growing number of churches ... the minister has been greatly undermined by the brand new idea that the elders of the church are all entirely equal, and that all of them are preaching elders. This novel arrangement has come about in the last twenty years and has gained popularity, curiously enough, in both Reformed and charismatic circles.'[12]

Some claim a distinction is drawn in 1 Timothy 5:17 between elders who rule and elders who rule and teach ('labour in the word and doctrine'). Though all elders must be 'able to teach', the amount of public preaching in which they engage will depend upon their ability, the time available for preparation and the demands of other duties. Charles Whitworth follows this line but raises another problem when he asserts: 'Clearly the amount of public ministry an elder in full-time employment will be able to undertake may be limited. But it would be a good rule of thumb that every elder

> Let the elders who rule well be counted worthy of double honour, especially those who labour in the word and doctrine
> (1 Tim. 5:17).
>
> Be diligent to present yourself approved to God, a worker who does not need to be ashamed, rightly dividing the word of truth
> (2 Tim. 2:15).

should have some part in the preaching ministry on a regular basis. Conversely, churches should not invite out of their membership to preach regularly those whom they are otherwise unwilling to endorse in the office of elder.'[13]

> I kept back nothing that was helpful, but proclaimed it to you, and taught you publicly and from house to house (Acts 20:2).

Pastors are to 'convince, rebuke, exhort, with all long-suffering and teaching' (2 Tim. 4:2). Their task is the 'equipping of the saints' so that the church is built up (Eph. 4:12) and believers are enabled and encouraged to 'grow in the grace and knowledge of our Lord and Saviour Jesus Christ' (2 Peter 3:18).

The people of God need to receive 'the pure milk of the word' (1 Peter 2:2), then 'solid food' (Heb. 5:14) and ultimately 'the whole counsel of God' (Acts 20:27).

Boldness and courage

Courage, says J. Oswald Sanders, is 'that quality of mind which enables men to encounter danger or difficulty with firmness, or without fear or depression of spirits'. He makes the following comments:

> The courage of a leader is demonstrated in his being willing to face unpleasant and even devastating facts and conditions with equanimity, and then acting with firmness in the light of them, even though it means incurring personal unpopularity. Human inertia and opposition do not deter him. His courage is not a thing of the moment, but continues until the task is fully done... People expect of their leaders courage and calmness in crisis. Others may falter and lose their heads, but not they. They strengthen their followers in the midst of shattering reverses and weakening influences.

A Spirit-filled leader will not shrink from facing up to difficult situations or persons, or from grasping the nettle when that is necessary. He will kindly and courageously administer rebuke when that is called for; or he will exercise necessary discipline when the interests of the Lord's work demand it.[14]

> For God has not given us a spirit of fear, but of power and of love and of a sound mind (2 Tim. 1:7).
>
> Speak these things, exhort, and rebuke with all authority. Let no one despise you (Titus 2:15).

Conclusion

> My brethren, let not many of you become teachers, knowing that we shall receive a stricter judgement (James 3:1).

Functioning as a church leader is 'a good *work*' (1 Tim. 3:1, emphasis added). It is not a task for the lazy or indolent. It is hard work. It takes time and effort. It is not to be taken up as if it were a hobby. A man's obligation to his business, career, or employment, may well preclude him from eldership even when all other requirements are ideally in place. Family commitments and health considerations may also rule out his appointment.

Elders are often appointed because of their age, because they have worked hard and faithfully over many years, because they are respected for their godliness, or simply because there is a vacancy that *someone* must fill. The qualifications of Scripture cannot be ignored without great damage ultimately resulting to the church of Christ. It is better not to appoint anyone than to appoint the wrong one. Church leadership is not a position of honour given for long service to the church. Nor is it to be regarded as an office for exercising power and authority over the paid elder, or over the church.

Church leadership necessitates maturity and experience. It is not a task for the beginner, no matter how enthusiastic and insistent he may be (1 Tim. 3:6). Maturity, spiritual understanding, emotional stability, humility and the fulfilment of all the other qualifications listed in 1 Timothy 3:1-7 and Titus 1:6-9 are required.

> Church leaders are answerable to God (see Heb. 13:17).

7.
The leader's personal life

The leader's personal life

How much time do you spend in private prayer?

....

Should you spend more time in private prayer?   Yes   No
If 'yes' what steps will you take?

....

....

Are you physically fit?   Yes   No
If 'no' what steps will you take?

....

....

Do you spend sufficient time alone with your wife?   Yes   No
If 'no' what steps will you take?

....

....

Do you spend sufficient time with your children?   Yes   No
If 'no' what steps will you take?

....

....

Identify and quantify the time you waste.

....

....

Recommended reading

The books and papers listed below are written from differing, and initially convincing, viewpoints and therefore will stretch and train thinking and ability in handling Scripture.

Adams, J. E. *Shepherding God's Flock: a preacher's handbook on pastoral ministry, counseling, and leadership* (Phillipsburg, New Jersey: Presbyterian and Reformed, 1980), pp.39-56.

Baxter, R. *The Reformed Pastor* (Edinburgh: Banner of Truth Trust), pp.53-86.

Berghoef, G. and De Koster, L. *The Elder's Handbook: a practical guide for church leaders* (Grand Rapids, Michigan: Christian's Library Press, 1979), pp.67-70.

Hamer, C. Being a Christian Husband; a biblical perspective (Darlington: Evangelical Press, 2005), pp. 61-73.

MacDonald, G. 'Squelched by Marriage: Have I nurtured my spouse's personality, or buried it?' *Christian Today International/Leadership Journal.* www.Leadershipjournal.net.

Marshall, C. 'A Flea in Your Ear: increasing your ministry,' *Briefing*, no. 186, pp.2-5.

Sanders, J. O. *Spiritual Leadership* (Basingstoke, Marshall Morgan and Scott), 1967, pp.75-93.

Smith, R. 'Making Decisions about Gospel Work,' *Briefing*, no. 186, pp.5-11.

The leader's personal life

'Take heed to yourself' (1 Tim. 4:16), for, as Robert Murray M'Cheyne says, 'According to the purity and perfection of the instrument, will be the success. It is not great talents God blesses so much as likeness to Jesus.'[1]

Even in your recreation remember that you are a church leader. When you are off parade you are still an officer in the army of Christ and you must conduct yourself as such.

Church leaders come under the severest attacks of Satan. As they are the ones most likely to do his kingdom the greatest damage, it is on them that he applies his greatest pressure. He may attack openly like a roaring lion in hostility, animosity and persecution (1 Peter 5:8). He may come subtly by transforming 'himself into an angel of light' (2 Cor. 11:14). When tempting to sin he has a ready ally within the heart (James 1:14-16). Woe betide us if we are 'ignorant of his devices'! (2 Cor. 2:11).

> Take heed to yourself and to the doctrine. Continue in them, for in doing this you will save both yourself and those who hear you (1 Tim. 4:16).
>
> Therefore take heed to yourselves and to all the flock, among which the Holy Spirit has made you overseers, to shepherd the church of God which he purchased with his own blood (Acts 20:28).

Personal holiness

> ... what manner of persons ought you to be in holy conduct and godliness, looking for and hastening the coming of the day of God (2 Peter 3:11-12).

While the Lord's graciousness is quite remarkable and outstanding in using unworthy vessels, nevertheless, as C. H. Spurgeon points out, 'We shall be likely to accomplish most when we are in the best spiritual condition ... we shall usually do our Lord's work best when our gifts and graces are in good order.'[2] Lead a life 'worthy of the calling with which you were called', writes the apostle Paul (Eph. 4:1), for the greatest hindrance to our leadership will be our lack of Christlikeness. Only as we are like him will we command the respect and earn the love of his people. Our personal character should agree in all respects with our profession of faith — in morality, honesty and integrity.

Elders are to be 'blameless' (1 Tim. 3:2). In this we must guard the 'inner man, that Christ may dwell in [our] hearts through faith' (Eph. 3:16-17). The presence of Christ's Spirit in the heart drives out all evils, since it is 'out of the heart' that 'proceed evil thoughts, murders, adulteries, fornications, thefts, false witness, blasphemies' (Matt. 15:19).

Take care in even the small details of your behaviour — unpaid debts, delayed payments, unpunctuality, gossiping, petty arguments, and all the other little vices which fill the ointment with flies.

> Dead flies putrefy the perfumer's ointment,
> And cause it to give off a foul odour;
> So does a little folly to one respected for wisdom and honour
> (Eccles. 10:1).

The first church leaders were 'full of the Holy Spirit' (Acts 6:3,5; 4:8,31; 13:9). All Christians are urged to 'be filled with the Spirit' (Eph. 5:18). The fulness of the Spirit is an essential and indispensable experience for spiritual leadership. The Spirit is not to be 'grieved' by our sinful behaviour (Eph. 4:30), nor is he to be 'quenched' by our resisting his promptings (1 Thess. 5:19).

Private prayer

If anyone is exhorted to 'pray without ceasing' (1 Thess. 5:17), it is certainly the church leader. He has peculiar temptations, special trials, singular difficulties and heavy responsibilities. In personal holiness, in preaching and teaching, in counselling and pastoral work, in projects and decisions, he needs the wisdom of God, and he knows how the deficiency is to be made up (James 1:5).

As Samuel Chadwick says, 'The reason so many people do not pray is because of its cost. The cost is not so much in the sweat of agonizing supplication, as in the daily fidelity to the life of prayer. It is the acid test of devotion. Nothing in the life of Faith is so difficult to maintain. There are those who resent the association of discipline and intensity with prayer...'[3]

Jacob was given the name 'Israel' because he 'struggled with God and ... prevailed' (Gen. 32:28). Elijah 'prayed earnestly' (James 5:17) — that is, literally, 'he prayed in praying'. His praying was real, sincere, heartfelt, full of faith. He provides the biblical illustration of

> The effective, fervent prayer of a righteous man avails much. Elijah was a man with a nature like ours, and he prayed earnestly that it would not rain; and it did not rain on the land for three years and six months. And he prayed again, and the heaven gave rain, and the earth produced its fruit (James 5:16-18).

> ## The content
> ## of prayer
>
> *ACTS* =
>
> *Adoration*
>
> *Confession*
>
> *Thanksgiving*
>
> *Supplication*

the truth that 'The effective, fervent prayer of a righteous man avails much' (James 5:16).

If any man were capable of living a life pleasing to God without prayer it would have been the Lord Jesus Christ. Yet the testimony to his prayer life is remarkable. He was pre-eminently a man of prayer (Mark 1:35; 6:46; Luke 5:16; 6:12; 9:28; John 17; Matt. 26:36-46). The Son of God, of the same nature as the Father, nevertheless 'was heard because of his godly fear' when 'he had offered up prayers and supplications, with vehement cries and tears' (Heb. 5:7).

J. Oswald Sanders says, 'True praying is a strenuous spiritual exercise which demands the utmost mental discipline and concentration.'[4]

The Master gave a clear pattern of prayer for his disciples to follow (Matt. 6:9-13). The first priority in prayer is always the honour and glory of God. Before any concerns for others or ourselves, his name, his will and his kingdom are of paramount importance. Only after prayers of worship, praise and thanksgiving do we request God's help for ourselves and others. The Saviour encourages our supplications when he says, 'Ask, and it will be given to you; seek, and you will find; knock, and it will be opened to you' (Matt. 7:7).

Coming 'boldly to the throne of grace ... we may obtain mercy and find grace to help in time of need' (Heb. 4:16). Church leaders come to the Father as *sons* of God first and then as *servants* of God. We are to be concerned about our *walk with* God before ever we are concerned about our *work for* God.

Prayer is essential to the life of faith. Once the Christian soldier is fully clad with spiritual armour, he is exhorted to be 'praying always with all prayer and supplication in the Spirit' (Eph. 6:18). We need the Holy Spirit's assistance in our prayer life (Rom. 8:26). His presence and power are to be sought through

> Now it came to pass, as he was praying in a certain place, when he ceased, that one of his disciples said to him, 'Lord, teach us to pray, as John also taught his disciples.' So he said to them, 'When you pray, say:
>
> 'Our Father in heaven,
> Hallowed be your name.
> Your kingdom come.
> Your will be done
> On earth as it is in heaven.
> Give us day by day our daily bread.
> And forgive us our sins,
> For we also forgive everyone who is indebted to us.
> And do not lead us into temptation,
> But deliver us from the evil one'
> (Luke 11:1-2).
>
> Matthew 6:13 adds:
> For yours is the kingdom and the power and the glory for ever.
> Amen.
>
> If you then, being evil, know how to give good gifts to your children, how much more will your heavenly Father give the Holy Spirit to those who ask him! (Luke 11:13).

prayer (Luke 11:13). We pray *for* the Spirit that we might pray *in* the Spirit (Jude 20).

Bible reading

Through prayer we speak to God; through Scripture God speaks to us. We cannot read, study, meditate upon and pray over God's Word too much. Here is the source of all godly counsel for ourselves and for those in our care (Ps. 1:1-2).

The church leader must distinguish, however, between the use of the Word of God for his private meditation and its use for public teaching. The one purpose is exclusively devotional, for the good of his soul; the other is at its best a mixture of devotional and expositional. The very real danger for those who regularly expound the Scriptures in public is that all study of Scripture may become sermon-related. Thus the reading for purely personal spiritual benefit can be neglected altogether. Martyn Lloyd-Jones warns: 'Do not read the Bible to find texts for sermons, read it because it is the food that God has provided for your soul, because it is the Word of God, because it is the means whereby you can get to know God. Read it because it is the bread of life, the manna provided for your souls' nourishment and well-being.'[5] But keep a small notebook always at hand to jot down anything that stands out or impresses itself upon you.

The Bible should be periodically read through from Genesis to Revelation. This is far more important than using Bible notes or consulting commentaries. Saturation with the Word of God is the best preparation for the church leader. It is vitally important 'to keep up the daily reading of considerable portions of the pure word of God, and so to keep Scriptural truth ... continually revolving in the mind'.[6]

The elder's personal walk with God, his preaching and teaching in the assembly and his private counsel and guidance will all be beneficially influenced by familiarity with 'the Word of life' (1 John 1:1).

> Oh, how I love your law!
> It is my meditation all the day...
> How sweet are your words to my taste,
> Sweeter than honey to my mouth!
> (Ps. 119:97,103).
>
> ... his divine power has given to us all things that pertain to life and godliness, through the knowledge of him who called us by glory and virtue, by which have been given to us exceedingly great and precious promises, that through these you may be partakers of the divine nature, having escaped the corruption that is in the world through lust (2 Peter 1:3-4).

Study

Self-discipline is essential to the church leader if he is to spend time in study. The financially supported elder, or the elder who has retired from secular employment, can so easily fritter away the time, since no one is watching his time-keeping and 'office hours' are non-existent. There will be no shortage of church members eager to spend (or waste) time with him, or to involve him in temporalities, if he is not extremely disciplined. The demands of family life can also easily encroach when a man lives without structure and discipline.

Church leaders who are also in secular employment have quite different demands on their time, but the need for self-discipline is no less urgent. Whereas the financially supported elder may organize his life so that his best hours are given to prayer and the study of God's Word, those without this privilege are forced into grasping a couple of hours here and there, usually at the end of a busy day!

All church leaders who desire to function well for God will work while others waste time, study while others sleep and pray while others play. This is the unwritten demand of eldership.

It takes considerable time and effort to study the Scriptures so as to 'shepherd [literally, 'feed as sheep'] the church of God' with the best spiritual food, 'the pure milk of the word' — that is, with 'sound doctrine' (Acts 20:28; 1 Peter 2:2; Titus 1:9; cf. 1 Tim. 4:13,15-16; 2 Tim. 2:15). Teaching the Word of God, and thereby pastoring the flock, is the major task of the elders. As

> Be diligent to present yourself approved to God, a worker who does not need to be ashamed, rightly dividing the word of truth (2 Tim. 2:15).

those who are 'able to teach', they need to be clear and accurate in communicating and applying doctrine, in order to nourish the sheep and the lambs (John 21:15-17; 1 Peter 5:2).

The indispensable quality which distinguishes the elder from the deacon is the ability to master Christian doctrine, to teach it, to recognize error and to debate effectively with those who teach falsehood (1 Tim. 3:2; Titus 1:9-16).

Time management

The busiest people seem to find time to do more things than do people who are not so busy. This is not simply because they delegate work, but because they have learned the secret of managing their own time well.

> See then that you walk circumspectly, not as fools but as wise, redeeming the time, because the days are evil. Therefore do not be unwise, but understand what the will of the Lord is (Eph. 5:15-17).
>
> To everything there is a season,
> A time for every purpose under heaven...
> (Eccles. 3:1).

Find out how you spend your time. Keep a careful record, over a three-week period, of how you spend the time not taken up by your job or profession. Analyse your findings in the light of scriptural priorities. The church leader must be meticulously careful in his selection of priorities: 'Think out a scale of values: the time required by your job, by your family, by essential recreation; the time due the Church, the community, your social obligations; the time required to stay alert to issues in the news, the issues in your country and community, to issues in the Church, the time essential to Bible study, meditation, and prayer. Consider essentials peculiar to your own circumstances, or those of your family, which require allocation of precious hours.'[7]

The chart on the next page identifies the numerous demands on a leader's time. Even so, it is the careful use of spare minutes that makes up the saved hours: 'Small spaces of time become ample and great by being regularly and faithfully employed. It is because time is wasted so regularly and uniformly, and not because it is wasted in such large amounts at once, that so much of human life runs to waste.'[8]

Where the demands upon your time are greater than the hours available it is necessary to delegate some responsibilities to others. Leadership is the art of ensuring that the work gets done — by someone! There is always sufficient time for us to do what God wills us to do. As the Lord Jesus challenges, 'Are there not twelve hours in the day?' (John 11:9).

Clifford Pond writes, 'A man's business commitments may be such that he would not be able to give the necessary time to this ministry unless he was willing and able to make changes. Health and family considerations may also be involved. A man may be entirely suitable and yet not be appointed if he is for some practical reason unable to fulfil this ministry.'[9]

To be a church leader in a manner that pleases the Lord requires great personal commitment and a readiness to make eldership a priority in Christian service. The demands are great: attendance at elders' meetings for prayer and discussion; thorough preparation for preaching and teaching; selected pastoral visitation; giving necessary leadership and guidance to congregational activities. A particular individual may have the character and gifts, and even the inclination to be an elder, but may not have the time.

Church leadership — demands on time

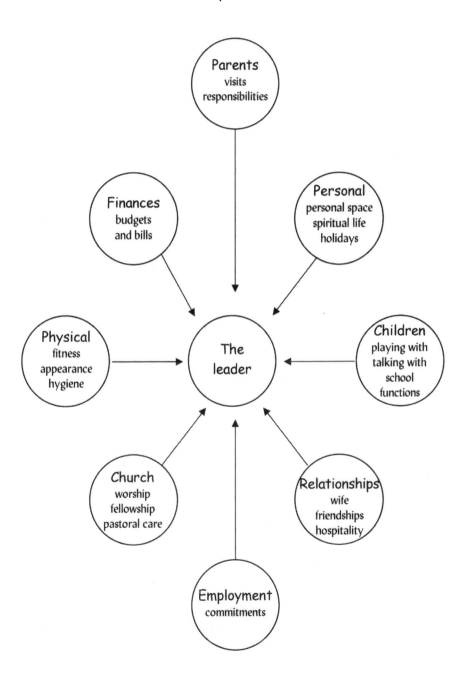

Few congregations will be able to guide as to the *wise* use of the church leader's time. Church members are notorious for making impossible demands upon their leaders. The only way for the elder to deal with the pressures of the work is for him to gain complete mastery over his time; otherwise he will soon find that:

1. The demands are unrealistic and cannot be met.
2. The result will be guilt for having failed to measure up to an unrealistic standard.
3. All of this may lead to confusion and frustration over the lack of appreciation and judgemental words and actions of others.[10]

Marriage

> Husbands, likewise, dwell with them with understanding, giving honour to the wife, as to the weaker vessel, and as being heirs together of the grace of life, that your prayers may not be hindered (1 Peter 3:7).
>
> Husbands, love your wives, just as Christ also loved the church and gave himself for her, that he might sanctify and cleanse her with the washing of water by the word, that he might present her to himself a glorious church, not having spot or wrinkle or any such thing, but that she should be holy and without blemish. So husbands ought to love their own wives as their own bodies; he who loves his wife loves himself. For no one ever hated his own flesh, but nourishes and cherishes it, just as the Lord does the church. For we are members of his body, of his flesh and of his bones (Eph. 5:25-30).

Church leaders lead by example. No area is more important than a leader's relationship with his wife. If he is not living with her in a considerate manner, then his relationship with his heavenly Father also suffers (1 Peter 3:7). Furthermore, everything that he may teach from the Scriptures about marriage, whether in public preaching or private pastoral care, will flounder if his own marriage is inconsistent with the Word. Here, as in so many areas, he must be able to say, 'Imitate me' (1 Cor. 4:16; cf. 11:1; Phil. 3:17; 1 Thess. 1:6).

In recent years the devil has successfully attacked the marriages of many church leaders. We are a prime target. When a church leader fails or falls he brings great dishonour upon the Lord, the gospel, the church, his family and upon himself. Brothers, 'love your wives, just as Christ also loved the church and gave himself for her' (Eph. 5:25).

'The wife is to give to her husband the submission she owes to Christ; but the husband is to give to his wife the love he receives from Christ... It is a love in which the husband will constantly sacrifice himself for the sake of his wife.'[11] As there is love in submission, so there is submission in love.

Lasting marriages are built neither upon a claustrophobic possessiveness nor upon uncommitted distance; finding and sustaining a balance between these two extremes which is comfortable for both parties 'requires patience, flexibility, forgiveness and understanding, and should never be taken for granted'.[12] Every satisfactory loving relationship has to work out 'a balance between availability and independence, dependence and autonomy, closeness and separation'.[13]

A married couple's experience of genuine oneness will be determined by the health of their communication system. A sound husband-and-wife relationship is impossible apart from good communication. 'Healthy marriages are those where couples communicate openly about issues and feelings they want discussed without fearing they will hurt or be unduly hurt in the process.'[14]

Good communication is essential. In every act of communication there are two components: the content of the message and the feeling behind what is said. Knowing what is in your wife's mind, without being told, requires you to be a clairvoyant; expecting her to know what is in *your* mind requires from her a mind-reading act.[15]

> Let the husband render to his wife the affection due her, and likewise also the wife to her husband. The wife does not have authority over her own body, but the husband does. And likewise the husband does not have authority over his own body, but the wife does. Do not deprive one another except with consent for a time, that you may give yourselves to fasting and prayer; and come together again so that Satan does not tempt you because of your lack of self-control (1 Cor. 7:3-5).
>
> Have you not read that he who made them at the beginning 'made them male and female', and said, 'For this reason a man shall leave his father and mother and be joined to his wife, and the two shall become one flesh'? So then, they are no longer two but one flesh. Therefore what God has joined together, let not man separate (Matt. 19:4-6).

Family life

How many church leaders have ruined their ministry through an unwillingness to train their children? 'A foolish son is the ruin of his father' (Prov. 19:13). Managing 'his own house well, having his children in submission with all reverence' (1 Tim. 3:4), is an essential prerequisite in the choice and appointment of an elder and it is equally necessary for him to *maintain* that management.

The first essential of family life is secure, loving relationships. A family holds together and functions effectively only where there is genuine love between its members.

The atmosphere of the home, the attitude and behaviour of parents towards each other and towards their children and the expressions of love and care should provide an ethos where a standard of behaviour is expected and deviation is not overlooked.

An elder should lead his children by example, expecting obedience, truthfulness and consideration from infancy.

Guidelines to child-raising

1. Spend time with your children (Deut. 6:7).
2. Avoid favouritism.
3. Avoid inconsistency (Matt. 5:37).
4. Maintain parental unity.
5. Expect obedience (Col. 3:20).
6. Discipline out of love (Heb. 12:6).
7. Discipline as soon as possible (Prov. 13:24).
8. Explain where possible (Prov. 29:15).
9. Avoid harsh punishment (Col. 3:21).
10. Avoid excessive discipline (Prov. 19:18).
11. Keep commands to a minimum (Eph. 6:4).
12. Allow freedom within bounds.
13. Do not withdraw love (1 Cor. 13:8).

Though an elder cannot convey saving grace to his children, at least he can enforce restraints where necessary and so be free of the charge of honouring his children more than he honours God (1 Sam. 2:29).

> Hear, O Israel: The LORD our God, the LORD is one! You shall love the LORD your God with all your heart, with all your soul, and with all your strength. And these words which I command you today shall be in your heart. You shall teach them diligently to your children, and shall talk of them when you sit in your house, when you walk by the way, when you lie down, and when you rise up (Deut. 6:4-7).
>
> And you, fathers, do not provoke your children to wrath, but bring them up in the training and admonition of the Lord (Eph. 6:4).
>
> Fathers, do not provoke your children, lest they become discouraged (Col. 3:21).

Relaxation and exercise

Our bodies are the dwelling place of the Holy Spirit. It is therefore imperative that we take good care of them, that we might 'glorify God' in our body and in our spirit, 'which are God's' (1 Cor. 6:20).

Taking good care of the body requires a balanced diet, an orderly and adequate pattern of sleep and regular exercise. It should be visibly evident to all that the church leader exercises self-control in regard to food. Avoiding obsessions, he will eat neither too much nor too little. He is to be governed by the principle: 'Whatever you do, do all to the glory of God' (1 Cor. 10:31).

Every workman knows the importance of keeping his tools in good order. In a very real sense pastors are their own tools. We cannot do our work well unless we keep ourselves in good condition.

While the apostle Paul drew a right comparison between bodily exercise and godliness (1 Tim. 4:8), he was not intending to decry the importance of bodily exercise. After all, he himself walked hundreds of miles in fulfilment of his evangelistic commission. Those who do not undertake physical exertion in their daily work should build into their schedule regular periods of appropriate exercise. You may even find the activity enjoyable! Once again the rule is to avoid obsession and resist becoming enslaved.

Engaging in sporting activity may also enable the church leader to interact with non-church folk, especially men who would not normally enter a church building. Two benefits then ensue: exercise and contact with the world. Care will need to be taken, since 'Evil company corrupts good habits' (1 Cor. 15:33). Nevertheless the Lord Jesus achieved the balance and earned a reputation as 'a friend of ... sinners' (Matt. 11:19), while yet remaining 'holy, harmless, undefiled, separate from sinners' (Heb. 7:26).

The mind needs recreation and refreshment as well as the body. There is no value in overworking ourselves into a state of physical, mental and emotional exhaustion. Prolonged fatigue makes Christians more vulnerable to Satan and the old sinful nature, more liable to error in pastoral duties, more susceptible to illness and disease and more likely to die prematurely.

A change of environment, change of pace and change of mind may be achieved by a holiday, a short activity break (such as a work-out, walking, or golf), or a weekly sports match. These activities may make all the difference to an elder heavily committed to his

---

Therefore, whether you eat or drink, or whatever you do, do all to the glory of God (1 Cor. 10:31).

I beseech you therefore, brethren, by the mercies of God, that you present your bodies a living sacrifice, holy, acceptable to God, which is your reasonable service (Rom. 12:1).

For bodily exercise profits a little, but godliness is profitable for all things, having promise of the life that now is and of that which is to come (1 Tim. 4:8).

I wrote to you in my epistle not to keep company with sexually immoral people. Yet I certainly did not mean with the sexually immoral people of this world, or with the covetous, or extortioners, or idolaters, since then you would need to go out of the world (1 Cor. 5:9-10).

And he said to them, 'Come aside by yourselves to a deserted place and rest a while.' For there were many coming and going, and they did not even have time to eat. So they departed to a deserted place in the boat by themselves (Mark 6:31-32).

work and also deeply engrossed in the problems and projects of the church. 'Returning refreshed, coming back to the work from a new perspective can change one's whole outlook.'[16]

Conclusion

Church leadership is the most important and the most demanding task entrusted to any Christian. We follow a Saviour who was able to say, 'I have finished the work which you have given me to do' (John 17:4). The apostle Paul also said, 'I have fought the good fight, I have finished the race, I have kept the faith' (2 Tim. 4:7). Each elder should be able to say that 'The Saviour "loved me and gave himself for me" (Gal. 2:20); consequently there is nothing that I would not do for him, and nowhere I would not go for him.' As David declared to the Lord, 'My times are in your hand' (Ps. 31:15). Time is so important that we need to measure it by days rather than years and to pray with Moses: 'So teach us to number our days, that we may gain a heart of wisdom' (Ps. 90:12).

The questions remain. Are you using the time entrusted to you, which is really Christ's time, to its best advantage? Are there ways in which you could reapportion your work to make more hours available for the specific work of ministry? What is more important than telling others the news of Christ and building his church? Are you choosing the soft option, rather than giving your maximum in the fulfilment of the purposes of God?[17]

We should live for the day when we hope to hear him say, 'Well done, good and faithful servant... Enter into the joy of your lord' (Matt. 25:23).

8.
Preaching and teaching

Preaching and teaching

Please answer these questions before reading the articles, chapters and notes that follow.

What sermons do you most remember and why?

....

....

....

Is preaching a special gift from God or a skill that may be learned?

....

....

....

Are you a preacher? .... How do you know? ....

....

....

....

What is the difference between preaching and teaching? (Cite Scripture in support of your answer.)

....

....

....

....

Recommended reading

The books and papers listed below are written from differing, and initially convincing, viewpoints and therefore will stretch and train thinking and ability in handling Scripture.

Adam, Peter. 'Arguing for Expository Preaching,' *The Rutherford Journal of Church and Ministry*, issue 13.1, Spring 2006, pp.4-7

Packer, J. I. 'Puritan Preaching', *Reformation Today*, no. 68, July/August 1982, pp.3-8.

Robinson, H. W. 'The Shapes Sermons Take', *Biblical Preaching: the development and delivery of expository messages* (Grand Rapids, Michigan: Baker, 1980), pp.115-34.

Robinson, H. W. 'How to Preach so People will Listen', *ibid.*, pp.191-208.

Sermons to analyse

Wesley, J. 'The Almost Christian,' *Fifty-Three Sermons* (London: Wesleyan Methodist Book-Room, no date), pp.18-26.

Wesley, J. 'The Use of Money' , *ibid.*, pp.702-15.

Preaching and teaching

'Who then is that faithful and wise steward, whom his master will make ruler over his household, to give them their portion of food in due season?' (Luke 12:42).

The primary task of shepherds is to feed sheep — to cause them 'to lie down in green pastures' (Ps. 23:2). 'Feeding' in this context means imparting 'knowledge and understanding' from God's Word (Jer. 3:15). The Word of God is often compared to food: honey (Ps. 119:103), milk (1 Peter 2:2; 1 Cor. 3:2, Heb. 5:12-13), solid food (1 Cor. 3:2; Heb. 5:12,14) and wheat (Jer. 23:28).

> Woe to the shepherds of Israel who feed themselves! Should not the shepherds feed the flocks? You eat the fat and clothe yourselves with the wool; you slaughter the fatlings, but you do not feed the flock. The weak you have not strengthened, nor have you healed those who were sick, nor bound up the broken, nor brought back what was driven away, nor sought what was lost; but with force and cruelty you have ruled them (Ezek. 34:2-4).

Equipping the saints

> And I will give you shepherds according to my heart, who will feed you with knowledge and understanding (Jer. 3:15).

Pastors and teachers are among the gifts given to the church of Christ. They are responsible 'for the equipping of the saints for the work of ministry, for the edifying of the body of Christ, till we all come to the unity of the faith and of the knowledge of the Son of God' (Eph. 4:12-13). This can only be achieved through the faithful preaching and teaching of the Word of God, thus educating the people in 'sound doctrine' (Titus 1:9; cf. 1 Tim. 4:13,15-16; 2 Tim. 2:15).

Pastors, as teachers, are 'stewards of the mysteries of God', trusted servants responsible for the distribution of 'food' to the Master's family (1 Cor. 4:1-2). The first benefit of such 'sound doctrine' is that the saints under their responsibility are built up in their faith and become less and less vulnerable to false teaching (Eph. 4:14). The second benefit is that they become more and more competent in the performance of their own ministries for the Lord, whether evangelizing the unsaved, instructing children, guiding youth, caring for the elderly, or preparing for their duties as the next church leaders.

C. H. Spurgeon once said, 'Reverently hearing the word exercises our humility, instructs our faith, irradiates us with joy, inflames us with love, inspires us with zeal, and lifts us up towards heaven.'[1]

Many professing believers appear to have lost confidence in preaching. Even those who are preachers appear to undervalue the importance of preaching as the means that God has appointed for communicating truth. Some church leaders have even convinced themselves that the ability to preach depends on having certain special qualities (e.g. fluency, sufficient Bible knowledge) which they say they do not possess. This deficiency does not drive them to greater endeavours and harder work, but serves as an excuse for lethargy.

Part of the explanation for this negative view of preaching may be, as Jim Packer asserts, that there has been much 'non-preaching' in our pulpits. Either there has been a failure to explain the Bible; or, if it is explained, a failure to apply its truths; or else, the preaching has consisted of a revealing of the preacher's opinion rather than declaring a message from God.[2]

Preaching and teaching

> Then Paul dwelt two whole years in his own rented house, and received all who came to him, preaching the kingdom of God and teaching the things which concern the Lord Jesus Christ with all confidence, no one forbidding him (Acts 28:30-31).
>
> For there is one God and one mediator between God and men, the man Christ Jesus, who gave himself a ransom for all, to be testified in due time, for which I was appointed a preacher and an apostle — I am speaking the truth in Christ and not lying — a teacher of the Gentiles in faith and truth (1 Tim. 2:5-7).

The difference between preaching and teaching is not immediately obvious in Scripture.

The word 'preach' translates two quite different words in the Greek: *kerusso* and *euangelizo*. The first word, *kerusso*, means 'to herald', 'to speak with authority', 'to announce demands', or 'to declare facts' (e.g. Luke 9:2). The word 'preacher' always translates *kerux*, which is the noun form of this verb, and hence means 'a herald' (1 Tim. 2:7; 2 Tim. 1:11; 2 Peter 2:5). The second word, *euangelizo*, focuses on the message as good news or glad tidings and is used for any verbal communication of the gospel of Christ (e.g. Luke 4:43; Acts 8:4; Rom. 1:15).

By contrast the word 'teach' (*didasko*) involves explanation, detailed instruction, and often close reasoning (Luke 13:10; Matt. 28:20).

> Paul and Barnabas also remained in Antioch, teaching and preaching the word of the Lord, with many others also (Acts 15:35).

'Preaching,' as either heralding or announcing good news, is God's revealed way of making himself and his salvation known to us (Mark 13:10; 1 Cor. 1:17-24; Rom. 10:13-14,17). 'Teaching' usually follows upon conversion and is more directed to discipleship, establishing converts in the faith (Matt. 28:19-20). A combination of preaching (as heralding and evangelizing) with teaching (as instructing the faithful) is desirable. Each sermon may have a different emphasis.

In the majority of church settings, because of the spiritual mix in the congregation, considerable skill is necessary if the task is to be undertaken to the glory of God. Church leaders/preachers need a knowledge and understanding of Scripture, a knowledge and understanding of the congregation and skill in communicating the one to the other. Teaching the Word without understanding the people produces an irrelevant ministry. Understanding the people without teaching the Word produces an unfaithful ministry.

A sermon is not a lecture: 'The lecturer speaks *about the Bible*; the pastoral preacher speaks *from* the Bible *about* the congregation. He tells them what God wants from them.'[3]

To quote James Montgomery Boice, A sermon 'is exposition of a text of Scripture in terms of contemporary culture with the specific goal of helping people to understand and obey the truth of God. But to do that well the preacher must be well studied. To do it exceptionally well he must have exceptional understanding of (i) the Scripture he is expounding, (ii) the culture into which he is expounding it, and (iii) the spirituality and psychology of the people he is helping to obey God's Word. These understandings do not come merely from native abilities or mere observance of life. They come from hard study as the preacher explores the wisdom of both the past and the present to assist him in his task.'[4]

Sermon objectives

Why are you speaking?

To challenge	'Go ... and make disciples of all the nations...'	Matt 28:19
To change	'... be transformed by the renewing of your mind, that you may prove what is that good and acceptable and perfect will of God'	Rom. 12:2
To comfort	'"Comfort, yes, comfort my people!" says your God. "Speak comfort ..."'	Isa. 40:1-2
	'... lest you sorrow as others who have no hope'	1 Thess. 4:13

To convert	'Turn, turn from your evil ways! For why should you die...?'	Ezek. 33:11
To convince	'... holding fast the faithful word as he has been taught, that he may be able, by sound doctrine, both to exhort and convict those who contradict'	Titus 1:9
To encourage	'... let us not grow weary while doing good, for in due season we shall reap if we do not lose heart'	Gal. 6:9
To equip	'... for the equipping of the saints for the work of ministry, for the edifying of the body of Christ'	Eph. 4:12
To feed	'... shepherds ... who will feed you with knowledge and understanding'	Jer. 3:15
To inform	'Let all the house of Israel know assuredly that God has made this Jesus, whom you crucified, both Lord and Christ'	Acts 2:36
	'For I have not shunned to declare to you the whole counsel of God'	Acts 20:27
To inspire	'... it is written, "Be holy, for I am holy"'	1 Peter 1:16
To instruct	'All Scripture is given by inspiration of God, and is profitable for doctrine, for reproof, for correction, for instruction in righteousness...'	2 Tim. 3:16
To persuade	'Knowing, therefore, the terror of the Lord, we persuade men'	2 Cor. 5:11
To plead	'We implore you on Christ's behalf, be reconciled to God'	2 Cor. 5:20
To motivate	'Now is the accepted time; behold, now is the day of salvation'	2 Cor. 6:2
To restore	'Return, you backsliding children, and I will heal your backslidings'	Jer. 3:22
To strengthen	'My soul melts from heaviness; strengthen me according to your word'	Ps. 119:28
To support	'Uphold me according to your word, that I may live'	Ps. 119:116

The ultimate objective

| To glorify God | 'Let the words of my mouth and the meditation of my heart be acceptable in your sight, O LORD, my strength and my redeemer' | Ps. 19:14 |
| | 'If anyone speaks, let him speak as the oracles of God. If anyone ministers, let him do it as with the ability which God supplies, that in all things God may be glorified through Jesus Christ, to whom belong the glory and the dominion for ever and ever. Amen' | 1 Peter 4:11 |

Rightly handling the Word

'People who "sit under" the right sort of expository preaching form the habit of living all week according to what they learn from the Bible. They begin to look on it as a contemporary book, grounded in history, full of light and power for today.'[5]

In order for a verse or passage of Scripture to be faithfully expounded, the preacher/teacher needs a good all-round grasp of biblical theology. For those brought up under regular expository ministry the groundwork will have been well laid over many years. Others without this foundation will need to engage in specific study to make up the deficiency. Biblical theology and systematic theology enable the teacher to avoid serious error in making one verse appear to contradict another.

When considering a portion of God's Word for ministry, read the text 'as a detective who has found a relevant but unclear scrap of paper in the wastebasket of the dead person's room. The success or failure of the whole enterprise – for the time being – rests on understanding this one clue, this text.'[6] To do the best work requires communion with God, knowledge and understanding of the people and patient and laborious study (1 Tim. 5:17).

> Be diligent to present yourself approved to God, a worker who does not need to be ashamed, rightly dividing the word of truth (2 Tim. 2:15).
>
> It is not desirable that we should leave the word of God and serve tables. Therefore, brethren, seek out from among you seven men of good reputation, full of the Holy Spirit and wisdom, whom we may appoint over this business; but we will give ourselves continually to prayer and to the ministry of the word (Acts 6:2-4).

Do not turn too quickly to commentaries. They are someone else's thoughts. Biblical scholars are good instructors, but the Author himself is far better, and prayer makes a direct appeal to him and enlists him in our cause. Rely on the Holy Spirit and the Word and do your own 'spade work'. Only then should you turn to commentaries to check out your interpretation and application. Where you differ from them be sure of your biblical reasons.

Seek the main theme, the main point. Does it present some aspect of the glory and majesty of God? Does it deal with the person, ministry, promises, suffering, death, or intercession of Christ? What is it revealing about the unique ministry of the Holy Spirit? Is it exposing the human condition in sin, blindness, antagonism or fear? Grapple with the text. Consider what it would mean to specific members of the congregation. 'Become passionately involved with the text.'[7]

'The preacher's business is simply to take what he finds in the Scriptures, and as he finds it, and press it down upon the understandings, hearts, and consciences of men. Nothing else is his business as a preacher.'[8]

Understanding people

You know, from the first day that I came to Asia, in what manner I always lived among you, serving the Lord with all humility, with many tears and trials which happened to me by the plotting of the Jews; how I kept back nothing that was helpful, but proclaimed it to you, and taught you publicly and from house to house, testifying to Jews, and also to Greeks, repentance toward God and faith towards our Lord Jesus Christ... Therefore I testify to you this day that I am innocent of the blood of all men. For I have not shunned to declare to you the whole counsel of God. Therefore take heed to yourselves and to all the flock, among which the Holy Spirit has made you overseers, to shepherd the church of God which he purchased with his own blood (Acts 20:18-21,26-28).

Christian preaching must be thoroughly grounded in Scripture, but it must also communicate with people. The preacher needs insight into the human condition. He must understand people. Preaching and pastoral work belong together. How an individual leader's time is allocated between preaching and pastoral work will depend upon his gifts and acumen. Pastoral contact is necessary even for those whose main responsibility is to preach and teach, since it is the means by which they gain understanding of the real lives of the people of God: the insights into their thinking, the awareness of the pressures which distress them, the problems which perplex them and the temptations which test them. Here the preaching pastor learns what he cannot discover from books. As Charles Bridges says, 'Preaching ... derives much of its power from connection with the Pastoral work; and its too frequent disjunction from it is a main cause of our inefficiency.'[9]

Pastoral work is a two-way process. It is the personal application of the pulpit ministry to individual needs, and it is learning to know the people so that the ministry of the Word may be appropriate and relevant. We must be well acquainted with their situation: spiritual state, home circumstances, pressures in employment, health, spiritual and natural gifts, and the many demands that are placed upon them.

Peter Lewis argues that the considerable and beneficial influence of Puritan preachers was based upon 'the learning of the study and the practicability of the market place. Their sermons savoured of close meditation in the closet and no less close observation in the street. Their preaching was lively because it dealt with life as it was.'[10]

When invited to preach to another congregation, the church leader should obtain as much information as possible: the make-up and size of the congregation, the purpose of the visit (evangelistic, teaching, motivating) and the setting and format (formal or informal, monologue, dialogue or seminar).

Sermon preparation

An address is a man talking *to* people; a sermon is a man speaking *from* God. Even so, the most demanding concentration, considerable time and strenuous effort need to be expended to structure and mould a sermon so that it will faithfully communicate a portion of the Word of God.

> Preach the word! Be ready in season and out of season. Convince, rebuke, exhort, with all long-suffering and teaching. For the time will come when they will not endure sound doctrine, but according to their own desires, because they have itching ears, they will heap up for themselves teachers; and they will turn their ears away from the truth, and be turned aside to fables (2 Tim. 4:2-4).

In choosing a text the golden rule is: 'Keep to centralities.' Peripheral matters, though often fascinating to the preacher, may be of little or no value to the congregation. Our task is not to amuse or entertain, nor to impress people with our skill in handling the obscure. There is no more serious business in the whole world than preaching. Just like Aaron, we stand between the living and the dead (Num. 16:48).

Every sermon must have a clear outline. A theme should be established which captures the central message of the text. What is the Lord saying here? What does *he* want the people to remember? What content will best achieve this end? Sangster said that 'The simplest people can take the best we have to give. It just requires not less but more time to get it ready: to make it plain, vivid, understandable.'[11]

Faithfulness in teaching implies being plain and simple. For preaching to be powerful it must be direct, and it cannot be direct when it is not understood by the people. According to Hamish Mackenzie, 'It takes a first-class mind, great purity of heart and much labour to achieve simplicity.'[12]

The preacher must take truths, some of which are deep and complex, and explain them in terms that are simple, dignified and clear. There can be no clear speaking without clear thinking. There can be no clear speaking if the hearers do not understand the words we use. Of Jesus it is said that 'The common people heard him gladly' (Mark 12:37).

The basic approach

Outline your message	Introduction
Deliver your message clearly and fully	Key points
Condense and apply your message	Conclusion

The introduction should be short and one that will arrest attention. Rick Warren suggests three things that always get the congregation's attention: things they value, things that are unique to them and things that threaten them. This fact has profound implications for those who preach and teach. If you want to capture the attention of an uninterested crowd you must tie your message to one of these three attention-getters.[13]

In the 'body' of the sermon, the order of the key points may be determined by the text. Alternatively the key points may be ordered so that they rise from the least important to most important. Unstructured sermons, or sermons which get out of control, use up all the time on the introduction or the first point. As a general rule this creates an unsatisfactory feeling in the congregation even when the material presented is good.

Long quotations from books other than the Bible are not easily understood by those who are listening, nor are numerous passages read from the Scriptures. Occasionally asking the congregation to turn to a specific passage in their own Bibles helps their concentration and 'grounds' the teaching solidly in the Word of God.

An apt illustration, especially a vivid personal anecdote (a short account of an incident), has great impact. If, however, people remember the illustration but not the important truth it is illustrating, it is of no value.

Interesting and faithful expository preaching has the great advantage of giving clarity to a particular passage or verse of Scripture. When members of the congregation, in their private reading, turn again to that passage or verse, they should be able to say, 'Now I understand more clearly what the Lord is saying here and how it affects my faith and life.' This may be the best lasting impact of any sermon.

In preparing a sermon constantly engage in what William Sangster calls 'prayer-thought' — that is, hold 'a conversation in the mind with God, and a conversation about that particular aspect of truth which the Holy Spirit has laid upon [you] as a message for the people'.[14]

Sermon planning and preparation

Decide the text
Define the theme
Determine the objective
Develop the key points
Detail the introduction
Deduce the conclusion

Halvorson has devised a 'hermeneutical circle' as a helpful way to look at a text.[15]

Exegetical — hermeneutical circle

1. What did it say?	3. To whom?	2. What does it say?
a. Read it personally, literally.	a. To whom was it written?	a. What is the theological centre?
b. Exegete, using tools of scholarship	b. To whom is it reaching for today?	b. What is the vulnerable point of modern attitude?
c. Listen to it, as one of those addressed — then and now.	c. What is the language style? Argumentative? Pastoral? Evangelistic? Poetic? Historical?	c. What are my pastoral concerns?
	d. What are the similarities and differences — then and now?	d. What excites me? Am I a type of my age, or different from my age?

Different methods can be adopted to make the sermon memorable. When regularly addressing the same congregation it is important to undertake a variety of approaches to avoid monotony and predictability. It is often helpful to use mnemonics (systems to aid the memory) to break down the sermon into manageable chunks. The two most common forms are acrostics and alliterations.

Acrostic

A series of words in which the first letter of each word forms another word when read in sequence — e.g.:

FAITH
Forsaking
All
I
Take
Him

GRACE
God's
Riches
At
Christ's
Expense

Alliteration

Beginning the headings with the same letter(s) — e.g.:

Text: 1 Peter 2:9-10

1. Communion	The Christian in relation to the Lord
2. Community	The Christian in relation to the church
3. Communication	The Christian in relation to the world

> But you are a chosen generation, a royal priesthood, a holy nation, his own special people, that you may proclaim the praises of him who called you out of darkness into his marvellous light; who once were not a people but are now the people of God, who had not obtained mercy but now have obtained mercy (1 Peter 2:9-10).

Easily remembered headings

While some preachers excel in the use of acrostics and alliterations, others settle for different divisions that may be easily remembered, for example:

Theme: The impact of the grace of God
Text: Titus 2: 11-12

1. The psychological impact	Teaching us to live soberly
2. The sociological impact	Teaching us to live righteously
3. The theological impact	Teaching us to live godly

> For the grace of God that brings salvation has appeared to all men, teaching us that, denying ungodliness and worldly lusts, we should live soberly, righteously, and godly in the present age, looking for the blessed hope and glorious appearing of our great God and Saviour Jesus Christ, who gave himself for us... (Titus 2:11-14).

The goal is to be plain and simple without being boring, to balance doctrine and practice, to communicate effectively and, above all, to be honouring to God.

As Peter Adam says, 'The response called for in the Bible to the hearing of the words of God is not mere assent, but faith in God who speaks the promise, obedience to the God who commands, faithfulness to the God who has made his covenant plain, return to the God who warns, and hope in the God who foretells the future. To respond to God's words is to respond to God: God is present in the speaking of his words.'[16]

Gospel preaching

'Preach the word' (2 Tim. 4:2). Preach the gospel. Preach 'Jesus Christ and him crucified' (1 Cor. 2:2). 'For we do not preach ourselves, but Christ Jesus the Lord' (2 Cor. 4:5). The saved will rejoice in hearing of their Saviour once more. The unsaved need to hear, 'for there is no other name under heaven given among men by which we must be saved' (Acts 4:12). We not only preach out of love for sinners, but out of love for our Saviour. Every preacher should desire that sinners will gladly respond to the gospel for the Saviour's glory as well as for the sinner's good.

> For 'whoever calls on the name of the LORD shall be saved.' How then shall they call on him in whom they have not believed? And how shall they believe in him of whom they have not heard? And how shall they hear without a preacher? And how shall they preach unless they are sent? ... So then faith comes by hearing, and hearing by the word of God.
> (Rom. 10:13-15,17).

Like Paul at Corinth, we must determine to lay aside all striving for 'excellence of speech', or for a show of human 'wisdom', and speak only of Jesus Christ. 'The need for this Christ is universal; the adequacy of this Christ is inexhaustible; the power of this Christ is immeasurable.'[17] The man of God will reject a thousand fine-sounding words for one that is likely to penetrate the conscience and reach the heart. Like John the Baptist, we would arrest the attention of the people and focus their thoughts on the Saviour: 'Behold! The Lamb of God who takes away the sin of the world!' (John 1:29).

In this unique and wonderful person is centred an inexhaustible amount of vital truth relating to God and humanity, life and death, time and eternity, heaven and hell. Everything we teach in the congregation, from wherever it is taken in the sixty-six books of the Bible, whether evangelistic or pastoral, should be explicitly or implicitly linked to the grace of God manifested supremely in the cross of Calvary and the salvation obtained there by Christ.

> 'The need for this Christ is universal; the adequacy of this Christ is inexhaustible; the power of this Christ is immeasurable'
> (J. I. Packer)

The greatest reward for the preacher is to carry a congregation by the power of God to the very heights of heaven, to sit together at the feet of the Lord Jesus Christ, beholding his beauty, his magnificence, his splendour, his matchless grace, and there to be lost in wonder, love and praise. To glorify God — that is the response we desire from the people.

> For we are to God the fragrance of Christ among those who are being saved and among those who are perishing. To the one we are the aroma of death leading to death, and to the other the aroma of life leading to life. And who is sufficient for these things? (2 Cor. 2:15-16).

If there is no passion in our hearts for the Saviour it is unlikely that others will be touched. Christian preaching should be undertaken with real warmth and conviction. The word is a matter of life and death.

This is the preacher's task: to preach about God, to show human beings their own true nature, to expose sin, to announce the way of salvation, to amaze people with the truth of the incarnation, to hold up in a hundred ways the wonder of atonement, to tell of the work of the Holy Spirit, and to proclaim all the wonders of God's grace.

A balanced ministry

The power of preaching is not only evident in conversions and changed lives, it is also demonstrated in the feeding of the hungry faithful, the challenging of the erring, the restoring of the backslider, the encouraging of those who are weary in well-doing, the supporting of those who are weak in the faith, the upholding of those who are severely tempted, the comforting of those who are distressed. Some of our best pastoral work is done through preaching and teaching!

Four dimensions of preaching

1. Evangelistic

Declaring the good news and calling for repentance and faith in Christ.

2. Pastoral

Words to comfort, encourage and inspire devotion, dedication, loyalty and discipleship to Christ.

3. Doctrinal

Imparting clear, understandable Christian teaching.

> For whatever things were written before were written for our learning, that we through the patience and comfort of the Scriptures might have hope (Rom. 15:4).
>
> Receive one who is weak in the faith, but not to disputes over doubtful things (Rom. 14:1).
>
> And let us not grow weary while doing good, for in due season we shall reap if we do not lose heart (Gal. 6:9).
>
> Therefore strengthen the hands which hang down, and the feeble knees... (Heb. 12:12).

4. Ethical

To build moral sensitivity and awareness and bring about a change in behaviour.

'In a year of preaching,' says Thomas Oden, these four aspects should all 'stand in a thoughtful balance'.[18]

Following the principle of Paul in endeavouring 'to declare ... the whole counsel of God' (Acts 20:27), many preachers welcome the discipline of systematically proceeding through a book of the Bible, or preaching a series on a particular theme. This ensures that we do not major on our 'pet' subjects.

Style of presentation

For centuries preachers have been aware of what is now termed 'body language' – that is, the importance of appearance, gestures and stance to aid the preacher's presentation.

Body language[19]

Stance

Feet should be firmly placed on the ground with weight towards the balls of the feet. This prevents involuntary movements. Once into presentation, movement creates interest – but move with control.

Hand gestures

Use hands to enhance and emphasize points of your presentation.

Eye contact

Always look at your audience. For thinking time, drop eyes to shoulder level and look between two people.

Facial expressions

Use facial expression to bring your presentation alive.

Note that, according to secular research:

7% impact on your audience is created by the words you use.

38% by the voice you use.

55% by the positive body language you use.

The wind was high,

the window shakes;

With sudden start, the Miser wakes!

C. H. Spurgeon wrote caustic words about the gestures, movements and mannerisms of a number of preachers of his day. While obviously insisting that the 'sermon itself is the main thing: its matter, its aim, and the spirit in which it is brought before the people', yet, 'In the service of God even the smallest things should be regarded with holy care.' He enters into some detail about unhelpful posture, action and gesture in preaching. He is mainly concerned about those gestures and actions which arise from a lack of confidence in the subject matter, excessive nervousness at facing a congregation, failure to find the next words to speak and a host of silly habits which have been allowed to develop unchecked: 'The posture of the minister should be natural, but his nature must not be of a coarse type; it should be a graceful, educated nature... Stand upright, get a firm position, and then speak like a man... Too many men assume a slouching attitude, lolling and sprawling as if they were lounging on the parapet of a bridge and chatting with somebody down in a boat on the river... A reverent and earnest spirit will not be indicated by a sluggish lounge or a careless slouch.'[20]

Along the silent room he stalks;

Looks back,

and trembles as he walks!

The sketches on the left are taken from Spurgeon's book and illustrate what he considers to be appropriate arm and body movements.

In marked contrast to the attention given by Spurgeon to matters of posture, action and gesture is the attitude of another highly gifted preacher, Martyn Lloyd-Jones. In his lectures on preaching he offers a strong word of warning to those who train preachers: '... if in your training you tend to make him become conscious of his hands, or what he does with his head, or anything else, you are doing him great harm. It should not be done, it should be prohibited! You cannot teach a preacher in these ways; and I feel that to attempt to do so is an injustice to the Word of God. What then is the young preacher to do? Let him listen to other preachers, the best and most experienced. He will learn a lot from them negatively and positively. He will learn what not to do, and learn a great deal of what he should do. Listen to preachers!'[21]

Movements and mannerisms that distract a congregation obviously hinder the preacher's work, so too does a stiff motionless form of presentation. While in the early stages of rectifying faults and introducing good posture, action and gesture into preaching, a man may feel self-conscious and awkward; this should diminish with practice and perseverance.

As well as 'body language', the preacher must give attention to another practical matter, termed these days as vocal or para-verbal communication.

Vocal effectiveness [22]

Pace

The change in pace holds attention. Change means variety. Try two or three different speeds of speaking.

Projection

Voice should be well projected to enable all to hear. Projection is simply the words expelled on a breath keeping an open throat.

Pitch

Variety in the rise and fall of the voice holds attention. Work at widening the voice band.

Pause

The pause when used correctly is very powerful in speech. Try to avoid using non-linguistic communication and "filler words" (e.g. 'you know,' 'er,' 'well,' 'anyway').

While language, skilfully chosen and used, wields a powerful influence, effective communication does not consist simply in the words that are spoken. Non-verbal communication is recognized as being exceptionally powerful in confirming, or in undermining, the content of speech. Basic issues connected with the

> Death and life are in the power of the tongue, And those who love it will eat its fruit (Prov. 18:21).

voice need careful attention: volume, stress, pitch, enuncia-tion, projection, pace, accent, dialect. There are many ways in which a glorious message can fail to be delivered. Good communication depends upon clear transmission and un-hindered reception — remember that the hard of hearing usually sit at the back of the hall!

Good diction, clear projection, and modulated tone ensure that the people hear, and are stimulated to 'listen' attentively. As with good posture, actions and gesture, the 'right' level is achieved when a congregation is unaware of their presence or absence!

Conclusion

No amount of training can make a preacher. The priorities are the love of God, the love of souls, a knowledge of the truth and the Holy Spirit within. These are the things that make the preacher.[23] Nevertheless a man may learn how to im-prove his skill and develop his gift: 'A preacher must learn ... skills in communi-cation. A preacher must learn ... how to read and interpret the Bible and how to think theologically. A preacher must learn ... how to read the human situation so the sermons are relevant. But these skills are strangely impotent if they are not employed by an authentic person... We are authentic when we are what we seem to be. We are not phoney.'[24]

The man of God has no interest in receiving adulation when the preaching is over. He wants backsliders restored, believers strengthened and the distressed comforted. Above all he wants sinners to turn to the only Saviour. In the words of James Henley Thornwell, 'Let us always remember that sinners must be eter-nally damned unless they obey the Gospel; let us preach for life and death; let us move heaven and earth in the great commotion; preach for the saving of souls, for the glory of God. Our work is not done unless sinners do obey the Gospel... We should have our eyes singly fixed upon it. We should never preach for the sake of preaching, but always for the sake of obedience. One great reason why we meet with so little success is that we do not expect success. Often it would surprise us to be told that sin-ners were cut to the heart under our ministry.'[25]

> This is a faithful saying and worthy of all acceptance, that Christ Jesus came into the world to save sinners (1 Tim. 1:15).

9.
Pastoral counselling

Pastoral counselling

Where should Christians turn when they have personal problems they cannot surmount?

....

....

Does the Bible provide answers for insurmountable personal problems?
Yes   No   If you answered 'yes', give two or three examples.

....

....

....

Is there a biblical case for female Christian counsellors?   Yes   No
Support your answer from Scripture.

....

....

Should all pastors/elders be competent to counsel?   Yes   No
Where do pastors turn when facing insurmountable personal problems?

....

....

What safeguards should the pastor put into place when counselling (a) a woman and (b) a child?

....

....

....

Recommended reading

The books and papers listed below are written from differing, and initially convincing, viewpoints and therefore will stretch and train thinking and ability in handling Scripture.

Adams, Jay E. *Competent to Counsel* (Presbyterian and Reformed, 1974), pp.41-64.

Adams, J. E. *Shepherding God's Flock: a preacher's handbook on pastoral ministry, counseling, and leadership* (Phillipsburg, New Jersey: Presbyterian and Reformed, 1980).

Crossley, Gareth. 'Counselling: Pastoral Care or Psychotherapy', *Foundations,* no. 29, Autumn 1992, pp.12-24.

Hughes, Selwyn. *The Christian Counsellor's Pocket Guide* (Eastbourne: Kingsway, 1977).

Hurding, Roger F. *Roots and Shoots: a guide to counselling and psychotherapy* (London: Hodder and Stoughton, 1985).

MacArthur, John. 'The Sufficiency of Scripture in Counselling,' *Our Inheritance,* Summer 1998, pp.8-10.

Nelson-Jones, Richard. *The Theory and Practice of Counselling Psychology* (London: Cassell Educational, 1982).

Pastoral counselling

'When *I* use a word it means just what I choose it to mean – neither more nor less.'[1] Humpty Dumpty's scornful words to Alice might well describe so many who write or speak upon the subject of 'counselling'. Within Christian circles no word is more abused or misused, misunderstood or misrepresented than the word 'counselling' – with the possible exception of the word 'Christian'!

What is counselling?

The term 'counselling', in the words of Tony Bolger, 'may cover a whole range of helping methods, from psychotherapy through behaviour modification, to befriending or advice-giving, and counsellors may use any or all of these methods'.[2] As well as the mainstream 'pedigree' approaches to secular psychotherapy, there are also numerous 'hybrids'. Eclecticism emphasizes 'borrowing freely from various sources', while integration emphasizes 'combining parts into a whole'.[3] 250 distinct approaches to secular counselling have been identified.

Counselling is concerned with problems of living. A problem arises through bereavement, illness, ignorance, failure, stress, sin, abuse, or a persistent bad habit. Help is required to comfort, support, encourage, guide, inform, challenge, correct or console someone who is in distress.

Friends, family and brothers and sisters in Christ often minister the necessary assistance in the normal everyday circumstances of life. Sometimes, however, there is a need to turn to a pastor to seek a remedy for what appears to be an insurmountable problem.

All counselling is aimed at changing people. Counselling aims to help those receiving the counsel to help themselves. The church leader's pastoral skills include the ability to form an understanding relationship and the competence to show Christians how to change specific aspects of their thinking, feelings or behaviour.

The question arises as to where the pastor learns his wisdom in order to be of more use to such people than the average church member. Is it his skill in understanding the various strands of secular counselling, his study of psychology, or the accumulated wisdom of experience, which makes him eminently useful in this area? Or might it be that his expertise lies in his aptitude in understanding, interpreting and applying the Word of God?

Is counselling biblical?

Christian 'experts' make numerous claims that they are presenting 'biblical counselling', yet there is by no means a consensus between these various 'authorities'. Their theories and practices range from thinly disguised secular techniques, on the one hand, to 'pray and trust God', or 'lay hands on for inner healing', on the other.

Does the Bible have anything to say about counselling? Are there principles, examples, illustrations and guidelines to lead the believer to a clear perspective on the subject?

> To the law and to the testimony! If they do not speak according to this word, it is because there is no light in them (Isa. 8:20).
>
> Beware lest anyone cheat you through philosophy and empty deceit, according to the tradition of men, according to the basic principles of the world, and not according to Christ (Col. 2:8).

No one turns to the Bible to learn mathematics, rock climbing or cooking, since it makes no claim to give instruction in these areas. There are, however, numerous claims in Scripture that it is the only reliable instruction on how to live life for God and how to deal with the problems of living. The apostle Peter declares that God's 'divine power has given to us all things that pertain to life and godliness' (2 Peter 1:3). In the Holy Scriptures there are not only those things 'which are able to make ... wise for salvation through faith which is in Christ Jesus', but also that which 'is profitable for doctrine, for reproof, for correction, for instruction in righteousness' (2 Tim. 3:15,16). Two specific areas of authority are asserted: firstly, the Bible alone teaches how penitent sinners are to be saved from the guilt and consequences of their sins; and, secondly, the Bible alone teaches how saved sinners are to live for God's glory.

In the opening words of the Psalms the value and benefit of the Scriptures are set over against the folly of taking the advice of unbelievers:

Blessed is the man
Who walks not in the counsel of the ungodly...

But his delight is in the law of the LORD,
And in his law he meditates day and night
(Ps. 1:1-2).

By clear implication the contrast highlights the Bible as the only source of godly counsel. This is the place to turn when there is need for comfort, support, advice, guidance, or instruction. The Bible is the manual for Christian living. Hence the pastoral counsellor who is competent to counsel will have a thorough working knowledge of the Scriptures. 'Theological and biblical training ... is the essential background for a counsellor.'[4]

> 'Theological and biblical training ... is the essential background for a counsellor; not training in psychology or psychiatry' (Jay Adams).

Ungodly counsel

> Blessed is the man
> Who walks not in the counsel of the ungodly,
> Nor stands in the path of sinners,
> Nor sits in the seat of the scornful;
> But his delight is in the law of the LORD,
> And in his law he meditates day and night
> (Ps. 1:1-2).

Similarities between some theories propounded by non-Christian counsellors and the teachings of Scripture have led a number of Christians to conclude that there is much to learn from secular practitioners. Sometimes Christians have been beguiled through their ignorance either of secular theories and practices, or of the true teaching of Scripture. A cursory perusal of such writings is dangerous since a believer may be led away from the pure Word of God.

Two illustrations will demonstrate the danger. Secular counsellor Carl Rogers propounded the core conditions of person-centred counselling as congruence, empathic understanding and unconditional positive regard.[5] Theologian Thomas Oden laboured to show the connection between these three core conditions of counselling and the Christian virtues of faith, hope and love.[6] While similarities can be argued, it is wiser to define the basic ingredients of Christian counselling from the context of Scripture alone.

The whole basis of Rogers' therapy is ungodly. Though brought up in a God-fearing home, he rejected Christianity and turned to existentialism in his mid-twenties. Consequently Rogers held a high view of human nature — contrary to the teaching of Scripture (Jer. 17:9; Ps. 51:5; Rom. 7:18; 8:7-8) — in which he insisted that people move in a basically positive direction. He used words such as 'positive', 'constructive', 'moving towards self-actualization', 'growing towards

> Behold, I was brought forth
> in iniquity
> And in sin my mother
> conceived me
> (Ps. 51:5).
>
> But we are all like an unclean
> thing,
> And all our righteousnesses
> are like filthy rags
> (Isa. 64:6).
>
> For I know that in me (that is,
> in my flesh) nothing good
> dwells; for to will is present
> with me, but how to perform
> what is good I do not find.
> For the good that I will to do,
> I do not do; but the evil I will
> not to do, that I practise.
> Now if I do what I will not to
> do, it is no longer I who do it,
> but sin that dwells in me. I
> find then a law, that evil is
> present with me, the one who
> wills to do good
> (Rom. 7:18-21).

maturity', 'growing towards socialization'.[7] The human organism, he argued, is not only moving in a positive direction, but it can also be relied upon to provide the individual with trustworthy messages. This is discernible in the physiological processes of the entire body and through the process of growth by which an individual's potentialities and capacities are brought to realization. He further argued that, left to itself, the 'organismic self' knows what it needs for its enhancement both from its environment and from other people.

'Person-centred' counsellors have a belief in the basic rightness, even goodness, of human nature. Mearns and Thorne (secular counsellors) claim that this is not the same as suggesting that humans are 'born pure and without defect ... but it is undoubtedly a point of view which runs counter to many of the pessimistic beliefs enshrined in certain religious and psychological systems. The "person-centred" counsellor believes that each individual has the potential to become a unique and beautiful creation, but that none of us can do this alone and unaided.'[8] They are implying that a counsellor is needed, not a Saviour.

Albert Ellis (a secular counsellor), in his 'rational-emotive therapy', teaches an ABC theory connecting events and emotions. 'A' is the activating event; 'C' is the consequent emotion and 'B' is the belief system. His basic premise is that the emotional response to any event is distinctly and inevitably dependent upon what we think about that event.[9] Say, for example, that your dog died. If you loved the animal and appreciated its company walking in the fields and woods, then the response would be grief. If you loathed the animal, found it a constant nuisance and irritation, but could not bring yourself to have it put down, then your response would be relief — two extreme reactions and responses to the same event, grief or relief, depending upon your 'belief' about that event.

The idea that what you believe affects your emotional response to events is close to biblical teaching. In the case of the loss of a loved one, confidence about the individual's spiritual state will have far-reaching implications and greatly affect the response of those who mourn (e.g. 1 Thess. 4:13-18, especially verse 13 — 'lest you sorrow as others who have no hope'). But Ellis himself refused to believe in an Absolute Being to whom we are all accountable and he insists that the idea of sin is 'highly pernicious and anti therapeutic'.[10]

Giving or receiving ungodly counsel must be avoided.

Theory and practice

Conversation is the most prominent activity in counselling. Words are used and exchanged, problems and feelings are described, understanding is sought, advice or suggestions given and sometimes received. All counsellors, whether Christian or secular, have a belief system that controls their attitudes, speech and behaviour. This belief system, or world view, includes assumptions or convictions about:

1. How humanity came into being.
2. How dysfunctional feelings, thoughts and behaviour are acquired.
3. How dysfunctional feelings, thoughts and behaviour are perpetuated or sustained.
4. How dysfunctional feelings, thoughts and behaviour can be changed.

These assumptions or beliefs are sometimes divided into just two categories: a model of humanity and a methodology of change. The 'model' posits *why* people behave the way they do and the methodology posits *how* to accomplish change. But knowing and understanding the theory is only the first step, since translating theory into practice often requires additional specialized skills, patiently and persistently applied: 'The jump from theory to practice is a large one, from the niceties of intellectual constructs to the complexities of real problems...'[11]

A psychological model of humanity may be elaborate because it comprises the basic nature, growth stages, aberrant behaviour and normal behaviour of human beings, analysed and categorized in great detail. Some of these models, such as Freud's psychoanalytic model, have been created through the observation of a limited number of atypical individuals. Few systems have been developed after observing a relatively normal segment of the population. Although *observations of behaviour* may be somewhat objective, *explanations for*

> 'The jump from theory to practice is a large one, from the niceties of intellectual constructs to the complexities of real problems ... from the systems of papers to the vagaries of people' (R. R. Carkhuff).

behaviour are generally subjective. Therefore, every man-made model is a subjective interpretation of man and his behaviour. Because it is presented in scientific-sounding language, a psychological model will generally appear more objective and accurate than it really is.[12]

Psychological malfunctions usually consist of, or stem from, problems such as guilt, anxiety, resentment, uncontrolled appetites, lack of self-acceptance, feelings of personal unworthiness, insecurity, wrong priorities and selfishness. Even the most casual reading of Scripture quickly reveals that it has a great deal to say about problems of this sort.[13] The *why* of human behaviour and the *how* to change it are already contained in Scripture. Therefore it is unnecessary and inadvisable to turn to any psychotherapeutic system.

The biblical model of humanity is the product of three major events: creation, separation and restoration. All human problems stem from the Fall. From the events recorded in Genesis 3 alone, we become aware of the human tendency towards 'blame-shifting, self-seeking, pride, desire/feeling orientation, rebellion against authority, guilt, fear, depression, shame, covering up, hiding, and the breakdown of communication'.[14] All human hope centres in the person of the Redeemer.

> But we all, with unveiled face, beholding as in a mirror the glory of the Lord, are being transformed into the same image from glory to glory, just as by the Spirit of the Lord (2 Cor. 3:18).
>
> Him we preach, warning every man and teaching every man in all wisdom, that we may present every man perfect in Christ Jesus (Col. 1:29).
>
> … till we all come to the unity of the faith and of the knowledge of the Son of God, to a perfect man, to the measure of the stature of the fulness of Christ… (Eph. 4:13).

The Bible presents a true revelation of God, an accurate picture of humanity as it is, and as it can be. Two pictures of humanity are delineated clearly: the first portrays human beings 'having no hope and without God in the world' (Eph. 2:12). The consequences of rebellion and sin are vividly presented. In this sense reading the Scriptures becomes 'like a man observing his natural face in a mirror' (James 1:23). At the same time another image is portrayed for believers. They see what Christ is and what they are to become (2 Cor. 3:18; 1 John 3:2).

In the Lord Jesus Christ, the Bible presents a living demonstration of mental-emotional soundness. Our ultimate 'model' is Christ; our 'methodology' is derived from the Word of God illuminated and applied by the Spirit of God. The Lord Jesus was constantly aware of his origin, purpose and destination. He knew where he had come from, why he was here and where he was going (John 13:3).

The Christian pastor has confidence in his pastoral counselling because he has answers the world cannot give. From the biblical revelation we too may know our origin, purpose and destination. From Scripture we learn where we have come from, why we are here and where we are going.

As with preaching, so with counselling – we determine not to know anything among the people 'except Jesus Christ and him crucified' (1 Cor. 2:2).

When God's love touches the soul, and begins to transform us into the likeness of Christ, the consequence is always 'an improved mental-emotional-behavioural life'.[15]

Ungodly practitioners tend to think that counselling is a recent phenomenon owing its origin largely to the work of Sigmund Freud. The reality is quite different. Christian pastors have been counselling the godly and the ungodly for centuries. In fact the activity of counselling, as discussion, advice, guidance, support and comfort to hurt, anxious or bewildered people, stretches back throughout the Old Testament period to the earliest days. In the wilderness Jethro counselled his son-in-law, Moses, to take his difficulties to God (Exod. 18:17-23). The living God has been, and still is, a ready Counsellor to those who will seek his aid (Ps. 32:8). The godly of all ages have been able to re-echo the words of Asaph as he expressed his confidence in the Lord: 'You will guide me with your counsel, and afterward receive me to glory' (Ps. 73:24). The Lord 'is wonderful in counsel and excellent in guidance' (Isa. 28:29).

The Son of God is also revealed as an excellent Counsellor. The remarkable prophecy of Isaiah announcing the forthcoming birth of a Son declares Messiah's name as 'Wonderful, *Counsellor*, Mighty God, Everlasting Father, Prince of Peace' (Isa. 9:6, emphasis added). The promise is given also that he will embody the 'Spirit of counsel' (Isa. 11:2).

As the Lord Jesus makes the final preparation for leaving his disciples, he promises another 'Helper' (John 14:16, the Greek word translated 'helper' may also be translated 'counsellor' [NIV, RSV] or 'comforter' [AV]).

> Listen now to my voice; I will give you counsel, and God will be with you: Stand before God for the people, so that you may bring the difficulties to God (Exod. 18:19).
>
> For unto us a Child is born,
> Unto us a Son is given;
> And the government will be upon his shoulder.
> And his name will be called Wonderful, Counsellor,
> Mighty God,
> Everlasting Father, Prince of Peace
> (Isa. 9:6).
>
> There shall come forth a Rod from the stem of Jesse,
> And a Branch shall grow out of his roots.
> The Spirit of the LORD shall rest upon him,
> The Spirit of wisdom and understanding,
> The Spirit of counsel and might,
> The Spirit of knowledge and of the fear of the LORD.
> His delight is in the fear of the LORD,
> And he shall not judge by the sight of his eyes,
> Nor decide by the hearing of his ears...
> (Isa. 11:1-3).

> But you have an anointing from the Holy One, and you know all things. I have not written to you because you do not know the truth, but because you know it, and that no lie is of the truth... But the anointing which you have received from him abides in you, and you do not need that anyone teach you; but as the same anointing teaches you concerning all things, and is true, and is not a lie, and just as it has taught you, you will abide in him (1 John 2:20-21,27).

The special work of the Holy Spirit that related to the apostles of Jesus Christ is of course no longer in operation. These days the Father and the Son give counsel to their people by means of the Holy Spirit working through the Word (1 John 2:20-21,27).

God also calls and equips men to function as counsellors to God's people through public preaching (2 Tim. 4:2) and private consultation (1 Tim. 5:1-2; 6:17-19; Titus 1:7-9).

Counsellors in the Bible

What does Scripture reveal about counsellors?

The Father is a Counsellor

I will instruct you and teach you in the way you should go;
I will guide you with my eye.
Do not be like the horse or like the mule,
Which have no understanding,
Which must be harnessed with bit and bridle,
Else they will not come near you

(Ps. 32:8).

The LORD brings the counsel of the nations to nothing;
He makes the plans of the peoples of no effect.
The counsel of the LORD stands for ever,
The plans of his heart to all generations

(Ps. 33:10-11).

The LORD will guide you continually,
And satisfy your soul in drought,
And strengthen your bones;
You shall be like a watered garden,
And like a spring of water, whose waters do not fail

(Isa. 58:11).

The Son is a Counsellor

Come to me, all you who labour and are heavy laden, and I will give you rest. Take my yoke upon you and learn from me, for I am gentle and lowly in heart, and you will find rest for your souls. For my yoke is easy and my burden is light (Matt. 11:28-29).

The Spirit of the LORD shall rest upon him,
The Spirit of wisdom and understanding,
The Spirit of counsel and might,
The Spirit of knowledge and of the fear of the LORD.
His delight is in the fear of the LORD,
And he shall not judge by the sight of his eyes,
Nor decide by the hearing of his ears...

(Isa. 11:2-3).

For unto us a Child is born,
Unto us a Son is given;
And the government will be upon his shoulder.
And his name will be called
Wonderful, Counsellor, Mighty God,
Everlasting Father, Prince of Peace

(Isa. 9:6).

What can we glean about counselling from the example of the Lord Jesus in such places as Mark 10:17-22; John 4:4-26; 21:15-17?

The Holy Spirit is a Counsellor

If you love me, keep my commandments. And I will pray the Father, and he will give you another Helper, that he may abide with you for ever — the Spirit of truth, whom the world cannot receive, because it neither sees him nor knows him; but you know him, for he dwells with you and will be in you (John 14:15-17).

It is to your advantage that I go away; for if I do not go away, the Helper will not come to you; but if I depart, I will send him to you. And when he has come, he will convict the world of sin, and of righteousness, and of judgement (John 16:7-8).

But when the Helper comes, whom I shall send to you from the Father, the Spirit of truth who proceeds from the Father, he will testify of me (John 15:26).

The Lord Jesus Christ calls the Holy Spirit 'the Helper' (John 14:16,26; 15:26; 16:7). This word translates the Greek noun *parakletos*. The verb form *parakaleo* 'is used 109 times in the New Testament, and covers a range of meanings: to summon, invite, ask, implore, exhort, beseech, comfort, encourage'.[16]

Pastors are to be counsellors too

But as for you, speak the things which are proper for sound doctrine: that the older men be sober, reverent, temperate, sound in faith, in love, in patience; the older women likewise, that they be reverent in behaviour, not slanderers, not given to much wine, teachers of good things — that they admonish the young women to love their husbands, to love their children, to be discreet, chaste, homemakers, good, obedient to their own husbands, that the word of God may not be blasphemed.

Likewise exhort the young men to be sober-minded, in all things showing yourself to be a pattern of good works; in doctrine showing integrity, reverence, incorruptibility, sound speech that cannot be condemned, that one who is an opponent may be ashamed, having nothing evil to say of you. Exhort bondservants to be obedient to their own masters, to be well-pleasing in all things, not answering back, not pilfering, but showing all good fidelity, that they may adorn the doctrine of God our Saviour in all things.

For the grace of God that brings salvation has appeared to all men, teaching us that, denying ungodliness and worldly lusts, we should live soberly, righteously, and godly in the present age, looking for the blessed hope and glorious appearing of our great God and Saviour Jesus Christ, who gave himself for us, that he might redeem us from every lawless deed and purify for himself his own special people, zealous for good works. Speak these things, exhort, and rebuke with all authority. Let no one despise you (Titus 2:1-15).

Preach the word! Be ready in season and out of season. Convince, rebuke, exhort, with all long-suffering and teaching (2 Tim. 4:2).

And we urge you, brethren, to recognize those who labour among you, and are over you in the Lord and admonish you, and to esteem them very highly in love for their work's sake. Be at peace among your-selves. Now we exhort you, brethren, warn those who are unruly, comfort the faint-hearted, uphold the weak, be patient with all (1 Thess. 5:12-14).

A pastor/counsellor learns from the Holy Spirit:

1. To draw near to another person (John 14:16) to com-fort, console, encourage, challenge, guide.
2. To bear witness to Jesus Christ (John 15:26).
3. To speak the truth (John 14:17).
4. To minister the Word of Christ (John 14:26).
5. To bring a convicting word about sin, righteousness and judgement (John 16:8).

> Let the word of Christ dwell in you richly in all wisdom...
> (Col. 3:16).

True Christian counselling is 'a creative, spiritual process involving a person who needs help and another person who will come alongside as God's channel of mercy and truth'.[17]

The art of listening

> He who answers a matter before he hears it,
> it is folly and shame to him
> (Prov. 18:13).
>
> Do not judge according to appearance, but judge with righteous judgement
> (John 7:24).
>
> A word fitly spoken is like apples of gold In settings of silver
> (Prov. 25:11).

Before counsel may be given it is necessary to ascertain the problem accurately. Doctors in general practice were often caricatured as filling in the prescription slip *before* they had recognized the patient or heard the symptoms. In a similar manner counsellors can be in such a great hurry to provide sound advice that they do not *listen effectively* to the person they are counselling, and consequently their diagnosis is wrong and the rem-edy is inappropriate.

'Listening is basic to all counselling. It requires that the counsellor be silent most of the time and use all his senses to get the total message. He listens with his ears to the words spoken and the tone of voice, with his mind to the underlying message, and with his eyes to the lan-guage of the body in its posture, bearing and gestures.'[18]

The goal of listening is to *understand* the person who has turned to you for help or assistance. As you gain understanding, and share that understanding with those whom you counsel, this can help them understand themselves more fully and put them in a better position to act constructively. The capacity to be a good and understanding listener is perhaps the most fundamental counselling skill of all.[19]

Active, total or complete listening involves three things:

1. Observing and reading non-verbal behaviour — posture, facial expression, movement, tone of voice, etc.
2. Listening to and understanding verbal messages.
3. Listening in an integrated way to the person in the context of both the helping process and everyday life.[20]

Applying Scripture

All counselling is aimed at changing people. Its objective is to help those on the receiving end to help themselves. The counsellor's skill includes forming an understanding relationship with the persons he counsels and helping them to change specific aspects of their feeling, thinking and behaviour. The Scriptures provide remarkable resource material:

> Your word I have hidden in my heart,
> That I might not sin against you...
> Your word is a lamp to my feet
> And a light to my path
> (Ps. 119:11,105).
>
> ...his divine power has given to us all things that pertain to life and godliness, through the knowledge of him who called us by glory and virtue
> (2 Peter 1:3).

1. If properly approached, the Bible is sufficient to provide a framework for thinking through every question a counsellor needs to ask.
2. A relationship with Jesus Christ provides resources that are utterly indispensable in substantially resolving every psychological (that is, non-organically caused) problem.
3. The community of God's people functioning together in biblical relationship is the intended context for understanding and living out God's answers to life's problems.[21]

Pastoral wisdom is formed by the interaction of four components: Scripture, tradition, reason and experience.[22]

'Scripture' is the Word of God addressed to us 'for doctrine, for reproof, for correction, for instruction in righteousness' (2 Tim. 3:16).

'Tradition' is used in the sense of the history of exegesis. The accurate interpretation and wise application of Scripture necessitate awareness and appreciation of the wisdom of the past. Great pastors like Luther, Calvin, Baxter, Owen, Wesley and Edwards provide invaluable help in the pastoral application of the Scriptures. In the interpretation of Scripture the pastor will take particular note of the accumulated wisdom of godly men, past and present. While the Word of God alone is a guide, we must take care to be humble whenever we are inclined to an interpretation that is not well attested in the history of the church of Jesus Christ. Traditions are not always bad or unhelpful (2 Thess. 2:15; 1 Cor. 11:2).

The use of 'reason' implies an effort to think 'constructively, rigorously, and consistently; to argue cogently; and to reflect systematically' on the balanced use of pastoral wisdom.[23]

Personal experience, when coupled with the accumulated wisdom of others, forms the fourth and final branch of the tree of pastoral wisdom. The best pastoral insight is derived from lived experience of ministry. All problems are not the same; all people are not the same. The skilful pastor learns to distinguish cases so that he might counsel in the most appropriate manner. He

> Then the apostles gathered to Jesus and told him all things, both what they had done and what they had taught (Mark 6:30).

learns also the importance of correct timing, since individuals are not always ready to receive all that we might wish to give them (John 16:12). 'The fabric of effective pastoral work involves the constant interweaving of scriptural wisdom, historical awareness, constructive theological reasoning, situational discernment, and personal empathy.'[24]

> 'The fabric of effective pastoral work involves the constant interweaving of scriptural wisdom, historical awareness, constructive theological reasoning, situational discernment, and personal empathy. It is best studied by examining case materials of concrete problems of pastoral counsel, viewed in the light of Scripture and tradition' (T. C. Oden).

There are two serious obstacles to the pastor/elder who takes this approach to caring for the Lord's people in their difficulties. The first comes from psychiatrists and professional counsellors, who often regard the Christian pastor as unskilled and irrelevant in dealing with serious problems. The second arises from the 'amateur' Christian counsellor who will regularly attempt to move in on suffering Christians and provide remedies and solutions that are distinctly unhelpful. Christian pastors need to be equipped with the knowledge and skill to resist both intrusions into their pastoral sphere. There is no need to turn to ungodly counsellors with their ungodly counsel. We have a fine Christian tradition of outstanding men in pastoral care, such as Augustine, Luther, Calvin, Edwards, Owen, Baxter, Shedd, Fairbairn and Bridges.

Christian pastors/elders must resist the pressure to feel intimidated. We are called of God to be physicians of the soul.

Case studies

The case studies should be read aloud with others and then discussed in the light of the questions that follow.

Case study no. 1: 'Luke'[25]

Luke: I have problems relating to people. They seem not to care about me. I've tried all sorts of ways to make friends but have failed.

                   I have doubts about my salvation, too. I don't seem to be able to do what the Bible tells me. Do you think that there is something wrong with me? [Luke asks this question for the second consecutive week.]

Counsellor: Yes, life can be a struggle, but before we talk about that, why don't you tell me about this one note that you wrote down in your homework about not being able to see men in any stage of undress?

Luke: Oh, that — well I was depressed when I wrote that. I was going to erase it. I get depressed because I can't do what God wants me to do and think about all sorts of things which cause it. It's nothing.

Analysis

1. Is Luke evading, or is he telling the truth?
2. What might be behind this entry in his homework?
3. Why didn't Luke erase the item?
4. What line of approach would you want to take?

Case study no. 2: 'Virginia'[26]

After having worked through the depression and other presentation problems (which had caused absence from her work as a dental receptionist) at the outset of this fourth counselling session, twenty-four-year-old Virginia announces (as soon as she is seated): 'I know that I am bitter and resentful. I am lonely and I don't like it. I know what my problem is. All that I really want is a husband!'

At this she breaks down and cries. Lifting her head, she continues with tears streaming down her face: 'What can I do? I am a Christian; I can't marry an unbeliever. Our church is small. There are hardly any prospects, and no one ever asks me out on a date.'

Analysis

1. How would you define Virginia's problem(s)?
2. What resources may you draw upon to help her meet her need?
3. If you were to suggest a timetable of activities for her, what would be the order of items on the list?

Case Study no. 3: 'Jim'[27]

Counsellor:	So the main problem you'd like help with is depression. We'll see what we can do about it, Jim.
Jim:	Good, I'm hoping to find some relief soon.
Counsellor:	First of all, Jim, do you know Jesus Christ as your own personal Saviour?
Jim:	Yes I do. I've been a Christian since I was a young child.
Counsellor:	So you've trusted in him for forgiveness of sins, and you know that God is your Father?
Jim:	Yes, that's right.
Counsellor:	Well then, as a child of God, it's important for you to know and meditate on the promises of God. Have you ever memorized Scripture?
Jim:	I guess I know a lot of familiar verses by heart, but I've never conducted a conscientious programme of memorization.
Counsellor:	Well, I'd like you to do just that. Philippians 4:4 says, 'Rejoice in the Lord always. Again I will say, rejoice!' When you start to get depressed remind yourself of this verse. As a Christian you have plenty to be joyful about.

Analysis

1. What do you think of this counsellor's approach?
2. If you disagree with his method of dealing with depression, suggest another.

3. The counsellor's heart and his concern are right. How can these concerns be maintained but more realistically applied to Jim's problem?

Conclusion

The goal of Christian counselling is to 'present every [human being] perfect in Christ Jesus' (Col. 1:28). As preaching applies God's Word collectively in the public arena, so Christian counselling seeks to apply God's Word individually in the private sphere. Counselling provides the environment for the closer application of Scripture to specific needs. This is not to be confused with the simple quoting of texts.

The pastor is always learning. Preparation for counselling lies in prayer, meditation upon the Scriptures and the painstaking formation and application of a solid biblical ethic.

'Christian ethics takes place in the dialogue between a biblically informed theology and a biblically shaped spirituality on the one hand, and the demands of living in the modern world, on the other.'[28]

> For the grace of God that brings salvation has appeared to all men, teaching us that, denying ungodliness and worldly lusts, we should live soberly, righteously, and godly in the present age, looking for the blessed hope and glorious appearing of our great God and Saviour Jesus Christ (Titus 2:11-13).

10.
Local church evangelism

Local church evangelism

Where are the opportunities for evangelism in your town and community?

....

....

What are the weaknesses or omissions in the evangelistic work of your church?

....

....

Why is evangelism failing in our present day?

....

....

What is the biblical basis for evangelism by the local church?

....

....

What is the biblical basis for personal evangelism?

....

....

How can Christians be motivated to evangelism?

....

....

Recommended reading

The books and papers listed below are written from differing, and initially convincing, viewpoints and therefore will stretch and train thinking and ability in handling Scripture.

Bolt, Peter. *Mission Minded: a tool for planning your ministry around Christ's mission* (London: St Matthias Press, 1992).

Thornwell, James Henley. 'The Sacrifice of Christ the Type and Model of Missionary Effort', *The Collected Writings of James Henley Thornwell*, vol. 2, 'Theological and Ethical' (Edinburgh: Banner of Truth Trust, 1974 [first published 1875]), pp.411-49.

Timmis, Steve and Chester, Tim. 'The Principles of Gospel Ministry', *The Briefing*, vols. 234-7, 2000–2001.

Local church evangelism

The Lord Jesus Christ will build his church, and nothing and no one will stop him (Matt. 16:18). His Great Commission to his people begins with the assertion: *'All authority has been given to me in heaven and on earth. Go therefore and make disciples of all the nations...'* (Matt. 28:18-19, emphasis added). The implications of this statement are profound and immense: there is no uncertainty concerning the outcome of evangelism because there is no limit to the authority of the Lord Jesus Christ; therefore there should be no hesitation in the obedience of the church.

> I will build my church, and the gates of Hades shall not prevail against it (Matt. 16:18).
>
> All authority has been given to me in heaven and on earth. Go therefore and make disciples of all the nations, baptizing them in the name of the Father and of the Son and of the Holy Spirit, teaching them to observe all things that I have commanded you; and lo, I am with you always, even to the end of the age (Matt. 28:18-20).

What is evangelism?

> Go into all the world and preach the gospel to every creature (Mark 16:15).
>
> Thus it is written, and thus it was necessary for the Christ to suffer and to rise from the dead the third day, and that repentance and remission of sins should be preached in his name to all nations, beginning at Jerusalem. And you are witnesses of these things (Luke 24:46-48).

'Evangelism, writes John Stott, 'is neither to convert people, nor to win them, nor to bring them to Christ, though this is indeed the first goal of evangelism. Evangelism is to preach the gospel.'[1]

J. I. Packer explains: 'According to the New Testament, evangelism is just preaching the gospel, the evangel. It is a work of communication in which Christians make themselves mouthpieces for God's message of mercy to sinners ... the way to tell whether in fact you are evangelizing is not to ask whether conversions are known to have resulted from your witness. It is to ask whether you are faithfully making known the gospel message.'[2]

To quote Stott again, 'Evangelism must not be defined in terms of the recipients of the gospel, nor in terms of the results, nor in terms of the methods adopted. Evangelism must be defined only in terms of the message.'[3]

Stuart Olyott put it like this: 'Evangelism is the relating of the Evangel [Good News], by means of the spoken word, and in the power of the Holy Spirit — in order that men may seek God, repent of their sins, and believe on the Lord Jesus Christ and be saved; and then order the whole of their lives by his Word.'[4]

> Paul, a bondservant of Jesus Christ, called to be an apostle, separated to the gospel of God which he promised before through his prophets in the Holy Scriptures, concerning his Son Jesus Christ our Lord, who was born of the seed of David according to the flesh, and declared to be the Son of God with power, according to the Spirit of holiness, by the resurrection from the dead... (Rom. 1:1-4).
>
> Do all things without complaining and disputing, that you may become blameless and harmless, children of God without fault in the midst of a crooked and perverse generation, among whom you shine as lights in the world, holding fast the word of life...
> (Phil. 2:14-16).

Evangelism is the proclamation of 'the gospel of God ... concerning his Son Jesus Christ', declaring both the unique person of Christ, his deity and his humanity, and his glorious saving work (Rom. 1:1-5). It is the good news of the incarnation, the atonement and the kingdom of Jesus Christ, the Son of God: his cradle, his cross and his crown. It is the news of how God prepared a body for his Son (Heb. 10:5) and how that Son came 'in the likeness of sinful flesh, on account of sin' (Rom. 8:3), to 'save his people from their sins' (Matt. 1:21), by bearing 'our sins in his own body on the tree' (1 Peter 2:24), suffering 'once for sins, the just for the unjust, that he might bring us to God' (1 Peter 3:18).

The goal of evangelism is that others may also come to 'believe that Jesus is the Christ, the Son of God, and that believing [they] may have life in his name' (John 20:31; cf. Rom. 10:13-15,17).

The gospel is not just the truth concerning the remission of sins and eternal life through faith in the substitutionary sacrifice of the Lord Jesus Christ at Calvary. It is the whole revelation given to us in the Bible: salvation through faith in Christ, the power of the Holy Spirit in believers, godly living in community, work, family and church, commitment to worship, and life and service in fellowship with a company of God's people.

> Do Christians in their daily witness see themselves as the principal agent in evangelism, or do they think that the chief responsibility lies with the preacher in his 'one-hour-a-week' gospel service?

Every Christian's responsibility

Preparation

It is the duty of every Christian to be prepared and willing to give a clear personal testimony to the saving grace of God through our Lord Jesus Christ (1 Peter 3:15).

It is the duty of church leaders to train Christians in the work of evangelism; it is a part of every member's ministry (Eph. 4:11-12).

> But sanctify the Lord God in your hearts, and always be ready to give a defence to everyone who asks you a reason for the hope that is in you, with meekness and fear...
> (1 Peter 3:15).

Proclamation

> At that time a great persecution arose against the church which was at Jerusalem; and they were all scattered throughout the regions of Judea and Samaria, except the apostles... Therefore those who were scattered went everywhere preaching the word (Acts 8:1,4).

All Christians should be able to bring the gospel of Christ naturally into everyday conversations with the unsaved (Acts 8:4). We are to tell people about Christ: his incarnation, his life, his ministry, his suffering, his crucifixion, his resurrection and the promise of his return.

The gospel needs to be preached clearly to the congregation not only with a view to the conversion of the unsaved, but also with the intention of instructing the saved, so that they learn how to express the glorious gospel by numerous different approaches.

Prayer

- Prayer for the presence of the Holy Spirit in power and grace (Acts 4:33; Ezek. 37:9; John 3:7-8)
- Prayer for liberty for gospel presentation (2 Thess. 3:1-2)
- Prayer for boldness in word and witness (Eph. 6:18-20; cf. Acts 4:29)
- Prayer for increased evangelistic opportunities (Col. 4:2-3)
- Prayer for more evangelists (Luke 10:2; Matt. 9:36-38)

> 'The great fault of the children of God is that they do not continue in prayer — they do not go on praying; they do not persevere. If they desire anything for God's glory, they should pray until they get it' (George Müller).

'We pray; but what is there of agony in our prayers? Who wrestles with God? Whose soul is burdened with the weight of a perishing world? Or who takes an hour from his sleep or foregoes a single meal in order that he may plead the cause of the millions upon millions that know not God?'[5]

Why are Christians not evangelizing?[6]

- Some lack a personal faith to share. There may be those who profess faith in Christ and yet have no living experience of him. They may have nothing more than 'a form of godliness but [deny] its power' (2 Tim. 3:5).
- Many do not think it is their responsibility to evangelize the lost.
- They may not be living close to God. A lack of prayer and personal Bible study may produce a sense of powerlessness and inadequacy.
- Evangelizing may be seen as too demanding of time and energy.
- They may be afraid to tell their work colleagues and friends. It seems that Timothy was timid and prone to fear (2 Tim. 1:6-7). How many Christians display the attitude of Joseph of Arimathea, who was 'a disciple of Jesus, but secretly, for fear of the Jews'! (John 19:38).
- A lack of knowledge may incline some to fear being beaten in a discussion; but the concern is not winning an argument, but winning a soul.
- A pessimistic view assuming a negative response.
- A ghetto mentality causes some to remain within the Christian circle and never to venture to talk about spiritual matters with anyone who is not already a Christian. Fellowship with believers takes priority over evangelistic contact with unbelievers.
- Blindness to the true state of the lost; they are unmoved by their 'having no hope and [being] without God in the world' (Eph. 2:12).
- Introverted evangelism concentrates the whole attention on reaching children with the gospel, particularly children of church members. But, 'A flourishing work among the young in one generation is no guarantee of a thriving adult church in the next.'[7] Furthermore, running children's clubs may be the 'soft option', instead of addressing adults with the gospel of Christ.

- A sense of inadequacy, like that of Moses, who told the Lord, 'I am not eloquent ... but I am slow of speech and slow of tongue'; to which the Lord replied, 'Who has made man's mouth? Or who makes the mute, the deaf, the seeing, or the blind? Have not I, the LORD? Now therefore, go, and I will be with your mouth and teach you what you shall say' (Exod. 4:10-12).
- Doctrinal hindrances may arise by misunderstanding the outworking of predestination and election and thinking that 'If God wills to save, people will be saved without my involvement.'
- False teaching about the ultimate end of the unsaved, such as second probation, annihilationism and universalism.[8]

The truth is, the apathy of the Christian Church to the condition of the heathen can only be explained by the supposition of a lurking scepticism in regard to the perils of their state. There is secret feeling, where there is not a developed conviction, that after all they shall not surely die. This plea may extenuate, but does not justify, the neglect of the Church, for it only denies without destroying the eternal misery of the heathen. [9]

Add further reasons/excuses that you have heard (or given) for not sharing the gospel with the unsaved.

....

....

....

Evaluating church life

Mission and ministry

The fact that an activity has worked in previous years is no reason to perpetuate it if it is no longer working: 'The greatest enemy to our success in the future is often the success of our past.' [10]

Analyse all the activities of your church on the basis of the principles set out by Peter Bolt in *Mission Minded* (see evaluation form on following page):

Evaluating the activities of your church

Activity	Evangelism				Edification			Support ministry
	Raising awareness	Initial contact	Pre-evangelism	Evangelism	Follow-up	Nurture	Training in ministry	

The principles of gospel ministry

Steve Timmis and Tim Chester have set out the following principles for the gospel ministry.[11] Indicate your agreement or disagreement with each principle, citing a biblical reference in support.

1. Mission — that begins on the doorstep and ends at the far corners of the world — is the central, defining purpose of the church in the world.

2. Church exists wherever there are believers covenanted together sitting under the Word of God in order to hear and obey it.

3. The model of church as extended family is to be taken seriously and worked out consistently.

4. A believing community is vital in terms of providing a persuasive apologetic for the gospel.

5. The most effective approach to gospel ministry is one that is long-term, low-key and relational.

6. Whenever believers come together, non-Christians are to be welcomed and helped to understand what is happening, even if they cannot fully participate.

7. People will be more willing to respond to the gospel if they are able to have a sense of 'belonging' before they feel the necessity to believe.

8. The truth that worship is a 'life-thing' rather than a purely, or even principally, a 'meeting-thing' should be taught, modelled and practised.

9. It is the privilege and responsibility of all believers to bear a credible witness to the good news that is Jesus, in whatever context they find themselves.

10. All possible means should be employed to ensure that Christians do not retreat into cosy, safe, evangelical ghettos.

11. Gospel ministry should be contemporary, daring, radical and should arise directly out of serious, careful and humble biblical and theological reflection.

12. Failure to undertake gospel initiatives, rather than the 'failure' of certain gospel initiatives, is the greater error.

13. Active involvement in society, and penetration into various subcultures, is best done with the knowledge, support, encouragement and where possible, participation of others.

14. Leadership is providing an environment in which the people of God are able to flourish.

15. Church activity is gift-led.

16. A local church should always be actively looking to plant other churches.

17. People are essential to a gospel ministry, while buildings are not.

18. All church structures and activities are to be evaluated by the imperative of the gospel.

The worship and service of the church of Jesus Christ

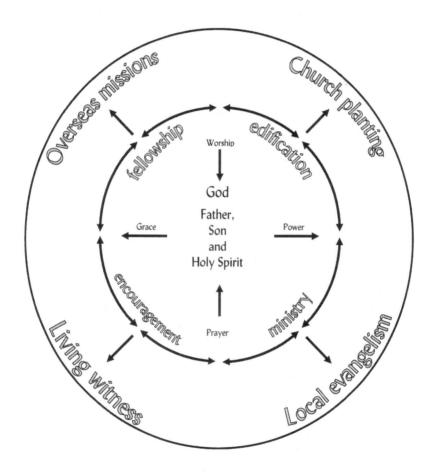

While evangelism is 'the central and defining purpose of the church in the world', as Steve Timmis and Tim Chester assert, it is not the central and defining purpose of its whole existence (Acts 2:42).

A clear strategy

Any work of evangelism should be evaluated according to the principles and practices derived from Scripture.

In evangelism there is need for the insight and perception of the children of Issachar, 'who had understanding of the times, to know what Israel ought to do' (1 Chr. 12:32). Vision, strategy and organizational skills are as essential as a fighting force itself.

> *Are we placing the responsibility on believers to go and evangelize, or on unbelievers to come and be evangelized?*

The gospel is not to be targeted at 'felt need'; it is not to be marketed as a commodity to enhance life. In the Acts of the Apostles people were told about Christ. They were informed that Jesus is Lord and were to respond accordingly. They were not told that God had sent his Son to make them happy. They were told that they stood before a King whom they had offended. This was God-centred proclamation, for God is worthy to be known and proclaimed for who he is.[12]

> But as we have been approved by God to be entrusted with the gospel, even so we speak, not as pleasing men, but God who tests our hearts (I Thess. 2:4).
>
> For though I am free from all men, I have made myself a servant to all, that I might win the more; and to the Jews I became as a Jew, that I might win Jews; to those who are under the law, as under the law, that I might win those who are under the law; to those who are without law, as without law (not being without law toward God, but under law toward Christ), that I might win those who are without law; to the weak I became as weak, that I might win the weak. I have become all things to all men, that I might by all means save some. Now this I do for the gospel's sake...
> (I Cor. 9:19-23).

Our object is not to please sinners but to save sinners (Gal. 1:10; 1 Thess. 2:4).

The responsibility lies upon Christians to *go out*, not upon non-Christians to *come in*. Our duty is 'to seek and to save that which was lost' (Luke 19:10). On behalf of the Good Shepherd we are seeking his lost sheep (Luke 15:4).

'Adaptation' and 'relevance' are key words in personal evangelism. When the Lord Jesus spoke with the woman of Samaria who had come to draw water from the well, he talked about 'living water' (John 4:10). In discussion with Nicodemus the Pharisee, ruler of the Jews and 'the teacher of Israel', he raised a vital theological issue (John 3:3,10). To country folk he told stories about seed (Mark 4:3-9,26-29; Matt. 13:24-32). To a multitude of people of all ages he spoke about eating bread (John 6:33,35). Addressing fishermen, the Saviour spoke of evangelists as being 'fishers of men' (Mark 1:17).

> Therefore, since we have this ministry, as we have received mercy, we do not lose heart. But we have renounced the hidden things of shame, not walking in craftiness nor handling the word of God deceitfully, but by manifestation of the truth commending ourselves to every man's conscience in the sight of God (2 Cor. 4:1-2).
>
> Knowing, therefore, the terror of the Lord, we persuade men... (2 Cor. 5:11).

Flexibility was evident in the evangelistic approach of the apostle Paul. He was sensitive to the people he addressed (1 Cor. 9:19-23). He reveals that he learned this approach from the example of the Lord Jesus Christ.

While the primary concern is to glorify God by declaring the person and work of his Son, the object of evangelism also necessarily includes the endeavour to elicit a response to these truths. It is communication with a view to conversion. It is an attempt to *win*, or *save*, or *catch*, our fellow citizens for Christ (1 Peter 3:1; 1 Cor. 9:19-22; Luke 5:10). We endeavour to persuade sinners (2 Cor. 5:11), though that must never deteriorate into browbeating.

Motivating the church

Ultimately the motivation comes from the Lord, since 'it is God who works in you *both to will and to do* for his good pleasure' (Phil. 2:13, emphasis added). Church leaders may, however, provide encouragement and stimulation for the people of God to initiate or to continue evangelistic enterprises.

Motives for evangelism

The glory of God

'The heavens declare the glory of God' (Ps. 19:1), but nowhere is his glory displayed as excellently as in the saving of sinners. In his redeemed church he will 'show the exceeding riches of his grace in his kindness towards us in Christ Jesus' (Eph. 2:7).

The example of Christ

There is no brightness in heaven that can transcend the glory of the cross. It is supremely through personal sacrifice that our Saviour demonstrates his love for God and his love for sinners. 'Is it our business to spread, as it was His business to purchase, salvation by sacrifice?'[13]

Obedience to the Master

The commands are to go and make disciples (Matt. 28:18-20), to invite strangers to God's celebration (Matt. 22:1-10), to be 'holding fast the word of life' (Phil. 2:16), to 'proclaim the praises' of our Saviour God (1 Peter 2:9) and to give an explanation to any enquirer (1 Peter 3:15). Christians are under obligation to make the Saviour known.

There are Christ-centred promises which inspire confidence that the harvest of saved humanity will be great (Luke 10:1-2), that the elect of God are a great multitude that no one can number (Rev. 7:9) and that evangelism will certainly succeed (Matt. 16:18; 28:18-20).

A love for sinners

'One might think that shame would drive us to our task. Do the commands of our Lord mean so little to us? Are we indifferent to him? Or, if not shame, pity on those who have not heard. Are we unconcerned at the cries of the heathen? Can we shed tears watching a film on the large screen or small, and yet sit dry-eyed before the needs of the lost?[14] As love for neighbour is a fulfilling of the law of God (Gal. 5:14), then the greatest expression of that love is to desire their salvation.

Robert Dabney reminds us that the 'heathen, like us, are depraved; they need a new birth. Therefore they cannot be saved without the gospel, which is the only instrument of regeneration.'[15]

Conclusion

The Great Commission placed upon his church by the ascending Lord was: 'Go ... and make disciples of all the nations' (Matt. 28:19). In recent years the influx into the United Kingdom, and other Western nations, of people from all over the world has resulted in evangelistic opportunities of unparalleled proportions. More Christians than ever before are able to respond to the commission of the Saviour by evangelizing the nations – on their own doorstep.

With the increasingly cosmopolitan composition of so many major cities and towns, a misguided popular notion has arisen that all religions are the same. Declaring the uniqueness of Christ in a pluralistic society is regarded with suspicion and brings accusations of intolerance. Yet since Jesus is the only way to the true God (John 14:6), 'nor is there salvation in any other, for there is no other

> Jesus said ... 'I am the way, the truth, and the life. No one comes to the Father except through me' (John 14:6).

> And this is eternal life, that they may know you, the only true God, and Jesus Christ whom you have sent (John 17:3).

name under heaven given among men by which we must be saved' (Acts 4:12), our God-given duty is to share the knowledge of Christ with them.

'For "whoever calls on the name of the LORD shall be saved." How then shall they call on him in whom they have not believed? And how shall they believe in him of whom they have not heard?' (Rom. 10:13-14).

11.
Missionary endeavour

Missionary endeavour

What is a missionary?

....

....

....

What is the relationship between local church evangelism, church-planting and missionary endeavour?

....

....

....

What is the call to missionary work? (Cite biblical references.)

....

....

....

What is the role of a missionary organization or agency?

....

....

....

Recommended reading

The papers listed below are written from differing, and initially convincing, viewpoints and therefore will stretch and train thinking and ability in handling Scripture.

Fortner, Don. 'Why should we Support Missionaries?', *The Church of God* (Darlington: Evangelical Press, 1991), pp.151-8.

James, Bill. 'A Missionary Policy', *Reformation Today*, no. 163, May/June 1998, pp.23-7.

Milsom, Peter. 'The Local Church and World Mission', *Foundations*, no. 44, Spring 2000, pp.30-36.

Roberts, Vaughan and Thornborough, Tim (eds). *Workers for the Harvest Field* (New Malden: Good Book Co., 2006).

Tait, Ian. 'The Local Church and Missionary work', *Local Church Practice* (Leeds: Carey Publications, 1978), pp.136-58.

Thornwell, James Henley. 'The Sacrifice of Christ the Type and Model of Missionary Effort', *The Collected Writings of James Henley Thornwell*, vol. 2, 'Theological and Ethical' (Edinburgh: Banner of Truth Trust, 1974 [first published 1875]), pp.411-49.

Missionary endeavour

'He who has no sorrow for the perishing state of sinners,' writes Robert Haldane, 'and especially of his kindred, is not a Christian. No man can be a Christian who is unconcerned for the salvation of others.'[1]

The word 'missionary' derives from the Latin *missionarius*, meaning a 'sent one'. Is he/she a church-planting evangelist, a pastor/teacher, a medical worker, a social worker, an educationalist, or an agriculturalist working with a church or a group of churches overseas, or supported by a missionary organization? Or should all Christians view themselves as missionaries?

Don Fortner argues that the biblical word for missionary is 'evangelist'.[2] He therefore considers that Paul and Barnabas were missionaries sent out from the church at Antioch to preach the gospel to the Gentiles (Acts 13:1-3), Philip the evangelist was a missionary (Acts 21:8) and God has given some to his church who are specifically called to be missionaries or evangelists (Eph. 4:11).

> I tell the truth in Christ, I am not lying, my conscience also bearing me witness in the Holy Spirit, that I have great sorrow and continual grief in my heart. For I could wish that I myself were accursed from Christ for my brethren, my countrymen according to the flesh...
> (Rom. 9:1-3).

> And he himself [the ascended Lord] gave some to be apostles, some prophets, some evangelists, and some pastors and teachers, for the equipping of the saints for the work of ministry, for the edifying of the body of Christ, till we all come to the unity of the faith and of the knowledge of the Son of God, to a perfect man, to the measure of the stature of the fulness of Christ...
> (Eph. 4:11-13).

Malcolm Watts seems to be at the other end of the spectrum when he calls upon every local church to become 'a missionary organization' with a wholehearted acceptance of the missionary principle that 'The mission of the church is to reach the masses of mankind.' He pleads for the missionary spirit, 'the *burning enthusiasm* of those who know that Jesus Christ lives and fully saves'.[3] Here Watts is using the word 'missionary' in its broadest context of evangelizing the lost at home and abroad.

Others see a meaning to the word 'missionary' which not only includes the planting of new churches but the strengthening of indigenous churches;

hence they send a church-planter, a pastor/teaching elder, or a deacon to fulfil a supporting role. The qualifications of 1 Timothy 3:1-13 and Titus 1:6-9 (cf. Acts 6:2-4) apply. According to this understanding, women may also serve as missionaries provided that their ministries are defined in terms of 'excluding roles which are the functional equivalent of eldership but including all manner of other ministries'.[4]

In this book a distinction has been drawn between evangelism conducted by the local church (see chapter 10) and church-planting, whether at home or abroad (see chapter 12). There is considerable overlap, but in this study the emphasis will fall upon Christian work abroad. The term 'missionary' will be understood in its broadest connotations, as any Christian activity carried out for the benefit of the church overseas.

The origin of missionary endeavour

Missionary outreach stems from eternity when the Father said to the Son:

Ask of me, and I will give you
The nations for your inheritance,
And the ends of the earth for your possession

(Ps. 2:8).

> I will build my church, and the gates of Hades shall not prevail against it (Matt. 16:18).
>
> Thus it is written, and thus it was necessary for the Christ to suffer and to rise from the dead the third day, and that repentance and remission of sins should be preached in his name to all nations, beginning at Jerusalem (Luke 24:46-47).
>
> All authority has been given to me in heaven and on earth. Go therefore and make disciples of all the nations, baptizing them in the name of the Father and of the Son and of the Holy Spirit, teaching them to observe all things that I have commanded you; and lo, I am with you always, even to the end of the age (Matt. 28:18-20).

In his covenant promise to Abraham, established 4,000 years ago, God declared his purpose to be universal: '... and in you all the families of the earth shall be blessed' (Gen. 12:3, cf. 18:17-18). The book of Revelation foresees the completed church of Christ as composed of 'a great multitude which no one could number, of all nations, tribes, peoples, and tongues' (Rev. 7:9).

Robert Dabney referred to Christ as 'the missionary of heaven',[5] for the church has the privilege of being engaged in the spiritual crusade of the Lord Jesus Christ.

John the Baptist understood the universal purpose of God when he directed attention to the Lord Jesus Christ: 'Behold! The

Lamb of God who takes away *the sin of the world*' (John 1:29, emphasis added). The New Testament writers clearly saw the global extent of the atonement: 'Jesus Christ the righteous ... is the propitiation for our sins, and not for ours only but also for the whole world' (1 John 2:1-2). The reader of the Bible cannot fail to see the worldwide scope of God's love and mercy.

The Lord Jesus commissioned his church to 'make disciples of all the nations' (Matt. 28:19).

A worldwide vision

'The church must be put on a missionary footing.'[6] The missionary interest of a local church should be more than a special Sunday, an occasional visit from a missionary on furlough, or a visit from a national representative of a missionary agency; it should also be more than the apportioning of funds to the work of missions. What is needed is a global view of the church of Christ that is always looking beyond itself to the lost sheep which the great Shepherd will call to himself, to the lost coin to be discovered, to the lost son to be brought back from the far country (Luke 15). The church needs to see the world significance of a gospel that is for all nations, peoples, races and tongues and a Christ who is the Saviour *of the world*, through whom *all the families of the earth* will be blessed.

A multifaceted ministry

Peter Milsom argues for a breadth of ministry in missionary endeavour. He notes that the early Christians spontaneously co-operated together in strategic areas and this contributed to the advance of the gospel: 'It is vitally important that, as local churches, we have a global vision of the greatness of God's purposes. We may live in small communities and belong to small fellowships, or live in remote parts of the world and see very little happening, but it is a tremendous encouragement to realize that we are part of the greatest enterprise in history.'[7]

International co-operation

This is seen in the early church, which is our example in the following areas:

The work of gospel proclamation and church-planting[8]

During his great missionary journeys Paul drew on gifted men from many churches, including those that were newly established (Acts 15:40; 16:1-3; 20:4). Today we need to draw on gifted men from many churches for the great task of reaching the world with the gospel.

The goal of missions is to plant new churches and to strengthen indigenous local churches so that they continue the work of gospel preaching and making disciples in their area (Acts 14:21-23).

A ministry of mutual care and encouragement

The apostles and others visited churches to encourage believers (Acts 8:14; 9:32; 15:41; 16:1-5). Churches around the world today need encouragement. Such a ministry does not imply either a continuing apostolate or the authority of one church over another.

> And Sopater of Berea accompanied him [Paul] to Asia — also Aristarchus and Secundus of the Thessalonians, and Gaius of Derbe, and Timothy, and Tychicus and Trophimus of Asia (Acts 20:4).
>
> And when they had preached the gospel to that city and made many disciples, they returned to Lystra, Iconium, and Antioch, strengthening the souls of the disciples, exhorting them to continue in the faith, and saying, 'We must through many tribulations enter the kingdom of God.' So when they had appointed elders in every church, and prayed with fasting, they commended them to the Lord in whom they had believed (Acts 14:21-23).

The provision of leadership, ministry and pastoral oversight

New Testament examples of this were Barnabas at Antioch, Timothy at Ephesus and Titus in Crete (Acts 11:22; 1 Tim. 1:3; Titus 1:5). This can be achieved today through 'experienced pastors visiting to assist in the vital task of training indigenous evangelists and teachers'.

Serving each other with gifts of love, both material and personal

The early churches sent financial gifts (Acts 11:29-30; 1 Cor. 16:1; 2 Cor. 8 – 9; Phil. 4:14-16) and people, such as those who gave help and encouragement to Paul when he was in prison (Phil. 2:25).

Defining and defending the truth in the face of error

This is seen at the Council of Jerusalem (Acts 15:1 – 16:4) where important doctrinal issues were discussed and the conclusions communicated to the churches.

Additional international co-operation can be given in the following areas:

Printing and distribution

A significant part of missionary endeavour is the publication of suitable material for the mission field. In the West we have a wealth of Christian literature, spanning centuries. Bible translations, commentaries and publications geared to the cultural and spiritual climate of each race make an invaluable contribution to the spiritual growth of national churches.

Radio broadcasting

Skilled and gifted Christians can spread the gospel in lands where missionaries are forbidden to enter and where open conversation about the Lord Jesus Christ would result in imprisonment or execution.

Cultivating a worldwide vision

How can local churches cultivate a worldwide vision?

By preaching worldwide mission

It is difficult to see how any expository ministry could miss the universal implications of the gospel. The great issue of the early church was 'the defining of a trans-racial and trans-cultural community who knows God in Jesus Christ'.[9] But the global spread of God's salvation did not begin with the arrival of his Son into the world. One of the notable characters of the Old Testament was Jonah, the rebellious missionary, whose story serves to illustrate the failure of Israel towards her neighbours.

A glance at the ancestry of the Lord Jesus shows the inclusion of Rahab the Canaanite and Ruth the Moabitess (Matt. 1:5). And what about the wise men from the East who came to Jerusalem looking for the newborn King of the Jews? (Matt. 2:1-2).

By promoting worldwide mission

If the task of elders is to discern within the church those 'faithful men who will be able to teach others also' (2 Tim. 2:2) and to equip 'the saints for the work of ministry, for the edifying of the body of Christ' (Eph. 4:12), then they have a duty to stimulate interest and encourage suitably gifted people for the mission field. Elders have an important ministry 'in bringing into being evangelists for both home and overseas'.[10]

By the selection of missionaries

> Trust in the LORD with all your heart,
> And lean not on your own understanding;
> In all your ways acknowledge him,
> And he shall direct your paths
> (Prov. 3:5-6).

In New Testament days divine guidance seems to have been more straightforward and clear than it is today. The Holy Spirit made his will known among the prophets and teachers at Antioch when Barnabas and Saul were to begin their missionary endeavours (Acts 13:1-3). Apostles Peter, James and John supported this ministry when they 'perceived the grace' given to Paul (Gal. 2:9). Timothy, on the other hand, was appointed as a result of specific prophecies (1 Tim. 1:18).

These days the Lord makes his will evident by ordinary means through his Word and Spirit. Two clear indicators are graces and gifts. One who is appointed by God to engage in missionary endeavour will have both the spiritual calibre and the necessary abilities for the work.

Christian character

There will be good evidence of conversion. The local church will be ideally suited to discern the grace of God evidenced in the fruit of the Spirit (Gal. 5:22-23).

- Is there a genuine concern for the glory of God?
- Is there an active interest in the salvation of the lost?
- If the role involves preaching, is there good evidence of the necessary gifts and disposition?
- How does the candidate relate to his/her family, Christian brothers and sisters, friends, neighbours and colleagues at college or work?
- Is the candidate subject to depression? How does he/she endure discouragement? Is he/she stable in a crisis?
- Is the individual's family life of good quality, and will it survive the pressures of a cross-cultural situation? If the candidate is single, does he/she have the resilience to survive in an isolated situation in a foreign land?[11]

Ian Tait outlines the essential qualities required when considering the appointment and support of missionaries:

Doctrine

Sound theology in a missionary is essential (see 1 Tim. 4:16; 2 Tim. 1:13; 2:2,15; 4:1-5).

Discipline

'The man who is not himself disciplined has no warrant to make disciples of others.'

Development

Maturity is essential: 'No missionary training nor theological degree is a substitute for maturity.'

Demonstration

'If a man has no aptitude to demonstrate in the work at home, he has none to take abroad.'[12]

By training missionaries

The leadership of a local church needs to identify and train gifted men and women. Peter Milsom asks the question: 'Are we raising up a generation of men who have proven skills in evangelism, Bible teaching, discipling and church leadership — men whose first commitment is to the cause of the gospel in the world? Does your church leadership reflect a spectrum of ages incorporating both the wisdom of age and the energy of youth?'[13] This is the best training and experience for those who will later engage in missionary work.

Cross-cultural missionary work is demanding. Not only does it involve learning a new language, but there is also the requirement to understand a new culture.

It is the task of the home church to train, support and encourage its missionaries. Such people may be wholly supported by their home church or a number of churches; they may engage in 'tent-ministry' to support themselves;

> This is a faithful saying: if a man desires the position of a bishop [overseer], he desires a good work. A bishop then must be blameless, the husband of one wife, temperate, sober-minded, of good behaviour, hospitable, able to teach; not given to wine, not violent, not greedy for money, but gentle, not quarrelsome, not covetous; one who rules his own house well, having his children in submission with all reverence (for if a man does not know how to rule his own house, how will he take care of the church of God?); not a novice, lest being puffed up with pride he fall into the same condemnation as the devil. Moreover he must have a good testimony among those who are outside, lest he should fall into reproach and the snare of the devil. Likewise deacons must be reverent, not double-tongued, not given to much wine, not greedy for money, holding the mystery of the faith with a pure conscience. But let these also first be proved; then let them serve as deacons, being found blameless. Likewise their wives must be reverent, not slanderers, temperate, faithful in all things. Let deacons be the husbands of one wife, ruling their children and their own houses well. For those who have served well as deacons obtain for themselves a good standing and great boldness in the faith which is in Christ Jesus (1 Tim. 3:1-13).

they may follow their career or profession to the benefit of the indigenous peoples. The aim of the missionary is to promote the work of God through a local church, where there already is one, or by seeking to make disciples and establishing a local church.

In many lands there is no freedom to propagate the gospel. Entry requirements are becoming more difficult for the missionary or evangelist. Other skills must be offered to gain access for the gospel. Countries closed to the missionary may, for example, be open to the teacher of English.[14]

The missionary and the local church

'Local churches are central to God's global purpose.'[15] The local church, the home church, is the sending church. Ian Tait says, 'If the New Testament is our authoritative guide in the work of God, it is an unquestionable fact that concerning the human aspect of sending forth missionaries — sent ones — the sending body is the local church, and not a missionary society.'[16]

Now in the church that was at Antioch there were certain prophets and teachers: Barnabas, Simeon who was called Niger, Lucius of Cyrene, Manaen who had been brought up with Herod the tetrarch, and Saul. As they ministered to the Lord and fasted, the Holy Spirit said, 'Now separate for me Barnabas and Saul for the work to which I have called them.' Then, having fasted and prayed, and laid hands on them, they sent them away (Acts 13:1-3).

Paul and Barnabas were sent out by the local church at Antioch, under the direction of the Holy Spirit (Acts 13:1-3). Having spent some time in missionary endeavour, they reported back to the local church at Antioch (Acts 14:26-28). They were sent by the church to Jerusalem to consult with the apostles (Acts 15:1-2). Upon their return they 'remained in Antioch, teaching and preaching the word of the Lord' (Acts 15:35). After some time Paul set out again, this time with Silas, to encourage the newly planted churches, 'being commended by the brethren to the grace of God' (Acts 15:40). Two years later he returned for a prolonged stay (Acts 18:22-23).

Bill James recommends that each local church should adopt a missionary policy, where the Great Commission is accepted as a responsibility laid upon every one of God's people — a responsibility 'not only to our immediate locality, but also to the wider world as we look for disciples in "all nations".'[17]

If power and control are exercised by a local church over its missionaries it will lead to serious problems. 'Mobilizing' missionaries may all too easily become 'immobilizing' missionaries: 'The church is brilliant at turning its missionaries into Inoperative Combat Personnel, casualties to frustration, discouragement and spiritual intimidation.'[18]

Missionaries may also fall into the trap of wanting to retain control over newly-planted churches. Paul demonstrated remarkable self-control, rather than church control, in dealing with newly appointed church leaders. This 'liberty of development is in sharp contrast to the practice of many missions even today who retain control in the hands of expatriate missionaries'.[19]

> And we urge you, brethren, to recognize those who labour among you, and are over you in the Lord and admonish you, and to esteem them very highly in love for their work's sake (1 Thess. 5:12-13).

Prayer support

> But that you also may know my affairs and how I am doing, Tychicus, a beloved brother and faithful minister in the Lord, will make all things known to you; whom I have sent to you for this very purpose, that you may know our affairs, and that he may comfort your hearts (Eph. 6:21-22).
>
> Yet I considered it necessary to send to you Epaphroditus, my brother, fellow worker, and fellow soldier, but your messenger and the one who ministered to my need... (Phil. 2:25).

Paul frequently urged the churches to pray for him — to strive together with him in prayer (Rom. 15:30) and to plead with God for the opening of doors for the gospel (Eph. 6:18-19; Col. 4:3).

Missionaries have a responsibility to their own local church. They must keep their brothers and sisters well informed with news and relevant matters for prayer. Regular communication helps the home church keep involved in the missionary endeavour.

New Testament missionaries kept in close contact with their supporting church (Col. 4:7-9; Eph. 6:21-22) and the churches enquired about their missionary endeavour and at times sent church officers to encourage them (Phil. 2:25-30).

Pastoral support

Who provides the pastoral care for missionaries? Paul urges the elders of the church in Ephesus: '... take heed to yourselves and to all the flock, among which the Holy Spirit has made you overseers, to shepherd [i.e. pastor] the church of God which he purchased with his own blood' (Acts 20:28). Ideally missionaries will have been part of the leadership team before moving out in mission (Acts 13:1-3), but whether they are considered as part of the leadership who have been seconded to the work of gospel outreach, or whether they are regarded as members of the body who have been sent out, either way, they are the pastoral responsibility of their own local church. Their well-being will be of paramount importance to the church. Brothers and sisters 'back home' will not only be concerned to see that they have adequate living accommodation, sufficient food, clothing, heat and light, books, education for their children and transport, but also holidays for relaxation and refreshment and enough money to cover the cost of the fare home at appropriate intervals.

Financial support

'The Lord has commanded that those who preach the gospel should live from the gospel' (1 Cor. 9:14). Provision for those sent out by your local church should take precedence in church finances over all other missionary and charitable giving.

> For you know the grace of our Lord Jesus Christ, that though he was rich, yet for your sakes he became poor, that you through his poverty might become rich
> (2 Cor. 8:9).
>
> Let him who is taught the word share in all good things with him who teaches. Do not be deceived, God is not mocked; for whatever a man sows, that he will also reap
> (Gal. 6:6-7).

Giving to support missionary endeavour is based upon the Christian's response to the 'indescribable gift' of God (2 Cor. 9:15; cf. John 3:16) and 'the grace of our Lord Jesus Christ' (2 Cor. 8:9). There is also the strong motivation in the enigmatic words of the Lord: '... make friends for yourselves by unrighteous mammon' (Luke 16:9). What better way to make friends than, in the providence of God, to assist in their conversion? Financing evangelistic missionaries is part of our 'fellowship in the gospel' (Phil. 1:5; cf. 4:15-16).

Ian Tait summarizes the teaching on financial support in 2 Corinthians by stating that Christian giving is:

- Willingly and joyfully carried out (2 Cor. 8:3,12; 9:7)
- Real, active and businesslike (2 Cor. 8:10-11; 9:3-4)
- Fair (2 Cor. 8:13-15)
- Openly honest (2 Cor. 8:16-21)
- Generous (2 Cor. 9:5-6; 8:3)[20]

Failure to give proper financial support to preachers of the gospel is a serious offence, akin to mocking God! (Gal. 6:6-8; cf. Mal. 3:8-10).

Where a local church cannot raise the support for its minister and its missionary there may be fellowship with likeminded churches: 'We acknowledge that support, training and preparation of members sent out from our own congregation may best be accomplished in fellowship with like-minded churches and other agencies.'[21]

Those who are giving their lives to missionary endeavour deserve the encouragement and fellowship of brothers and sisters. When the apostle John wrote to his beloved friend Gaius (3 John) he warmly commended him for his generous treatment of missionaries.

Peter Barnes outlines from the Third Epistle of John the reasons for supporting Christian missionaries and evangelists:

> Now you Philippians know also that in the beginning of the gospel, when I departed from Macedonia, no church shared with me concerning giving and receiving but you only. For even in Thessalonica you sent aid once and again for my necessities. Not that I seek the gift, but I seek the fruit that abounds to your account (Phil. 4:15-17).

1. Missionaries and evangelists work in Christ's name (3 John 7).

2. Missionaries and evangelists are released from any temptation to solicit support from unbelievers (3 John 7).

3. We become fellow workers in the cause of the gospel (3 John 8; cf. Matt. 10:41).[22]

Conclusion

Next to the privilege of being directly engaged in missionary endeavour is the joy of sharing 'fellowship in the gospel' (Phil. 1:5). 'One sows and another reaps' (John 4:37); one plants and another waters (1 Cor. 3:6-8); one labours in the gospel and another supports that labour in prayer, fellowship and finance (Phil. 4:15-17; Luke 6:38). Whatever our contribution to the missionary crusade of Christ, we shall all share in the great reward (1 Cor. 3:8).

12.
Church-planting

Church-planting

What is an evangelist according to the Scriptures?

....

....

....

Is the office of New Testament evangelist for today?

....

....

....

What are the different methods for establishing new churches today?

....

....

....

What is the relationship between elders and evangelists?

....

....

....

What are the gifts necessary for an evangelist? (Cite Scripture in support of your answer.)

....

....

....

Recommended reading

The books and papers listed below are written from differing, and initially convincing, viewpoints and therefore will stretch and train thinking and ability in handling Scripture.

Crossley, Gareth. *Everyday Evangelism* (Welwyn: Evangelical Press, 1987), pp.139-70.

Hay, Alex. R. *New Testament Order for Church and Missionary* (Wirral, Cheshire: New Testament Missionary Union, 1947), pp.78-116.

Shakespeare, John. *Studies in New Testament Evangelism* (Walsall: Midland Road Strict and Particular Baptist Church, 1980), p.17.

Church-planting

'And he himself [the ascended Christ] gave some to be apostles, some prophets, some evangelists, and some pastors and teachers, for the equipping of the saints for the work of ministry, for the edifying of the body of Christ, till we all come to the unity of the faith and of the knowledge of the Son of God, to a perfect man, to the measure of the stature of the fulness of Christ...' (Eph. 4:11-13).

Over the years false ideas have arisen in the church in regard to the office and function of the evangelist. If our principle is *Sola Scriptura* (By Scripture alone), then the only right question is, 'What do the Scriptures say?'

> Preach the word! Be ready in season and out of season. Convince, rebuke, exhort, with all long-suffering and teaching. For the time will come when they will not endure sound doctrine, but according to their own desires, because they have itching ears, they will heap up for themselves teachers; and they will turn their ears away from the truth, and be turned aside to fables. But you be watchful in all things, endure afflictions, do the work of an evangelist, fulfil your ministry (2 Tim. 4:2-5).

What are evangelists?

> And Jesus came and spoke to them, saying, 'All authority has been given to me in heaven and on earth. Go therefore and make disciples of all the nations, baptizing them in the name of the Father and of the Son and of the Holy Spirit, teaching them to observe all things that I have commanded you; and lo, I am with you always, even to the end of the age.' Amen (Matt. 28:18-20).

In modern usage the term 'evangelist' refers to someone who preaches to the unsaved. In practice the evangelist addresses a large mixed company of saved and unsaved in a school hall, church building, marquee, or any other suitable location. Modern-day evangelists travel extensively but rarely stay anywhere for more than a week or two, often only spending one or two evenings in one place. These are not evangelists in the New Testament sense, but simply preachers who have been gifted by God to preach salvation through repentance and faith to the lost. It is likely that some of those termed evangelists in the modern sense are really called to the full ministry of the evangelist in the New Testament sense, but are fulfilling only a part of their ministry.[1]

Because the term 'evangelist' occurs only three times it has generally been thought that the Bible has little to say on the subject. This misunderstanding has been further strengthened by commentators misnaming the letters of Paul to Timothy and Titus 'The Pastoral Epistles'.[2] Consequently, or coincidentally, it is a common misconception that these letters are addressed to 'pastors', or 'ministers of the gospel'. It is difficult to understand why they were ever called 'Pastoral Epistles', for neither their objective nor their content gives any ground for such a designation.[3] Not one biblical passage can be adduced to show, or even hint, that Timothy was a pastor or elder, yet this is the traditional view strongly asserted by many commentators and preachers today. While Lenski argues that Timothy and Titus were not pastors, he nevertheless assigns to them a unique irreplaceable role as 'representatives of Paul for the guidance of the churches'.[4]

In a similar way Bannerman maintains that New Testament evangelists 'are exhibited to us in the Scripture narrative rather as the attendants upon the apostles in their journeys and their assistants in planting and establishing the churches, acting under them, as their delegates, carrying out their instructions. If the contributions of one church were to be carried to another to supply its more urgent need, it was an evangelist that was selected as the messenger of the church. If an inspired letter was to be conveyed to the Christian community to whom an apostle had addressed it, an evangelist was the bearer of the precious record. If an apostle had converted many to the faith of Christ in one particular locality and hastened on to other labours and triumphs, an evangelist was left behind to organize the infant church.'[5]

In seeing evangelists as having such a restricted role, as being nothing more than 'attendants upon the apostles' and 'their assistants in planting and establishing the churches', there is a failure to understand the functions of the evangelists in their own right. With such a limited view of evangelists, it is not surprising that their office and function have been largely lost to the church through the years. Linking evangelists so closely with New Testament apostles inevitably leads to the demise of the former office when the latter is understood to have terminated with the end of the apostolic age (at the death of the apostle John).

In the New Testament the name 'evangelist' *is* applied to pioneers, groundbreaking men who travelled from place to place (Acts 21:8; cf. 8:5,26,40), to proclaim the gospel of God concerning his Son Jesus Christ to unbelieving individuals, groups or nations, but their ministry was not fulfilled until they had gathered the converts together as an assembly of the body of Christ and delivered to them the whole counsel of God. They were the extension agents, the church-planters, the missionaries responsible for establishing the church in unevangelized regions, and the continuing counsellors to those churches once they had been established. All these assertions will be substantiated from the biblical record.

In the first place, the twelve apostles were commissioned to be evangelists, or, as Jesus called them, 'fishers of men' (Matt. 4:19). Their apostleship evidently included a strongly evangelistic element. When we seek to build a concept of New Testament evangelists, cognizance has to be given to this evangelistic aspect of the apostles' function. They were apostles *and* evangelists. All the apostles were evangelists, but not all New Testament evangelists were apostles (e.g. Acts 21:8; Eph. 4:11; 2 Tim. 4:5). Distinctions must be drawn between each office and its corresponding function.

Secondly, and contrary to the traditional view, it is evident that both Timothy and Titus were evangelists, not elders, pastors or bishops, and Paul's letters were addressed to them in that capacity. They were operating the 'after-sales service' aspect of evangelism – preaching, consolidating and setting in order. Each was left behind by Paul to deal with churches until they could be independent.[6] The letters of Paul to Timothy and Titus would be better designated 'The Missionary Epistles' or 'A Manual for Evangelists'. Timothy and Titus were not pastors; they were evangelists, pioneers, receiving from their mentor instruction and counsel regarding their specific ministry. In 2 Timothy 4:5 Timothy is not being urged to be a pastor with evangelistic zeal, but to be an evangelist with pastoral concern.

The arguments against Timothy and Titus being regarded as elders (pastors) are as follows:

1. They had no local church to which they were answerable, but were under the direct authority of the apostle *and* evangelist Paul (1 Cor. 4:17; 1 Thess. 3:2).

2. They travelled extensively and for prolonged periods that would militate against pastoral responsibilities in one church (Acts 19:22; Phil. 2:19).

3. They functioned as assistants to evangelists, as pioneers performing whatever tasks were necessary in the founding and establishing of new churches (Titus 1:5; 1 Thess. 3:2).

> Therefore, when we could no longer endure it, we thought it good to be left in Athens alone, and sent Timothy, our brother and minister of God, and our fellow labourer in the gospel of Christ, to establish you and encourage you concerning your faith... (1 Thess. 3:1-2).

4. They functioned as pioneer evangelists in their own right and had evident authority over elders in local congregations (2 Tim. 4:5; Titus 1:5).

Although 1 and 2 Timothy and Titus contain teaching regarding elders and deacons and those who walk disorderly, they also emphasize the need for personal faithfulness in ministry and for being content with just the basic necessities of food and clothing. While these directives are applicable to supported ministers of the gospel, they are even more appropriate for evangelists (cf. Luke 10:1-12). Paul, the mature, experienced evangelist and church-planter (1 Cor. 3:6-11), was thoroughly acquainted with the difficulties, dangers and temptations of the evangelist's life and ministry. He knew only too well how tough the work could be — the subtlety of the enemy, the special dangers and temptations that beset the evangelist and the need for constant vigilance and preparedness.

The New Testament contains three references to evangelist(s) — literally, 'preacher(s) of good news':

> Therefore those who were scattered went everywhere preaching the word. Then Philip went down to the city of Samaria and preached Christ to them (Acts 8:4-5).
>
> On the next day we who were Paul's companions departed and came to Caesarea, and entered the house of Philip the evangelist, who was one of the seven, and stayed with him (Acts 21:8).
>
> And he himself [Christ] gave some to be apostles, some prophets, some evangelists, and some pastors and teachers, for the equipping of the saints for the work of ministry, for the edifying of the body of Christ, till we all come to the unity of the faith and of the knowledge of the Son of God, to a perfect man, to the measure of the stature of the fulness of Christ (Eph. 4:11-13).

1. Philip is called 'the evangelist' (Acts 21:8). He is first mentioned as one of the seven men appointed in Jerusalem to deal with the daily distribution to the widows in the church (Acts 6:2-6). He did not continue in that role but moved on to become an evangelist (Acts 8:5-8,26-40). Such a call to a wider ministry often occurs in Christian service.

2. The second occurrence is among the list of 'gifts' of the ascended Christ to his church: 'And he himself gave some to be apostles, some prophets, some evangelists, and some pastors and teachers' (Eph. 4:11). The context is one of church growth. The reference to the gifts which Christ gave to his church (vv. 7-8,11) may mean either, 'He gave some men gifts *to be* apostles...', or 'He gave the church gifts, *some of which were* apostles...' Whichever it is makes no material difference and the goal is clear. Church growth is the key

(v. 13). It is both quantitative and qualitative — the enlargement of the church through conversions (the work of apostles and evangelists), and the enrichment of the church through increased knowledge (the work of pastors and teachers). The church grows in quantity and quality through the Word.

3. The third reference is in the second letter to Timothy where Paul urges his young colleague, 'Be watchful in all things, endure afflictions, do the work of an evangelist, fulfil your ministry' (2 Tim. 4:5).

> But you be watchful in all things, endure afflictions, do the work of an evangelist, fulfil your ministry (2 Tim. 4: 5).

The function of pioneer evangelists

Evangelists work towards the formation of new churches. That church-planting is the goal of all evangelists 'is so obviously the case in the New Testament', writes John Shakespeare, 'that it is no wonder Satan has sought to disrupt it, this being the ordained means for the kingdom's growth and establishment. The whole pattern has become horribly distorted.'[7]

Evangelists are preachers

1. Evangelists are heralds of the gospel

Evangelists are public preachers who aim for the conversion of sinners through heralding the gospel of God (2 Tim. 4:2-5; Acts 14:21; Rom. 10:13-15). Evangelistic preaching is God's ordained method of saving sinners (1 Cor. 1:17-21).

As we saw in chapter 8, in the New Testament three verbs are used, at times almost interchangeably, for the activity of preaching, proclaiming, heralding good news about the Lord Jesus Christ. They are *euangelizo* ('to bring good news'), *kerusso* ('to herald') and *katangello* ('to herald or proclaim the message'). Paul twice speaks of himself as a *kerux* — a herald, each time distinguishing this work from his apostolic office and function as a teacher: 'I was appointed a preacher [*kerux*] and an apostle ... a teacher of the Gentiles in faith and truth' (1 Tim. 2:7); 'I was appointed a

> For 'whoever calls on the name of the LORD shall be saved.' How then shall they call on him in whom they have not believed? And how shall they believe in him of whom they have not heard? And how shall they hear without a preacher? And how shall they preach unless they are sent? ... So then faith comes by hearing, and hearing by the word of God (Rom. 10:13-15,17).

preacher [*kerux*], an apostle, and a teacher of the Gentiles' (2 Tim. 1:11). Noah is also referred to by Peter as a *kerux* of righteousness (2 Peter 2:5). A *kerux* is a herald who is invested with public authority to convey official messages. In relation to the Christian gospel, a herald is evidently one who is invested with *divine* authority to convey *God's* messages.

2. Evangelists are flexible public preachers

According to 2 Timothy 4:2, Timothy's 'proclamation is to be characterized by urgency, opportunism and changing response to the needs of his audience'.[8] There are five recorded accounts of evangelistic preaching — that is, proclamations of good news concerning Christ to those who did not know it (Acts 2:14-40; 3:12-26; 10:34-43; 13:16-41; 17:22-31). They are no doubt only summaries, but inspired summaries nevertheless, and therefore totally accurate.[9]

3. Evangelists preach privately

In contrast to his public preaching (literally, heralding) of Christ (Acts 8:5), Philip the evangelist was directed by the Holy Spirit to engage in private evangelism of the Ethiopian Minister of Finance (Acts 8:26-39). It is abundantly clear from the New Testament that evangelism includes addressing large or small groups, public or private gatherings, families or individuals. When speaking with the elders from Ephesus, the apostle Paul reminds them of his public and private work in their city (Acts 20:20-21).

> Preach the word! Be ready in season and out of season. Convince, rebuke, exhort, with all long-suffering and teaching (2 Tim. 4:2).
>
> I kept back nothing that was helpful, but proclaimed it to you, and taught you publicly and from house to house, testifying to Jews, and also to Greeks, repentance toward God and faith toward our Lord Jesus Christ (Acts 20:20-21).
>
> Go into all the world and preach the gospel to every creature (Mark 16:15)

4. Evangelists preach wherever there is an audience

They preach in town (Acts 2:14-39), in the market place (Acts 17:17), in the open countryside (Matt. 5:1; John 6:25), by the lakeside (Mark 4:1), in synagogues (Mark 1:39; Acts 13:14; 14:1; 17:1-2; 18:4; 19:8), in a school (Acts 19:9-10) and in homes (Acts 5:42; 11:12; 16:32; 20:20;28:30-31).

5. Evangelists preach widely

Paul covered a considerable area in his preaching work (Rom. 15:19). He was ambitious for God (Rom. 15:20), and he was an originator, an initiator, a pioneer evangelist. His goal was 'to preach the gospel, not where Christ was named, lest [he] should build on another man's foundation, but as it is written: "To whom he was not announced, they shall see; and those who have not heard shall understand"' (Rom. 15:20-21; cf. Isa. 52:15).

6. Evangelists strategically choose their locations

According to Jim Petersen, Paul's 'sphere of ministry was to establish beachheads of new believers. He didn't do everything; he just established beachheads. Then he counted on the continued growth of his offspring to enlarge that sphere. The entire success of Paul's effort depended on the continued growth and subsequent expansion of the gospel through his spiritual children.'[10]

Evangelists are teachers

1. Evangelists seek to instruct and establish the new converts in the faith (Matt. 28:20; Acts 14:21-22; Titus 2)

It is part of their work to equip 'the saints for the work of ministry, for the edifying of the body of Christ' (Eph. 4:12). To this end Paul preached fully, dealing with his subject in depth (Acts 20:27).

2. Evangelists gather new converts together as a local assembly of believers

They teach and instruct the assembly so that as a church it becomes a self-sufficient and independent body, answerable to God alone, having its own spiritual leaders, life, structure, discipline and teaching (Titus 1:5-9; Acts 14:23). Where Paul had to move on before the church was fully established, he left behind, where possible, some of his fellow evangelists to complete the work (Titus 1:5).

3. Evangelists stay in one location until a viable church is established

Paul stayed at Ephesus for three years (Acts 20:31; cf. 1 Cor. 16:5-9), and at Corinth for eighteen months (Acts 18:11). Sometimes evangelists were asked to move on (Acts 16:39-40) or even forced to leave (Acts 17:5-14). Occasionally in the New Testament period the Holy Spirit made the next destination obvious (Acts 16:6-10).

Evangelists share the gospel with the poor and needy

> Defend the poor and fatherless;
> Do justice to the afflicted and needy.
> Deliver the poor and needy;
> Free them from the hand of the wicked
> (Ps. 82:3-4).

A testimony to Messiah's ministry was that 'the poor have the gospel preached to them' (Matt. 11:5; Luke 7:22). Jesus declared that the scripture was being fulfilled which said:

> The Spirit of the LORD is upon me,
> Because he has anointed me
> To preach the gospel to the poor
> (Luke 4:18; cf. Isa. 61:1).

Evangelists are supervisors

1. Evangelists exercise supervision over the newly established churches (1 Tim. 4:11-13,16)

Their responsibilities include rebuke (1 Tim. 1:3; 5:19-21; Titus 1:13-14; 2:15) and the rejection of any whose life, teaching, or beliefs are not according to sound doctrine (Titus 3:10-11; Acts 15:1-2; 1 Tim. 1:3-4).

2. The authority of evangelists is solely the Word of God and their influence is entirely spiritual

In no case can they make a demand based upon their own authority, but they can insist upon compliance with what is taught in the Word of God. 'It is written,' is the evangelist's authority. Those who are spiritual will obey the Word of God (1 Cor. 14:37), and separate themselves from all who cause divisions and offences (Rom. 16:17).

> For I received from the Lord that which I also delivered to you...
> (1 Cor. 11:23).
>
> If anyone thinks himself to be a prophet or spiritual, let him acknowledge that the things which I write to you are the commandments of the Lord (1 Cor. 14:37).

3. Evangelists exercise a constant ministry of prayer for the newly established churches (Col. 1:9)

Paul said that his 'deep concern for all the churches' weighed heavily upon him 'daily' (2 Cor. 11:28).

The qualifications of pioneer evangelists

A two-tier structure for New Testament evangelists is evident: evangelists and assistant, or trainee, evangelists.

Senior evangelists

In order to be qualified for church-planting, pioneer evangelists must fulfil the qualifications for eldership and have some years of experience in church leadership.

Senior evangelists need to be spiritually mature and to possess a wide Christian experience. Because evangelists plant churches (Acts 2:41-42,47; 14:21-23; 15:36; 18:7-11; 20:17-35; 1 Tim. 3:1-13; Titus 1:5-9), their gifts and qualifications consist in more than simply the ability to communicate with and persuade unbelievers, but also in 'sufficient maturity, understanding and discernment to care for churches in their infant state'.[11] Experienced men, such as Barnabas and Saul (i.e. Paul), who were part of the established leadership of the church at Antioch, were separated by the Holy Spirit and were appointed as the team leaders (Acts 13:1-3). When Barnabas and Paul separated to form two teams, Paul chose Silas (Acts 15:40), one of the 'leading men among the brethren' at the Jerusalem Council (Acts 15:22). While evangelists were equal in rank, a senior leader was recognized in each team — presumably on the basis of experience and proven ability.

> This is a faithful saying: If a man desires the position of a bishop [overseer], he desires a good work. A bishop then must be blameless, the husband of one wife, temperate, sober-minded, of good behaviour, hospitable, able to teach; not given to wine, not violent, not greedy for money, but gentle, not quarrelsome, not covetous; one who rules his own house well, having his children in submission with all reverence (for if a man does not know how to rule his own house, how will he take care of the church of God?); not a novice, lest being puffed up with pride he fall into the same condemnation as the devil. Moreover he must have a good testimony among those who are outside, lest he fall into reproach and the snare of the devil (1 Tim. 3:1-7).

Assistant evangelists

Assistant evangelists work with the senior evangelists. They are in training, undergoing a practical apprenticeship — men like Timothy, Titus and Mark.

Timothy

Timothy 'was well spoken of by the brethren who were at Lystra and Iconium' (Acts 16:2). He was probably converted under Paul's ministry (1 Tim. 1:2,18). The Holy Spirit gave 'prophecies' regarding Timothy's work (1 Tim. 1:18). It is also recorded that 'Paul wanted to have him go on with him' (Acts 16:3). Timothy gained invaluable 'in-service' training from the apostle Paul (2 Tim. 1:13), who had every confidence in his young colleague (Phil. 2:19-23). Timothy travelled extensively between the newly formed churches (1 Cor. 4:17; Phil. 2:19; 1 Thess. 3:6) and was sent on many important and often highly sensitive missions (1 Cor. 4:17; 1 Thess. 3:2). He had authority to correct false teaching in the churches (1 Tim. 1:3) and was also authorized and encouraged to train suitable Christian men as teachers (2 Tim. 2:2). The men he trained would probably later be appointed as elders.

Titus

Titus travelled extensively between the churches (2 Cor. 7:6-7). Paul had a high regard for him. On one occasion Paul was actually hindered in preaching the gospel at Troas because Titus, whom he expected to be in the town, was not there, so Paul moved on to Macedonia (2 Cor. 2:13). Like the apostle Paul, Titus had a care for the churches (2 Cor. 8:16-17). Paul describes Titus as 'my partner and fellow worker' and he and the other members of the evangelistic team as 'messengers of the churches, the glory of Christ' (2 Cor. 8:23). Titus was instructed to 'appoint elders in every city' (Titus 1:5).

Mark

John Mark was taken along by Barnabas and Paul, in a similar capacity to that of Timothy and Titus (Acts 12:25). Unlike Timothy and Titus, he returned home prematurely and was the cause of a strong difference of opinion between Barnabas and Paul (Acts 15:36-40). John Mark obviously regained the esteem of Paul, as he is included in the second letter to Timothy, where Paul writes, 'Get Mark and bring him with you, for he is useful to me for ministry' (2 Tim. 4:11).

The appointment of pioneer evangelists

Evangelists are appointed by God

1. The Lord Jesus personally appointed his twelve apostles as 'fishers of men' (Matt. 4:19).

2. The Holy Spirit communicated his appointment of Barnabas and Saul (Acts 13:2). Saul had already demonstrated himself as an able teacher (Acts 11:26). In the absence of further information it is difficult to deduce just how the Holy Spirit makes his choice known to the church today.

3. God sends out his heralds (Rom. 10:15).

Evangelists maintain links with their supporting church

1. Prayer support is vital. Paul's evangelistic work among the Gentiles began in a prayer meeting in the church at Antioch. He was separated to the work after they had 'fasted and prayed' (Acts 13:2-3). He constantly appealed to the churches for prayer support (Eph. 6:18-20; Col. 4:2-4; 1 Thess. 5:25; 2 Thess. 3:1-2; Rom. 15:30-32).

> Continue earnestly in prayer, being vigilant in it with thanksgiving; meanwhile praying also for us, that God would open to us a door for the word, to speak the mystery of Christ… (Col. 4:2-3).

2. Evangelists have the respect of their 'home' churches. When Barnabas and Paul separated to form two teams, 'Paul chose Silas and departed, being commended by the brethren to the grace of God' (Acts 15:40). Silas, as we have noted, was one of the 'leading men among the brethren' at the Jerusalem Council (Acts 15:22). It seems reasonable to conclude that no man should be appointed as a senior evangelist unless he fulfils the following requirements: first, he should already be a 'leading man' among the brethren, having evident gifts that suit him for the work of an evangelist — considerable experience in dealing with sinners and saints, and a demonstrated spiritual maturity; secondly, he is commended to the work by his own church.

3. Evangelists are 'ordained', or 'separated', to their work by their sending church through the laying on of hands (Acts 13:3; 1 Tim. 4:14; 2 Tim. 1:6).

> From there they sailed to Antioch, where they had been commended to the grace of God for the work which they had completed. Now when they had come and gathered the church together, they reported all that God had done with them, and that he had opened the door of faith to the Gentiles. So they stayed there a long time with the disciples (Acts 14:26-28).

4. Evangelists report back to their sending church. Paul was careful and accurate in the accounts he gave of his work (Rom. 15:18; cf. 2 Cor. 10:13-18). Evangelists may return for an extended period to their 'home' or 'sending' church (Acts 14:26-28; cf. 13:1-3). When they recommence their evangelistic enterprises they are again 'commended' by the church (Acts 15:40). This process may be repeated (Acts 18:22-23).

5. Evangelists may choose fellow-evangelists (Paul chose Silas, Timothy and Titus). Those who are chosen must be well thought of by their own church, and separated to the work with their blessing.

The pioneer evangelistic team

Teams may consist of evangelists, assistant evangelists and fellow workers (male and female). The members of the team may not be together for the whole evangelistic period. There is considerable mobility and flexibility. Paul and Silas set off together (Acts 15:40), enrolled Timothy (Acts 16:3) and were joined along the way by Luke (Acts 16:10).

When mention is made in the New Testament letters of numerous 'fellow workers' or 'fellow labourers', it is not always clear whether these refer to evangelists, assistant evangelists, hard-working Christians in their own communities, or travelling traders and business people who made opportunities to spread the gospel during their journeys.

Paul speaks of Philemon as a 'beloved friend and fellow labourer' (Philem. 1); of Priscilla and Aquila as his 'fellow workers in Christ Jesus, who risked their own necks' for his life (Rom. 16:3-4); of Titus as his 'partner and fellow worker' (2 Cor. 8:23); of Timothy as 'our brother and minister of God, and our fellow labourer in the gospel of Christ' (1 Thess. 3:2). The apostle also refers to Tychicus as 'a beloved brother, faithful minister, and fellow servant in the Lord' and links his name with those of Onesimus, Aristarchus, Mark and Jesus Justus, calling them all his 'fellow workers' (Col. 4:7-11). Demas and Luke are also spoken of as 'fellow labourers' in the letter to Philemon (v. 24).

> Evangelists may be accompanied by their wives (1 Cor. 9:1-5)

Little information is given to piece together an adequate job description of these fellow workers. They prayed for the new converts (Col. 4:12). They delivered up-to-date reports about the evangelistic work, and sought information concerning the well-being of the new churches (Col. 4:7-9). They were messengers of the churches, and they 'ministered' to the evangelists (Phil. 2:25). Aquila and Priscilla were highly competent teachers of the Word of God (Acts 18:24-26). No distinction is drawn between men and women as 'fellow workers'. Paul seems to have continued the practice of the Lord Jesus in being accompanied by a loose-knit band of men and women. As in the mixed band which accompanied the Saviour there is specific mention of women who 'ministered' to him (Mark 15:40-41) and 'many others who provided for him from their substance' (Luke 8:1-3), so there is a high profile given by Paul to those women who laboured with him in the cause of the gospel (e.g. Rom. 16:3-16).

There was a high degree of mobility on the part of this loose-knit band of evangelists and fellow workers. As well as Paul, Silas, Luke, Timothy and Titus, there were others like Phoebe who travelled considerable distances (Rom. 16:1-2). Aquila and Priscilla were also highly mobile. They moved from Italy to Corinth, then on to Ephesus, and later back to Rome (Acts 18:2,18-19; Rom. 16:3).

Liberal scholar Susanne Heine recognizes the apostle Paul's positive attitude towards women when she writes, '... not only does he nowhere question working with these women but he confirms, values and at times stresses it — more often and more explicitly than any other author in the New Testament. And this is evidence of something else, namely, that at this time women had an undeniable and unmistakable significance.'[12]

About a quarter of the workers mentioned by name in the letters of Paul are women. In alphabetical order these are: Apphia, Eunice, Euodia,

Yet I considered it necessary to send to you Epaphroditus, my brother, fellow worker, and fellow soldier, but your messenger and the one who ministered to my need; since he was longing for you all, and was distressed because you had heard that he was sick... Receive him therefore in the Lord with all gladness, and hold such men in esteem; because for the work of Christ he came close to death, not regarding his life, to supply what was lacking in your service toward me (Phil. 2:25-26,29-30).

Now a certain Jew named Apollos, born at Alexandria, an eloquent man and mighty in the Scriptures, came to Ephesus. This man had been instructed in the way of the Lord; and being fervent in spirit, he spoke and taught accurately the things of the Lord, though he knew only the baptism of John. So he began to speak boldly in the synagogue. When Aquila and Priscilla heard him, they took him aside and explained to him the way of God more accurately. And when he desired to cross to Achaia, the brethren wrote, exhorting the disciples to receive him; and when he arrived, he greatly helped those who had believed through grace; for he vigorously refuted the Jews publicly, showing from the Scriptures that Jesus is the Christ (Acts 18:24-28).

Julia, Junia, Lois, Mary, Nympha, Persis, Phoebe, Priscilla, Syntyche, Tryphaena and Tryphosa.

Priscilla was obviously a significant person, frequently referred to before her husband Aquila; she was clear in her understanding of Christian truth, joined with Aquila in putting Apollos right, was a practical support in the job of tent-making and seems to have been an outstanding person in the church.[13] From Romans 16:3-5 we learn, firstly, that she was one of Paul's 'fellow-workers'; secondly, that she was loved, respected and appreciated by Paul and 'all the churches of the Gentiles'; and, thirdly, that for a time she had a church gathering in her own home.

Mary was a hard worker in ministering to the evangelistic team (Rom. 16:6). The mother of Rufus was loved and respected by Paul. She was like a mother to him (Rom. 16:13). Euodia and Syntyche, who laboured with Paul in the gospel (Phil. 4:2-3) must have been strong-minded, active women, and it is interesting to see that, though they were creating difficulties in the church, Paul in no way treats them with the heavy hand of masculine authority. He pleads with them, as he always does in every situation, to remember that they should be living 'in the Lord'.[14]

The women presented in the writings of Paul and Luke were not illiterate or suppressed. Lydia, Priscilla, Phoebe, Lois and Eunice were capable, hard-working women of intelligence, education and culture. They made an invaluable contribution to the spread of the gospel.

Evangelists, trainee evangelists and fellow workers, male and female, travelled in loose-knit association. Their goal was the extension of the kingdom of God, the increase of the church of Jesus Christ. They were highly committed to the advancement of the gospel. They evidently contributed their skills, time and energy, and 'ministered' to each other, to newly planted churches, to new converts and to the unsaved in whatever way they could. Unconcerned about 'office' or 'status', they were devoted to 'function'. Whatever was needed, that they could supply for the fulfilment of the Great Commission, they would perform.

There are several reasons why a group of evangelists and fellow workers labour together:

1. For the mutual encouragement and support that each one gives to the others. Jesus always sent his workers out in twos (Mark 6:7; Luke 10:1; cf. Mark 14:13). He was usually accompanied by a 'team' of fellow-workers – men and women (Luke 8:1-3; cf. Mark 15:40-41). Paul enjoyed the companionship of a large number of co-workers (Rom. 16:1-16,21-24). They did not all travel *en bloc* but in small groups, or in

pairs, as, for example, in the case of a married couple, or even alone (Acts 17:10,14-15; 18:2-3,18-19; 1 Cor. 16:17).

2. No evangelist possesses all the gifts necessary for sowing, reaping, planting and nurturing a new church.

3. As the number of churches grows, the need for a large group of flexible, highly mobile and competent evangelists also grows.

Support for pioneer evangelists

Prayer support for pioneer evangelists

1. Prayer for more evangelists, trainees, and fellow workers (Matt. 9:36-38; Luke 10:2) and for discernment in their appointment.

2. Prayer for courage, boldness and faithfulness to be constantly granted to the evangelistic team for the fulfilment of their task (Eph. 6:18-20).

3. Prayer for doors of opportunity to be opened for the evangelists (Col. 4:2-4).

> The harvest truly is great, but the labourers are few; therefore pray the Lord of the harvest to send out labourers into his harvest (Luke 10:2).
>
> Continue earnestly in prayer, being vigilant in it with thanksgiving; meanwhile praying also for us, that God would open to us a door for the word, to speak the mystery of Christ, for which I am also in chains, that I may make it manifest, as I ought to speak (Col. 4:2-4).

Financial support for pioneer evangelists

Whereas elders *may* be supported by the church they serve (1 Tim. 5:17-18; Gal. 6:6), *the Lord has commanded the support of evangelists* (1 Cor. 9:14) and he says, 'The labourer is worthy of his wages' (Luke 10:7). In practice, however, churches fail in this responsibility and it falls to the evangelist himself to raise support by visiting numerous churches or enlisting the help of sympathetic Christian friends.

The apostle Paul experienced times of considerable need which he viewed spiritually as an opportunity to learn contentment in Christ (Phil. 4:11-13). He was, however, appreciative of any financial aid given by the people of God and expressed his gratitude to the Christians at Philippi for their generous and sacrificial support (Phil. 4:14-18). He further reassures them that the Lord will supply all their need 'according to his riches in glory by Christ Jesus' (Phil. 4:19).

All Christians need discernment about their financial giving, whether in support of workers in their local church, charitable giving at home or abroad, missionary support, or the support of those in full-time evangelism anywhere in the world. The guideline is a minimum of one tenth of income, but the actual amount and the dispersal are a personal and private matter for the believer. The principles of charitable giving might be applied to the support of elders or evangelists: 'Let each one give as he purposes in his heart, not grudgingly or of necessity; for God loves a cheerful giver' (2 Cor. 9:7).

Solomon presents a 'spiritual law of economics' when he says:

Honour the LORD with your possessions,
And with the first-fruits of all your increase;
So your barns will be filled with plenty,
And your vats will overflow with new wine

(Prov. 3:9-10).

> Do you not know that those who minister the holy things eat of the things of the temple, and those who serve at the altar partake of the offerings of the altar? Even so the Lord has commanded that those who preach the gospel should live from the gospel (1 Cor. 9:13-14).
>
> 'Bring all the tithes into the storehouse,
> That there may be food in my house,
> And try me now in this,'
> Says the LORD of hosts,
> 'If I will not open for you the windows of heaven
> And pour out for you such blessing
> That there will not be room enough to receive it.
> And I will rebuke the devourer for your sakes,
> So that he will not destroy the fruit of your ground,
> Nor shall the vine fail to bear fruit for you in the field,'
> Says the LORD of hosts
> (Mal. 3:10-11).

In the days of Malachi the prophet, the Israelites were invited to 'try', or 'prove', the Lord by giving their tithe and trusting him to provide a more than adequate harvest later (Mal. 3:10-11).

There may be circumstances when evangelists do not make use of the rightful financial support from the churches (1 Cor. 9:15). At other times necessity may demand a 'tent-making ministry' where evangelists support themselves through a trade or profession (2 Thess. 3:8-9).

The apostle Paul was able to work at times in tent-making and provide not only for himself but for those with him (Acts 20:33-35). This is not a practice that can be emulated everywhere, since in some countries the level of income generated would be wholly inadequate.

Conclusion

The need for a return to biblical patterns of evangelism is all too evident. In many parts of the world, vast areas are bereft of churches that are faithful to the teaching of the Bible, and therefore of effective gospel witness. Even where 'new' churches have arisen, these are often little more than the drawing together of believers who live in a particular locality and who hitherto have travelled some distance to worship in other places. Such churches tend to perpetuate errors and extra-biblical teaching and practices because they generally lack a skilled and experienced evangelist to act as church-planter and counsellor. Often they lack the benefit of being supported by elders from another church who, though they may not have any experience in founding a church, could at least have provided some experienced leadership.

A return to biblical patterns of evangelism would, in the providence of God, establish travelling groups of church-planters composed of evangelists, trainee evangelists and fellow workers. New converts would be gathered into new local assemblies, taught and trained, organized and structured as independent churches with their own emerging leadership. The evangelists would continue a 'supervisory brief' and be available for counsel and advice, arbitration or mediation, according to the emerging needs of the new elders and the new congregations.

13.
Elders and deacons

Elders and deacons

What is the relationship between elders and deacons?

....

....

....

Has the role of a deacon been devalued? If so, please explain in what way.

....

....

....

To whom are deacons answerable?

....

....

....

Can women be deacons? Explain your answer with biblical references.

....

....

....

Recommended reading

The books and papers listed below are written from differing, and initially convincing, viewpoints and therefore will stretch and train thinking and ability in handling Scripture.

Fortner, D. 'The office of deacon', *The Church of God* (Evangelical Press, 1991), pp.68-76.

Kuiper, R. P. 'The office of the deacon', *The Glorious Body of Christ* (Edinburgh: Banner of Truth Trust, 1967), pp.150-57.

Morrison, A. 'Rulership and service: a biblical understanding of Christian ministry for men and women', *Diakrisis*, Spring/Summer 1998, issue 5, pp.69-77.

Prime, D. *A Christian's Guide to Leadership – for the whole church* (Darlington: Evangelical Press, 2005), pp. 131-52.

Elders and deacons

Service to others is a fundamental part of commitment to the Lord Jesus Christ. We are called upon 'through love' to 'serve [douleuo] one another' (Gal. 5:13). We are to follow the wonderful example of our Saviour: 'For even the Son of Man did not come to be served, but to serve [diakoneo], and to give his life a ransom for many' (Mark 10:45). All Christians are to be servant-like: 'As each one has received a gift, minister [diakoneo] it to one another, as good stewards of the manifold grace of God' (1 Peter 4:10). The word 'deacon' derives from the Greek diakonos.

Loving service is the outworking of the second greatest commandment, since 'Love your neighbour' is one of the two fundamental laws of the Old and New Covenants (Matt. 22:35-40) and 'Love is the fulfilment of the law' (Rom. 13:10). The Lord Jesus gave a further dimension to this love, especially as it relates to fellow-believers, when he said, 'A new commandment I give to you, that you love one another; *as I have loved you*, that you also love one another' (John 13:34, emphasis added). And Paul sums up the Christian virtues of faith, hope and love by insisting that 'The greatest of these is love' (1 Cor. 13:13). Kuiper declares: 'The diaconate is accurately described as the office of love, the greatest of Christian virtues.'[1]

> For you, brethren, have been called to liberty; only do not use liberty as an opportunity for the flesh, but through love serve one another. For all the law is fulfilled in one word, even in this: 'You shall love your neighbour as yourself' (Gal. 5:13-14).
>
> ... but, speaking the truth in love, may grow up in all things into him who is the head — Christ — from whom the whole body, joined and knit together by what every joint supplies, according to the effective working by which every part does its share, causes growth of the body for the edifying of itself in love (Eph. 4:15-16).

What is a deacon?

The difficulty in determining the office and function of a deacon is complicated by the apparently arbitrary manner in which the Greek words *diakonos, diakoneo* and *diakonia* are translated into English as, respectively, 'deacon', 'minister' and 'servant'; 'to minister', 'to minister to' and 'to serve'; 'ministry' and 'ministration'. The word *diakonos* is used repeatedly 'in the New Testament in the simple sense of *servant* without any reference to an office in the church'.[2]

> Now in those days, when the number of the disciples was multiplying, there arose a complaint against the Hebrews by the Hellenists, because their widows were neglected in the daily distribution. Then the twelve summoned the multitude of the disciples and said, 'It is not desirable that we should leave the word of God and serve [*diakoneo*] tables. Therefore, brethren, seek out from among you seven men of good reputation, full of the Holy Spirit and wisdom, whom we may appoint over this business; but we will give ourselves continually to prayer and to the ministry of the word'
> (Acts 6:1-4).

> You know that those who are considered rulers over the Gentiles lord it over them, and their great ones exercise authority over them. Yet it shall not be so among you; but whoever desires to become great among you shall be your servant [*diakonos* = deacon]. And whoever of you desires to be first shall be slave of all. For even the Son of Man did not come to be served, but to serve [*diakoneo*], and to give his life a ransom for many
> (Mark 10:42-45).

The basic meaning of the verb *diakoneo* is to serve (Acts 6:2). It is used of those who served wine at the wedding in Cana of Galilee (John 2:5); of Martha's work, in contrast to her sister Mary's sitting and listening (Luke 10:40); and of the one who serves at table, as opposed to the one who sits at table (Luke 22:27).

From this rather specific application to serving at tables it is evident that the term came to be used in a more general sense to describe a whole variety of services rendered to others, whether under compulsion or voluntarily, freely or for payment or reward.

The Lord Jesus Christ used the noun *diakonos* when teaching his disciples the nature of true greatness (Mark 10:42-44). In the same context he also used the verb *diakoneo* in describing his own ministry (Mark 10:45).

Literally, in the following examples, Paul glories in his 'diaconate' (Rom. 11:13), refers to Apollos and himself as 'deacons' through whom the Christians at Corinth had come to faith (1 Cor. 3:5), declares Timothy to be a brother and 'deacon' of God (1 Thess. 3:2), describes Epaphras as a faithful 'deacon' of Christ (Col. 1:7) and Tychicus as a beloved brother and faithful 'deacon' (Col. 4:7).

'In the overwhelming number of cases the terms refer, not to a specific office, but to various kinds of service or to particular people serving in varied capacities either inside or outside the church.'[3]

The function of deacons

Different understandings of the role of deacons

What deacons did in New Testament days is nowhere stated in detail. The only place where a function is specifically mentioned is in Acts 6, where the distribution of church funds for the support of widows is the only matter requiring attention. The noun *diakonos* is not found in the passage, though the verb *diakoneo* is used (v. 4), resulting in a difference of opinion among scholars as to whether this passage should be seen as the inauguration of the office of deacon, or simply the finding of men for the job in hand.

Ministries of mercy

On the basis of the appointment in the Jerusalem Church of seven spiritual and wise men to attend to the distribution of church funds to poor widows, the emphasis is seen to fall upon the ministry of mercy. In this view, 'Deacons represent Christ in His office of mercy.'[4]

John Murray writes, 'Ministry to the poor in material things is an important function of the church (cf. Rom. 15:25,26; Gal. 2:10). It is reasonable to infer that to the deacons is committed this ministry, and other activities of a similar character in the sphere of mercy.'[5]

R. P. Kuiper comments: 'If a particular church has no poor of its own, it should by all means through its deacons come to the assistance of other churches that have many ... should contribute generously to the relief of countless suffering saints in many churches and many lands. In that way the diaconate will give expression to a beautiful Biblical ecumenicity.'[6]

> Therefore, as we have opportunity, let us do good to all, especially to those who are of the household of faith (Gal. 6:10).

Assisting the eldership

There are differing views as to how this should be applied:

1. By sharing pastoral oversight

Herbert Carson points to Paul's greetings to the church at Philippi and suggests that 'The overseers and the deacons are bracketed together in such a way, that it would seem to be a legitimate deduction that the deacons are there to assist the overseers in the discharge of their task of pastoral oversight.'[7]

> Paul and Timothy, bondservants of Jesus Christ, to all the saints in Christ Jesus who are in Philippi, with the bishops and deacons: Grace to you and peace from God our Father and the Lord Jesus Christ (Phil. 1:1-3).

2. By relieving the one and only pastor

For those who, like Don Fortner, visualize a church with only one elder/pastor assisted by a number of deacons, the role of the latter is 'to see that their pastor has no worldly concern to distract him from, or interfere with, the work of the gospel ministry'.[8] When deacons faithfully discharge their responsibilities, then Don Fortner is confident that the church will grow, since he believes the remarkable growth of the early church in Jerusalem occurred 'because seven faithful men served as deacons in the church at Jerusalem'.[9]

3. By relieving a plural eldership

The similarity in the high qualifications required of elders and deacons, coupled with the significance of the first appointment of spiritual and wise men to 'serve tables' (Acts 6:2), leads to the conclusion that deacons work alongside elders and perform all necessary tasks to ensure that the elders 'give [themselves] continually to prayer and to the ministry of the word' (Acts 6:4).

> *'If an elder has special gifts as an evangelist, church-planter, missionary, writer, radio-broadcaster or any other specialized field, then it is the duty of the church-officers to lead the local church in facing up to the reality of sharing those special gifts with other churches'* (J. K. Davies).

The elders of the church are to be released from all responsibilities which are not directly related to pastoral care, spiritual oversight and the teaching/preaching aspect of church life: 'A deacon therefore should always be sympathetic and sensitive to assist in every way to relieve the pressures placed on elders.'[10]

'My contention,' writes John Benton, 'is that the works of elders and deacons are not to be seen as separate. The deacons were the general arm of the eldership. They were entrusted with various jobs to relieve pressure on the elders, but were in the happy position of not holding ultimate responsibility. The buck does not stop with the deacons, but with the elders!'[11]

The relationship between elders and deacons may be any of the following:

1. Each office has its separate and distinct responsibilities.
2. There is some overlap and an area of joint activity.
3. Deacons are integrated into aspects of the elders' duties, assisting where appropriate.

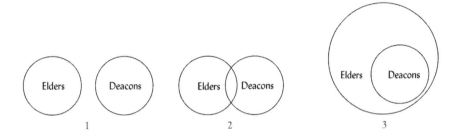

John Benton suggests that 'Perhaps we should contemplate the possibility that elder/deacon pairs might form a most helpful approach to the work. But most important of all there must be the closest possible links of affection and confidence between elders and deacons. It is a matter of vital importance. The warmth and mutual regard in the relationship is seen by the rest of the flock and will set an example to them, for good or for bad.'[12]

4. By supervision or delegation of non-eldership matters

The deacons were not the overseers; they did not act as pastors and spiritual leaders of the flock. According to Lenski, 'The best we can say is that they assisted the overseers by performing the minor services and attending to incidental matters such as collecting and distributing alms, looking after the physical needs of the sick... We must, therefore, be content with the little information that we have.'[13]

According to this view, deacons perform all tasks associated with finance, buildings and church organization. Ownership of a building or buildings involves enormous responsibilities: maintenance inside and outside, security (including liaison with police), access to buildings, insurance, fire precautions, disposal of rubbish, heating and lighting, ventilation, security of vehicles. Other duties include accountancy and confidential records of giving for tax purposes; recording the minutes of church meetings;

> If anyone speaks, let him speak as the oracles of God. If anyone ministers [*diakoneo*], let him do it as with the ability which God supplies, that in all things God may be glorified through Jesus Christ, to whom belong the glory and the dominion for ever and ever (1 Peter 4:11).

visiting the sick; keeping a general and close eye on the material needs of the poorer church members; practical matters such as seating arrangements and the organization of baptismal, communion and funeral services; the provision of Bibles; stewarding; the overall supervision of catering, transport and hospitality for students; leaflet distribution; the announcement of church activities, whether in the service or displayed on a notice board; arranging hospitality and payment of expenses for visiting preachers; crèche facilities, children's work, youth work, work with the elderly and within the community. Some churches remunerate someone to head up diaconal work under the title of 'church manager'.

5. By being deacons without being a diaconate

Alan Morrison challenges the view that there is such a body as the 'diaconate': 'Deacons are to be appointed on an individual basis to perform individual responsibilities as Deacons. There is no support in the Bible whatsoever for the creation of a body of Deacons working together as a unit in an autonomous group.'[14]

While recognizing that there is a power-holding body known as 'the eldership' or 'presbytery' (1 Tim. 4:14), Morrison insists that there is no body in the Scriptures referred to as 'the diaconate', whether power-holding or otherwise.[15] It is when deacons hold meetings, make decisions together and function as a distinct group that a third power base arises in the church – i.e. elders, church and deacons. Conversely where deacons function as servants, serving the church in individual tasks, each one answerable to the elders and to the church, there is no further power base and a much larger proportion of the church is involved. Not only the regular functions, such as secretarial tasks, accountancy and building maintenance, but also ministries of mercy, youth leadership, child-care and the like would be diaconal activities. All these responsibilities would require the qualifications necessary for a deacon and would be open to both men and women. There would be no deacons' meetings; therefore no female authority would be exercised 'over a man' (1 Tim. 2:12). All discussion and decision-making would be located in the eldership or the church meeting.

The qualifications for deacons

The instructions regarding deacons focus upon the exacting qualifications required of them rather than their function. It seems right therefore to infer that these qualifications must be met in their entirety by any member of the church undertaking any task whatsoever, either in the church or on behalf of the church.

In the vast majority of areas there is no distinction between the qualifications of a deacon and those of an elder (see chapter 6). In Christian graces, attitude and behaviour, the men are to be uniformly examples to the flock. In the home, church and community they are required to be blameless.

> Likewise deacons must be reverent, not double-tongued, not given to much wine, not greedy for money, holding the mystery of the faith with a pure conscience. But let these also first be tested; then let them serve as deacons, being found blameless. Likewise, their wives must be reverent, not slanderers, temperate, faithful in all things. Let deacons be the husbands of one wife, ruling their children and their own houses well. For those who have served well as deacons obtain for themselves a good standing and great boldness in the faith which is in Christ Jesus (I Tim. 3:8-13).

Comparison of qualifications for elders and deacons

Elders			Deacons		
	I Tim. 3:1-7	Titus 1:6-9		Acts 6:3	I Tim. 3:8-13
Blameless	✓	✓	Blameless		✓
Husband of one wife	✓	✓	Husband of one wife		✓
Temperate	✓				
Not quick-tempered		✓			
Sober-minded	✓	✓			
Of good behaviour	✓		Reverent		✓
Lover of what is good		✓	A pure conscience		✓
Just		✓			
Holy		✓	Full of the Holy Spirit	✓	
Hospitable	✓	✓			
Able to teach	✓				
A steward of God		✓			
Of sound doctrine		✓	Holding ... the faith		✓
Able to correct error		✓			
Not given to wine	✓	✓	Not given to much wine		✓
Not violent	✓	✓			
Not greedy for money	✓	✓	Not greedy for money		✓
Gentle	✓				
Not quarrelsome	✓				
Self-controlled		✓			

Elders	I Tim. 3:1-7	Titus 1:6-9	Deacons	Acts 6:3	I Tim. 3:8-13
Not covetous	✓				
Ruling the home well	✓		Ruling the home well		✓
Submissive children	✓		Ruling children well		✓
Faithful children		✓			
Mature — not a novice	✓		Full of wisdom	✓	
			Tested first		✓
A good testimony outside	✓		Of good reputation	✓	
Not self-willed		✓			
			Not double-tongued		✓

Deacons must be of good Christian character

> Since you have purified your souls in obeying the truth through the Spirit in sincere love of the brethren, love one another fervently with a pure heart... (1 Peter 1:22).
>
> But the fruit of the Spirit is love, joy, peace, long-suffering, kindness, goodness, faithfulness, gentleness, self-control (Gal. 5:22-23).
>
> But those who desire to be rich fall into temptation and a snare, and into many foolish and harmful lusts which drown men in destruction and perdition. For the love of money is a root of all kinds of evil, for which some have strayed from the faith in their greediness, and pierced themselves through with many sorrows (1 Tim. 6:9-10).

'Likewise deacons must be reverent ... holding the mystery of the faith with a pure conscience ... blameless' (1 Tim. 3:8-10).

There will be a marked seriousness in their behaviour — dignified, not frivolous; a sincerity and consistency in speech — neither favouring friends nor fearing foes.

Faith in God is demonstrated in a life of good works (Eph. 2:10; Titus 2:14). 'For as the body without the spirit is dead, so faith without works is dead also' (James 2:26). 'You know what kind of men we were among you for your sake. And you became followers of us and of the Lord' (1 Thess. 1:5-6).

To function as a deacon requires spiritual maturity, emotional stability, personal discipline, practical benevolence and generosity.

Deacons must be good husbands

Deacons are to be the 'husbands of one wife' (1 Tim. 3:12; see earlier comments relating to elders on page 99). As with elders, there is more implied than simply faithful monogamy. A married church leader is to be a role model as a husband and father. He will put a special value on his wife. He will 'treat her as something precious, which she is in and of herself'.[16] Husband and wife should be 'united in their profession of the Christian faith and their desire to live for our Lord Jesus Christ'; otherwise it will be difficult to run the home on Christian principles.[17] There will also be inevitable pressures on the husband that will affect the discharge of his duties for the church if his wife is an unbeliever.

> Husbands, love your wives, just as Christ also loved the church and gave himself for her (Eph. 5:25).
>
> Husbands, likewise, dwell with them with understanding, giving honour to the wife, as to the weaker vessel, and as being heirs together of the grace of life, that your prayers may not be hindered (1 Peter 3:7).

Deacons must be good home managers

> And you, fathers, do not provoke your children to wrath, but bring them up in the training and admonition of the Lord (Eph. 6:4).

Deacons, like elders, must be 'ruling their children and their own houses well' (1 Tim. 3:12). The Greek word translated 'ruling' is *proistemi*, meaning management, which involves 'planning, organization, enlistment, training and deployment of personnel, administration and discipline'.[18] Management skills are necessary in the home to ensure a careful balance of responsibilities as husband, father, worker and church member.

The difference between the two offices of elder and deacon is not so much in graces as in gifts.

Deacons must possess doctrinal clarity

Unlike elders, deacons are not required to be 'able to teach' (1 Tim. 3:2), but they are nevertheless to be men 'holding the mystery of the faith with a pure conscience' (1 Tim. 3:9). Any church could easily be destroyed were a deacon or deacons to be at variance with the eldership over matters of doctrine. The well-being of a local church largely depends upon the harmony that exists between its elders and deacons. Doctrinal differences would preclude them from being 'of one mind' (2 Cor. 13:11; 1 Peter 3:8). They are to be those who 'stand fast in one spirit, with one mind striving together for the faith of the gospel' (Phil. 1:27) and 'like-minded, having the same love, being of one accord, of one mind' (Phil. 2:2).

They not only require clarity in doctrine — 'holding the mystery of the faith' — but also consistency of life, since that faith is to be held 'with a pure conscience'. Christians serving in the church, or on behalf of the church, are to be under the authority of the Word of God. 'Isolated texts are no substitute for a thorough knowledge of the Bible, and are no evidence of submission to what the Bible teaches.'[19]

Deacons have an important role in being an example of respect and submission to those who have the rule over them (Heb. 13:17; 1 Thess. 5:12-13). All who are deacons 'will aim to enlarge the exercise of the elders' pastoral care by committing themselves to a widespread ministry in which practical administration, financial affairs, compassionate concern and general pastoral care will blend into a pattern of fruitful service'.[20]

The ministry of women

> Likewise their wives must be reverent, not slanderers, temperate, faithful in all things
> (1 Tim. 3:11).

Among the qualifications for elders and deacons set out in 1 Timothy 3, there appears the intriguing qualification traditionally understood to refer to the wives of deacons, that they must be 'reverent, not slanderers, temperate, faithful in all things' (1 Tim. 3:11). There are, however, serious questions that may be raised against this interpretation:

1. The Greek word translated 'wives' may also be translated 'women'. In the Authorized / King James Version the root word and its derivatives are translated 129 times as 'woman' (e.g. John 19:26; Acts 5:14; 8:3) and ninety-two times as 'wife'. Only the context can determine whether the word is to be understood to mean 'woman' or 'wife', 'women' or 'wives'.

2. No word is present in the original text to warrant the introduction of the English word 'their'. The original simply reads: 'Women [or wives], in like manner reverent...' The addition has been made by interpretation rather than translation, to link the women to the deacons of verse 10.

3. The use of the word 'likewise' suggests that a new category is being introduced (cf. 1 Tim. 3:8).

4. It is unlikely that Paul is referring to the wives of deacons, since the qualifications would be equally applicable to the wives of elders, who are not mentioned in the section on the eldership. It is just as important, if not even more important, that the wives of elders behave in a fitting manner.

5. There is good reason for Paul not to use the word for 'deaconess', since the word *daikonos* may be applied to either men or women (cf. Phoebe, in Romans 16:1, where *daikonos* is translated 'servant'). The word 'women' is therefore used in 1 Timothy 3:11 to distinguish them from male deacons.[21]

From these and other considerations Patrick Fairbairn concludes 'that not deacons' wives, but female deacons, are meant' in verse 11. 'Possibly the matter was so put as intentionally to include women of both classes; at once wives to the deacons who occasionally shared with their husbands in diaconal ministrations, and women who were themselves charged by the church with such ministrations ... it ought to be understood of women who, in the one character or the other, were actively engaged in the kind of work which was proper to deacons.'[22] This would explain, firstly, why the wives of elders are not included, since they cannot directly engage in eldership work with their husbands, and, secondly, why the qualifications required by these women are more related to diaconal duties than to domestic responsibilities.

Examining the evidence of the New Testament and early church history for the ministry of women, Morrison concludes that '... the Deaconess exercised a personal ministry to widows, the poor, the aged, the sick and the handicapped; she delivered alms to the needy; she read Scripture to the sick and housebound; she provided guidance to the young, especially young mothers; she was involved in teaching women and children; she took part in the instruction of women before baptism; she assisted the Elders as a practical support to the ruling and teaching ministry.'[23]

That there are ministries of mercy for *all* members of the church is evident from our Lord's warning about sheep and goats. Distinction is made on the grounds of feeding the hungry, giving drink to the thirsty, providing hospitality for strangers, clothing the naked, visiting the sick and the imprisoned (Matt. 25:31-46). Clearly there is here no gender-specific instruction, and no special office of 'female deacon' need be created to ensure that these ministries of mercy are fulfilled. All the tasks of a church can be fulfilled by women except those prohibited by God's Word.

Conclusion

The smooth running of church life requires the whole body to be responsible for a wide range of tasks: teaching, pastoral care, finance, buildings and church organization. The New Testament pictures Christians as exercising a variety of

> Having then gifts differing according to the grace that is given to us, let us use them: if prophecy, let us prophesy in proportion to our faith; or ministry, let us use it in our ministering; he who teaches, in teaching; he who exhorts, in exhortation; he who gives, with liberality; he who leads, with diligence; he who shows mercy, with cheerfulness (Rom. 12:6-8).

ministries, or works of service, for the good of the church (1 Cor. 12:7; Eph. 4:12; Rom. 12:6-8). How these ministries are designated, how they are apportioned and how they are co-ordinated and harmonized is not detailed in the Scriptures. Consequently each local church is free, within the general guidelines of principles laid down in Scripture, to determine its own method of organization. As with worship, the practical ministries of the church should undertaken 'decently and in order' (1 Cor. 14:40).

Wherever the division of responsibilities is set between elders and deacons, 'Communication, cooperation and co-ordination are vital and measures must be devised to achieve them, as appropriate to each local situation... The deacons must never become a rival leadership group in church life, for this will promote disharmony and division.' [24]

Epilogue

Church leaders are not trained in a few weeks, a few months, or even a few years. Competence in pastoral work, in all its varied aspects, requires the interplay of natural talents, spiritual graces, insight, reading, reflection and interaction with others. Considerable time and effort are required and many years of experience. The pressures are immense: maintaining spiritual priorities, balancing responsibilities in work, home, church and community, and training the mind by reading, meditation and prayer.

The tasks facing church leaders are daunting, to say the least. The oversight of any group of believers is not for the faint-hearted. Few people these days have an inherent respect for leaders, whether in society or church. It is more fashionable for each one to do 'what [is] right in his [or her] own eyes' (Judg. 17:6). Respect is hard won and easily lost.

While there are exceptional individuals who in youth display gifts, graces, wisdom and skill which far exceed their years, the majority of us struggle to make the most of what we have been given and to gain from the expertise of older and wiser men. A plurality of elders is the ideal in any church. A good mix of ages should ensure that younger men gain from the experience of older men.

Where there are a number of men working side by side in church leadership each one's gifts and skills may be utilized for the good of the whole. One may surpass others in preaching and teaching ability; another may excel in counselling skills, or in training the next generation of leaders; yet another may be gifted in communication with the church membership publicly or privately. Recognition of varied gifts often results in greater respect within the team and from the church to the team.

The hardest leadership situation of all is that of the lone elder. Not only has he the responsibility of all functions of church leadership, but he is often also liable for most, if not all, of the diaconal duties too. This man needs the support and encouragement of leaders from other churches. There is value in leaders from small churches forming fraternals, which may cover a large geographic area. In these gatherings the issues of leadership, as outlined in this manual, may be examined in detail. Too many existing gatherings are meetings addressed by a speaker or preacher giving a monologue. The urgent need is for true conferences, where church leaders thoroughly discuss their work and gain from the pooled resources of a number of godly men. Pastoral cases are becoming more varied and more complex; running a church is becoming more exacting, and the temptations to sin are becoming more insidious.

Only the man convinced by God dare take upon himself the role of a church leader. As the apostle Paul said, in a somewhat different context, '... who is sufficient for these things?' (2 Cor. 2:16).

Though the local church appoints her leaders (1 Tim. 3:2-7; Titus 1:5-9), the ultimate appointment is made in heaven. It is the Holy Spirit who ordains 'overseers, to shepherd the church of God' (Acts 20:28). Church leaders are therefore answerable to God and one day must give account (Heb. 13:17). Left to their own resources, whether of wisdom, talents, skills or experience, they would find oversight a formidable task. No one would be capable of adequately functioning for the glory of God. What a blessing that the Lord not only gives the responsibility but also provides the resources, not only gives the gifts but also the graces! (Rom. 12:6). Where wisdom is lacking, believers have only to 'ask of God' (James 1:5).

There is more. The Lord not only equips his people, but he also ensures their success according to his own will. This is a source of immeasurable comfort and reassurance to any Christian worker. It is also extremely humbling. The Lord will achieve his purposes with or without his people! He 'works all things according to the counsel of his will...' (Eph. 1:11).

> I planted, Apollos watered, but God gave the increase. So then neither he who plants is anything, nor he who waters, but God who gives the increase (I Cor. 3:6-7).
>
> So likewise you, when you have done all those things which you are commanded, say, 'We are unprofitable servants. We have done what was our duty to do' (Luke 17:10).

In evangelism and church-planting the apostle Paul was constantly aware that, while he could plant and others could water, success was entirely and only in the hands of the Lord (1 Cor. 3:6-7). So too in Christian service in general, when believers have been as faithful as they can be, they nevertheless acknowledge that they are unprofitable servants. They have simply done what it was their duty to do (Luke 17:10). They take no credit. The honour is to the Lord. For in all Christian service the saying is consistently true: ' "Not by might nor by power, but by my Spirit," says the LORD of hosts' (Zech. 4:6).

So then, in the final analysis, the success of any church leadership lies in the hands of God. The best — that is, the most biblical — procedures may be followed throughout; the most able and gifted of men may serve the church with tireless devotion, and years may be spent studying and training for pastoral office, and yet it may end in failure. There is constant need of humility, dependence upon God and an unwavering recognition that he is responsible for any good that is achieved in his church. His thoughts are not our thoughts; his ways are not our ways (Isa. 55:8).

Now to the King eternal, immortal, invisible, to God who alone is wise, be honour and glory for ever and ever. Amen (1 Tim. 1:17).

Appendices:
Specialist counselling

Appendix I
Counselling and depression

Counselling and depression

'In a sense,' writes Dr Martyn Lloyd-Jones, 'a depressed Christian is a contradiction in terms, and he is a very poor recommendation for the gospel... Nothing is more important, therefore, than that we should be delivered from a condition which gives other people, looking at us, the impression that to be a Christian means to be unhappy, to be sad, to be morbid...'[1]

There are two forms of depression: reactive (or exogenous) and endogenous. The first may arise in response to a sudden bad situation like bereavement, disappointment, discovery of serious illness, frustrated ambition or a sense of personal inadequacy: 'When we have faced the crushing blow of bereavement, when we have suffered a heart-breaking disappointment like a broken engagement or sudden unemployment, when we face a serious and unexpected illness — we may quietly submit to God's dealings as Job did and find peace; or we may feel thoroughly indignant and in our bitterness of soul plunge ... into the slough of depression.'[2]

The second arises from within the personality and has no connection with external events.

Symptoms of depression

A video made available to patients in the United Kingdom attending doctors' surgeries indicates that 20% of the population are understood to suffer from 'depressive illness' at some time in their lives. According to the author of the video, a person is suffering from 'depressive illness' when low feelings are severe, when they are not affected by what happens, when they interfere with a person leading a normal life, and when they do not go away for several weeks or even months. The definition of 'depressive illness' is when five of the symptoms listed below, one of which must be either item 1 or 2, are present for two weeks or more:

1. A depressed mood – for most of the day, every day, for at least two weeks.

2. Loss of interest or pleasure – for most of the day, every day, for at least two weeks.

3. Weight loss or gain.

4. Sleep disturbance – insomnia and drowsiness.

5. Feeling agitated or slowed down.

6. Lack of energy.

7. Feeling worthless or guilty (in modern terminology, 'low self-esteem').

8. Loss of concentration.

9. Frequent thoughts of death or suicide.[3]

Causes of depression

Determining the reason for depression in individual cases is generally very difficult, since the same symptoms may be displayed as a result of a various causes.

Physical factors

People function best when they follow regular patterns of behaviour – rising each morning at the same time, eating regular meals and retiring to bed at the same time. Regular exercise also has a significant effect on the health of the mind. When there is insomnia, the tendency is to resort to tablets to promote sleep, but these only serve to mask the problem and often adversely affect life the following day.[4] Indiscipline and disorderliness can also lead to depression.

Social factors

Loneliness is a fertile breeding ground for depression. Often lonely people begin to despair. Failure to form good human relationships can result in a feeling of rejection. Resentment towards others may then give rise to a person's becoming more and more withdrawn, then plummeting into depression.

Psychological factors

Stress experienced through the pressures of life can lead to physical and mental exhaustion, resulting in depression.[5]

Medical factors

'Scores of medical problems can lead to depression: Parkinson's disease, multiple sclerosis, lupus, hepatitis, electrolyte abnormalities from anorexia, and others. The most frequent physical cause of depression is the side effects of prescription medication. Blood pressure and heart medication, antibacterial drugs, and psychiatric drugs are common culprits.'[6]

Genetic factors

'Research indicates that genetic factors are involved in people who are depressive, as is also an insecure upbringing.'[7]

Spiritual factors

Spiritual depression takes many forms and includes many different spiritual issues. The Word of God provides examples to guide in the counselling of those suffering from this condition.

1. Guilt over sin

> When I kept silent, my bones grew old
> Through my groaning all the day long.
> For day and night your hand was heavy upon me;
> My vitality was turned into the drought of summer...
>
> (Ps. 32:3-4).

> O LORD, do not rebuke me in your wrath,
> Nor chasten me in your hot displeasure!
> For your arrows pierce me deeply,
> And your hand presses me down.
> There is no soundness in my flesh
> Because of your anger,

Nor any health in my bones
Because of my sin.
For my iniquities have gone over my head;
Like a heavy burden they are too heavy for me...
I am troubled, I am bowed down greatly;
I go mourning all the day long.
For my loins are full of inflammation,
And there is no soundness in my flesh.
I am feeble and severely broken;
I groan because of the turmoil of my heart

(Ps. 38:1-8).

These psalms, along with Psalm 51, 'speak of the same kind of anxiety, the same sort of depression, the same type of physical distress, and the same class of emotional visceral responses. All three describe the anxiety of a man who is guilty over his sin and who is crushed by that anxiety ... hiding sin causes distress both of soul and of body.'[8]

2. Fear or anxiety

Why are you cast down, O my soul?
And why are you disquieted within me?
Hope in God;
For I shall yet praise him,
The help of my countenance and my God

(Ps. 42:11).

Depression shows in the countenance, writes Lloyd-Jones: 'The man who is dejected and disquieted and miserable, who is unhappy and depressed always shows it in his face. He looks troubled and he looks worried. You take one glance at him and you see his condition.' So David says about the Lord, in the context of depression, that he is 'the help of my countenance and my God' (Ps. 42:11; cf. v. 5). 'He is weeping and tearful, and all because he is in this state of perplexity and of fear. He is worried about himself, he is worried about what is happening to him, he is troubled about these enemies who are attacking him and insinuating things about him and his God. Everything seems to be on top of him. He cannot control his feelings.' He has lost his appetite: 'My tears have been my food day and night' (Ps. 42:3).[9]

3. Satanic attack

Satan is capable of great hostility, as is evident in his promotion of persecution towards the people of God. Here he is 'like a roaring lion, seeking whom he may devour' (1 Peter 5:8). He also 'transforms himself into an angel of light' (2 Cor. 11:14) and works through respected members of the visible church who may ultimately prove to be apostates. The apostle Paul is able to say of the Evil One, 'We are not ignorant of his devices' (2 Cor. 2:11).[10] How necessary then for those in pastoral care to be aware of the craftiness and guile of Satan! The 'god of this age has blinded' the minds of those who are perishing (2 Cor. 4:4). He also brings confusion to the minds of those who are being saved. He no doubt stirs in all issues leading to depression in the people of God. Once Christians are depressed, he capitalizes upon the condition 'by encouraging a defeatist mentality, so that we can only see our own weakness and failure'.[11]

4. Failure to obey the Word of God

Welch notes that depression is sometimes related to being wronged by another person, or not getting one's own way. In these cases, 'A common response is anger toward the perpetrator and, ultimately, anger against God for giving hardships that "I don't deserve".'[12]

When the Lord confronted Adam with his unbelief and disobedience, Adam responded by blaming others: 'The woman whom you gave to be with me, she gave me of the tree, and I ate' (Gen. 3:12). Adam refused to accept responsibility for his own wrongdoing. He blamed Eve for his downfall. He went further; he blamed God: 'The woman *whom you gave* to be with me...' In other words, 'This is your fault, Lord, because this is the woman you gave me and she is responsible for leading me astray.'

Distress leading to depression may arise through failure to deal appropriately with sin: 'Moreover if your brother sins against you, go and tell him his fault between you and him alone. If he hears you, you have gained your brother. But if he will not hear, take with you one or two more, that "by the mouth of two or three witnesses every word may be established". And if he refuses to hear them, tell it to the church. But if he refuses even to hear the church, let him be to you like a heathen and a tax collector' (Matt. 18:15-17). 'Therefore if you bring your gift to the altar, and there remember that your brother has something against you, leave your gift there before the altar, and go your way. First be reconciled to your brother, and then come and offer your gift' (Matt. 5:23-24).

To these sources of depression numerous other spiritual causes may be added: depression resulting from failure in prayer and personal devotions;

failure in the face of severe temptations; loss of the sense of God's presence and grace; guilt over feeling depressed; reaction after great blessing; fear of the future; judging by personal feelings; dwelling on vain regrets; being troubled by false teaching; growing weary in doing good, etc. These have been thoroughly dealt with by William Bridge and Martyn Lloyd-Jones.[13]

Since Lloyd-Jones declares that 'The ultimate cause of all spiritual depression is unbelief,'[14] we will do well to heed the warning of Christian psychiatrist, John White: 'To read Bridge and Lloyd-Jones alone may cause us to assume something which neither author intended, that all depression is "spiritual" in the sense that bodily infirmity is never its source and that it has only "spiritual" remedies. To read my book with its emphasis on bodily processes may lead us to err in the opposite direction.'[15]

Diagnosing depression

Accurate diagnosis is essential in all cases of depression. If we mistake physical symptoms for spiritual ones, we are likely to hold people morally responsible for something over which they have no control whatsoever. If we mistake spiritual symptoms for physical ones, we remove responsibility, may be guilty of excusing sin, or, at the very least, remove hope of a cure.

Appropriate questioning, or a preparatory questionnaire, can readily identify basic characteristics and establish whether a simple explanation may be uncovered, such as lack of sleep, irregular eating habits, a disorderly lifestyle, loneliness, failure in interpersonal relationships, stress from one or many sources, or possible side-effects from prescription drugs. Elders without medical training and qualifications must strongly advise the person to go to his or her doctor for a thorough medical examination to ensure that there are no medical reasons for the depressed condition.

> If there is any doubt whatsoever, the pastor is well advised to ensure that a medical examination is undertaken.

Dr Law, qualified in medicine and psychiatry, writes, 'There are usually fairly clear indications when the problem is not psychological but medical. We would not wish to have the counsellor attempt medical diagnoses but wherever there are specific *physical* symptoms — pain, headaches, trembling, great tiredness, loss of sensations, vomiting, etc. — *then a medical check is essential.*'[16]

Counselling the depressed

When the Lord Jesus visited the pool of Bethesda, he asked a man there who had been paralysed for thirty-eight years, 'Do you want to be made well?' (John 5:6). The question was by no means irrelevant or unnecessary, since being healed would necessitate a totally new way of life for this man. Once cured, he would have to face new demands on him. In a similar way, being healed of depression brings with it new opportunities but also new responsibilities. Life delivered from depression may not be so attractive for some. As Dorothy Rowe observes, 'Inside the safety of depression you can refuse to confront all the situations that you find difficult. You can avoid seeing people, going to places and, most of all, making decisions.'[17] Consequently there may be a great resistance to being freed from depression. This particular reaction will not be immediately obvious in counselling.

Counselling the depressed begins where all good counselling begins, with careful, accurate listening and observation. Listen to the depressed: do not assume that your definition of depression will be accurate to the person who sits before you. Allow the depressed person to explain what it means to him. According to Edward Welch, 'When you do listen, you will hear pain, fear, hopelessness, dread of the future, terror, silent screams, and emptiness that threatens to destroy.'[18]

Christian specialists advocate different methods in counselling the depressed. Some counsellors argue for a head-on challenge: 'In dealing with depression,' say Law and Bowden, 'one of the important questions to ask is "What disappointments, annoyances or frustrations have you had that you have not been able to have your own way or get people to agree with you or approve of what you have done?" This may need some probing to reach the truth.'[19]

For Law and Bowden, '... the depressive is self-centred and self-pitying',[20] and the solution is clear, since according to the Scriptures we are required to love God and love our neighbour : 'He now needs to deliberately seek to love others by caring for them and thinking more of their needs than his own. His daily routine should be gone through to see where he can do something for others, preferably in the company of others, no matter how small ... it is important to stress that he must do these acts *irrespective of any negative feelings or unwillingness he may experience.*'[21] They advocate five steps to health:

1. Responsibility (an acceptance of blame).
2. Repentance (a wholehearted turning from myself and my way and turning to God and his way).

3. Restitution (to any whom I have robbed or wronged).
4. Reconciliation (to God, to my neighbour and to my situation).
5. Rebuilding on Christ (he is Lord over the whole of my life).[22]

While recognizing that genetic factors and the family environment may predispose people to depression, nevertheless Law and Bowden are emphatic: 'Medical illnesses do not make us sin.'[23] 'Temperament is never a valid excuse for sin or unacceptable behaviour.'[24]

John White, a Christian psychiatrist, warns against a simplistic approach towards depression: 'Depression has many faces. It cannot be relieved on the basis of one simple formula, arising as it does by numerous and complex mechanisms, and plummeting sometimes to depths where its victims are beyond the reach of verbal communication. There are mysteries about it which remain unsolved. No one theoretical framework is adequate to describe it.'[25]

When the cause of the depression is sin, according to Jay Adams, 'The downward cycle of sin moves from a problem to a faulty, sinful response, thereby causing an additional complicating problem which is met by an additional sinful response, etc. That pattern needs to be reversed by beginning an upward cycle of righteousness resulting in further righteousness.'[26]

Cain and Abel brought offerings to the Lord. Cain's offering was rejected. Cain complicated the problem by responding wrongly to the rejection — he became angry and depressed: 'And Cain was very angry, and his countenance fell' (Gen. 4:5). The Lord drew attention to this wrong response and warned Cain of the dire consequences of allowing anger and depression to control him. He would plunge into deeper sin: 'If you do well, will you not be accepted? (Gen. 4:7). 'God offered hope by saying that he could reverse the spiral and rule over sin by breaking out of the sinful pattern through repentance and a subsequent change of behaviour... Nursing his grudge, self-pity, and anger were all elements of the depressed look on Cain's face about which God strongly warned him.'[27]

'If depression were some strange, unaccountable malady that has overcome him, for which he is not responsible and consequently about which he can do nothing, hope would evaporate ... though he may not be responsible for the initial problem (e.g., physical illness or a bad turn in his financial picture), he is responsible for *handling this initial problem God's way*. Because he hasn't, but instead has sinfully reacted to the problem (e.g., neglecting duties and chores; becoming resentful; complaining in self-pity), subsequently, *as a result of this reaction* he has become depressed.'[28]

In other cases of depression practical steps can be taken to alleviate the condition.

Firstly, warns Jim Winter, 'We must ... be careful not to dwell on what would be considered as a negative factor in our past. We may have committed some great sin; we may have failed in a relationship; we may have been abused by another person; or we may feel that we have let God down. Past events may have been traumatic and left their residue within our personality, but it does us no good to dwell on them other than to deal with them in a proper and effective way. Past experiences still retain great power within us.'[29]

The principle of putting off and putting on is crucial in controlling the mind and the behaviour (Eph. 4:22-24). What we think about is under our control. Our minds can be trained to ignore negative thoughts and think more positively: '... whatever things are true, whatever things are noble, whatever things are just, whatever things are pure, whatever things are lovely, whatever things are of good report, if there is any virtue and if there is anything praiseworthy — meditate on these things' (Phil. 4:8).

Christians are urged to 'gird up the loins of your mind' (1 Peter 1:13), to bring 'every thought into captivity to the obedience of Christ' (2 Cor. 10:5), to be transformed by the renewing of their minds, and so to 'prove what is that good and acceptable and perfect will of God' (Rom. 12:2).

Practical steps for helping the depressed

1. Understand the experience of depression.
2. Make tentative distinctions between physical and spiritual symptoms.
3. Focus on heart issues; point to Christ; encourage faith; guide in the battle with sin.
4. If the pain of depression is excessive, consider using medical treatments as a possible means of easing the pain.[30]

Generally it is good to talk. With competent pastoral counselling the people of God will successfully work through particular problems and difficulties. The listening ear, the loving concern and the right application of Scripture bring relief to many who are depressed. Two problems, however, are particularly related to counselling depressed persons. On the one hand, elders may so identify with the sufferer that they become depressed themselves. On the other hand, it is possible to be so sympathetic as to make the position worse by encouraging self-pity and promoting excessive dependency.[31]

Practical steps for the depressed Christian

Martin Luther was all too familiar with depression for most of his adult life, for 'spiritual anxiety, satanic temptation and constitutional factors met and mingled in debilitating confusion'.[32] Luther's recommendations to the depressed were these: 'Better banish the whole subject, seek company and discuss some irrelevant matter ... shun solitude ... seek out some Christian brother, some wise counsellor. Undergird yourself with the fellowship of the church. Then, too, seek convivial company, feminine company, dine, dance, joke and sing. Make yourself eat and drink even though food may be distasteful. Fasting is the very worst expedient.'[33]

Puritan pastor Richard Baxter urges: 'Make as full a discovery as you can, how much of the trouble of your mind doth arise from your melancholy and bodily distempers [i.e. natural temperament or physical sickness], and how much from discontenting afflictions in your worldly estate, or friends, or name, and according to your discovery make use of the remedy... For melancholy [i.e. depression], I have by long experience found it to have so great and common a hand in the fears and troubles of mind, that I meet not with one of many [i.e. I have found hardly a single instance among all those I have met], that live in great troubles and fears for any long time together; but melancholy is the main seat of them; though they feel nothing in their body, but all in their mind. I would have such persons make use of some able godly physician, and he will help them to discern how much of their trouble comes from melancholy. Where this is the cause, usually the party is fearful of almost every thing; a word, or a sudden thought will disquiet them. Sometimes they are sad, and scarce know why: all comforts are of no continuance with them.'[34]

Baxter gives the following advice:

If you would have these fears and troubles removed, apply yourself to the proper cure of melancholy.

(i) Avoid all passion of sorrow, fear, and anger, as much as you can...

(ii) Avoid much solitariness, and be most commonly in some cheerful company ... keep company with the more cheerful sort of the godly. There is no mirth like the mirth of believers, which faith doth fetch from the blood of Christ, and from the promises of the word, and from experiences of mercy, and from the serious fore-apprehensions of our everlasting blessedness. Converse with men of strongest faith, that have this heavenly mirth, and can speak experimentally of the joy of the Holy Ghost; and these will be a great help to the reviving of your spirit, and changing your melancholy habit, so far as without a physician it may be expected...

(iii) Also take heed of too deep, fixed, musing thoughts; studying and serious meditating be not duties for the deeply melancholy...

(iv) To this end, be sure that you avoid idleness and want of employment; which as it is a life not pleasing to God, so is it the opportunity for melancholy thoughts to be working, and the chiefest season for Satan to tempt you ... and that time which you redeem for spiritual exercises, let it be most spent in thanksgiving, and praises, and heavenly conference. These things may do much for prevention, and abating your disease, if it be not gone too far; but if it be, you were best have recourse to the physician, and expect God's blessing in the use of means; and you will find, when your body is once cured, the disquietness of your mind will vanish of itself.[35]

Practical steps for the church

The people of God are called upon to share in each other's joys and sorrows (Rom. 12:15). We are to 'bear one another's burdens, and so fulfil the law of Christ' (Gal. 6:2) that we love one another as he has loved us (John 13:34). While loneliness may produce, or exacerbate, depression, depression can also produce intense loneliness. Sufferers withdraw and close in upon themselves. Unable to cope with relationships, they seek isolation. Alone they may suffer with inertia, a lack of motivation which leads to failure in the duties and responsibilities of life. Here the people of God can rally round and give the needed encouragement. Visits should be practically orientated: house-cleaning, audible prayer, reading the Scriptures, washing the dishes (together), walking, or cycling.

When someone is depressed there is a tendency to stay away from worship. Here the exhortation of Scripture is apt, not to forsake the assembling of ourselves together (Heb. 10:25). Worship lifts the believer's mind to heaven (Col. 3:2), concentrates our thoughts upon Christ and provides mutual encouragement (Col. 3:16).

Conclusion

'Seeing depression as an illness with a physiological cause can be a great comfort, both to the patient and the doctor,' says Dorothy Rowe, 'for the patient can feel absolved of responsibility, and the doctor can prescribe pills and not have to enquire too deeply about the patient's life and the pain and despair he is feeling... [Seeing] depression as an error in a person's way of living places the burden of responsibility on the person, but it also provides a way out.'[36]

At times life's circumstances get all Christians down. Sadness is not depression, and depression is not despair. With careful diagnosis, wise counsel and a faithful application of the Scriptures, depressed persons may be delivered from their distress: 'We are hard pressed on every side, yet not crushed; we are perplexed, but not in despair; persecuted, but not forsaken; struck down, but not destroyed...' (2 Cor. 4:8-9).

'Therefore strengthen the hands which hang down, and the feeble knees, and make straight paths for your feet, so that what is lame may not be dislocated, but rather be healed' (Heb. 12:12).

Appendix II
Counselling and abuse

Church leaders and abuse
Scripture and sexual abuse
Child abuse
Damage caused by child sexual abuse
Counselling survivors
The healing process
The church and child abuse

Counselling and abuse

'Due to the prevalence of childhood sexual abuse in the histories of individuals who seek counselling and the possible pervasive and long-term effects that stem from the abuse,' writes Claire Burke Draucker, 'it is important that all counsellors become adept at addressing the unique and complex needs of survivors.'[1]

The phenomenal rise in the number of people revealing experiences of childhood abuse may be accounted for in numerous ways; nevertheless none can doubt the evidence that these devastating occurrences are serious and widespread throughout society. The constructed air of secrecy, the unwillingness to admit its presence, the sense of shame and guilt to all concerned, makes abuse hard to detect, hard to disclose and hard to prove. Research sources in the UK and the USA suggest that one in four girls and one in nine boys experience some form of abuse in childhood.[2]

Before we consider the specific issue of childhood abuse, attention needs to be given to the matter of abuse among church leaders. Since those who have sufficient courage to disclose their painful past to elders are particularly vulnerable individuals, it is essential that the leaders themselves are men of blameless conduct, proven ability and emotional stability, satisfying their own needs appropriately with spouse, family and friends.

Church leaders and abuse

Leadership in the church of Jesus Christ is open to corruption. Tragically there have been a number of cases in recent years of men who have betrayed their trust and dishonoured their office. The higher that men are held in the esteem of the church, the more vulnerable they are to an abuse of power: 'It is the popular leader, not the social pariah, who is the typical abuser.'[3] This abuse may involve spiritual, emotional and psychological manipulation and control for personal aggrandizement, extracting detailed descriptions of sexual incidents for voyeuristic satisfaction, inappropriate touching, or seducing, or being seduced into a liaison.

Jane Chevous comments: 'The starting point for non-abusive leadership is the recognition of the imbalance of power in all positions of authority, but especially those of religious leaders and anyone engaged in public ministry. In this latter category we can include youth and children's workers, lay ministers, those involved in pastoral care and counselling, healing and prayer ministries, house-group and fellowship leaders, lay readers, evangelists and worship leadership.'[4]

The leadership style of the Lord Jesus Christ, in his teaching and in his example, is in marked contrast to that of others. He demands from his followers a gentle, respectful, humble form of leadership that empowers rather than overpowers: 'You know that the rulers of the Gentiles lord it over them, and those who are great exercise authority over them. Yet it shall not be so among you; but whoever desires to become great among you, let him be your servant. And whoever desires to be first among you, let him be your slave – just as the Son of Man did not come to be served, but to serve, and to give his life a ransom for many' (Matt. 20:25-28).

Self-awareness

Church leaders are urged to be concerned about themselves, as well as to be concerned about the people of God in their care: 'Take heed to yourselves and to all the flock, among which the Holy Spirit has made you overseers, to shepherd the church of God which he purchased with his own blood' (Acts 20:28). An elder is to be caring for himself, caring for his colleagues and caring for the flock. His character and behaviour as a Christian are of paramount importance, after which comes the quality of his functioning in leadership. Unlike the Pharisees in our Lord's days on earth, godly leaders will cleanse 'the inside of the cup and dish, that the outside of them may be clean also' (Matt. 23:26).

Self-awareness involves knowing one's own personal strengths and weaknesses. It is essential to be aware of areas of vulnerability to the temptations of Satan and of the weaknesses of the flesh. With all the care in the world, it is still wise to remember the exhortation: 'Let him who thinks he stands take heed lest he fall' (1 Cor. 10:12).

During all interaction with the people of God there should be the ability in the leader to reflect upon his own behaviour, recognize within himself his own agenda and evaluate his own performance. This is particularly important when engaged in counselling the vulnerable.

Practical steps when counselling women

There must be a measure of caution. As Herbert Carson points out, there have, sadly, been many disasters when pastors have discovered too late that a caring and advising role has led beyond the warmth of pastoral care to an increasingly intimate relationship.[5]

Jay Adams advises: 'All discussion of sexual relations in counselling, since it involves both parties intimately, should be in the presence of *both* the husband and the wife. Discussing such matters *privately* with a wife alone can lead to un-necessary temptations and/or accusations. If in very rare circumstances sexual matters must be discussed with the woman alone, it is always wise to do so in a team counselling situation.'[6]

Team counselling is also valuable in other ways: counsellors can learn from each other and there is a third-party witness to what is said, which 'precludes almost all of the provocative conversation and action which is the stock-in-trade of some female clients'.[7] Young, handsome, single ministers are particularly at risk from the female predator who has a 'crush' on the pastor.

Though exceptions may be appropriate in cases of serious illness, infirmity or old age, pastors will not normally visit a woman alone in her own home. Counselling should be conducted in the home of the elder, with his wife con-spicuously present, though not necessarily in the same room.

Boundaries

All human beings have the right to their own personal space (about eighteen inches, or 500 centimetres from the nose). This space should not be invaded: 'Any touching between a leader and someone they are serving should take place only in public. Even then touch should be age-appropriate and initiated by the person being helped rather than by the leader. Touching should be related to the person's needs rather than the leader's.'[8] Some church leaders are more comfortable with a policy of 'no touch'.

The ability to distinguish appropriately between personal and professional boundaries is a vital skill in safe practice. Clear boundaries provide safety and security, but they also provide freedom: 'For someone new and inexperienced in leadership ... being able to recognize, draw and maintain clear boundaries of role, agenda, and attachment is a core skill.'[9]

Supervision

Plurality in eldership provides many benefits for the exercise of pastoral care. Experienced elders may be paired to provide mutual support and supervision and an environment to reflect upon issues raised in specific counselling cases. A new or inexperienced pastor can be teamed up with a more experienced colleague who will be able to provide invaluable insight and guidance.

With these provisions in place, church leaders are better prepared to face the complex and heart-rending world of those who have experienced childhood abuse.

Scripture and sexual abuse

Church leaders should also ensure that great care is exercised in the public reading of Scripture. History is often recorded in the Word of God without comment upon the spiritual or moral content. Christians, and especially those appointed to teach the Scriptures, are expected carefully to assess and evaluate events in the light of God's clearly revealed moral code. Reading without explanation and interpretation may do the devil's work rather than the Lord's!

An example of this is the account of Lot offering his daughters to the citizens of Sodom (Gen. 19:8). As Annie Imbens and Ineke Jonker point out, those who lead worship are to remember that 'Children do not consider that a certain teaching might have been written in another context and was meant for use in a different situation from the one in which they find themselves.'[10] Reading this passage of Scripture without comment might give the impression that Lot's action was commendable, when it was in fact deplorable! To quote H. C. Leupold, 'The kindest interpretation of Lot's willingness to sacrifice his daughters to the depraved lusts of these evildoers stresses that it was done with the intent of guarding his guests... Delitzsch's summary still covers the truth ... as ... an attempt to avoid sin by sin ... we cannot but feel the strongest aversion to so unpaternal an attitude.'[11]

Calvin expresses his horror even more strongly: 'He [Lot] does not hesitate to prostitute his own daughters, that he may restrain the indomitable fury of the people. But he should rather have endured a thousand deaths, than have resorted to such a measure ... he inconsiderately seeks to remedy one evil by means of another... But when reduced to the last straits, let us learn to pray, that the Lord would open to us some way of escape.'[12]

An early indication of great anger on the part of the people of God regarding sexual abuse is seen in the events following the rape of Dinah (Gen. 34:2), the daughter of Jacob and Leah. While Dinah was not a child, nevertheless she suffered serious abuse. Though the deceit of Jacob's sons cannot be condoned (Gen. 34:13), nor the ruthless revenge of Simeon and Levi (Gen. 34:25-26), which was so distasteful to Jacob (Gen. 34:30; 49:5-7), nevertheless, as John Murray observes, '... we cannot fail to appreciate the indignation and deep sense of violated honour which Jacob's sons entertained when the purity of their sister Dinah had been desecrated by Shechem... We rightly detect the accents of a highly developed ethic when we read' the following account: 'And Jacob heard that he [Shechem] had defiled Dinah his daughter. Now his sons were with his livestock in the field; so Jacob held his peace until they came... And the sons of Jacob came in from the field when they heard it; and the men were grieved and very angry, because he had done a disgraceful thing in Israel by lying with Jacob's daughter, a thing which ought not to be done' (Gen. 34:5,7). [13]

The Lord's attitude towards child sexual abuse is clear in his unequivocal condemnation of incest. This includes all sexual contact between those who are prohibited from marriage: 'None of you shall approach anyone who is near of kin to him, to uncover his nakedness: I am the LORD' (Lev. 18:6). There follows a list of prohibited sexual relationships. The seriousness of these sanctions is indicated by the passing of the death sentence on violators (Lev. 20:11-14,17-21).

In the light of these laws it is evident what the Lord's judgement would have been upon David's son Amnon when he raped his half-sister Tamar (2 Sam. 13:1-22). Matthew Henry comments: 'We have here a particular account of the abominable wickedness of Amnon in ravishing his sister, a subject not fit to be enlarged upon nor indeed to be mentioned without blushing, that ever any man should be so vile, especially that a son of David should be so... Amnon's lust was unnatural in itself, to lust after his sister, which even natural conscience startles at and cannot think of without horror... Can he entertain the thought of betraying that virtue and honour of which, as a brother, he ought to have been the protector? She calls him brother, reminding him of the nearness of the relation, which made it unlawful for him to marry her, much more to debauch her. It was expressly forbidden (Lev. 18:9) under a severe penalty (Lev. 20:17). Great care must be taken lest the love that should be among relations degenerate into lust.'

Then, 'He basely turned her out of doors by force; nay, as if he now disdained to touch her with his own hands, he ordered his servant to pull her out and bolt the door after her (v. 17). Now, the innocent injured lady had reason to resent this as a great affront, and in some respects (as she says, v. 16) worse than the former; for nothing could have been done more barbarous and ill-natured, or more disgraceful to her.'[14] Here is an illustration of what often seems to happen in cases of incest and abuse – lust satisfied turns to loathing.

While Tamar's father, King David, 'was very angry' on hearing about the dreadful incident (2 Sam. 13:21), he nevertheless took no action to punish his son Amnon. Tamar's full brother Absalom counselled his sister to remain silent and he himself held a silent grudge and 'hated Amnon, because he had forced his sister Tamar' (2 Sam. 13:22). Two years later, Absalom was to take revenge by arranging the murder of his half-brother Amnon (2 Sam. 13:28-29). David's sin of polygamy and his failure to deal with Amnon in accordance with the law of God, coupled with his general indulgence of his sons, brought devastating consequences into his family and upon the nation of Israel.

In recent years criticism has been levelled at evangelical churches for adherence to the teaching of the Bible regarding gender role and relationship. In upholding male headship and female submission in marriage, the church has been accused of encouraging an environment which permits, if not promotes, abuse. Imbens and Jonker, in their study in the Netherlands of women raised in Christian homes who survived incest, concluded that 'Religion can be a factor that is conducive to incest and compounds trauma.'[15] They argue that, 'through their religious upbringing', these girls 'were made easy prey to sexual abuse in the (extended) family. Moreover, their religious upbringing caused them problems in working through their experiences.'[16]

Chevous adds her voice in attacking evangelical Christians: '... blame may be placed on pathology, culture, gender, stress, the victim's personality or behaviour, the environment or social construction. *In the Church, the fundamentalist mindset and the dangers of power have been identified as key factors*' (emphasis added).[17]

Reading through the cases cited by Imbens and Jonker, it becomes clear that the perpetrators of abuse did not use any biblical teaching to justify their wicked behaviour. Furthermore it is evident that the girls themselves were not intimidated by the teaching of Scripture to remain silent. However, the failure of church leaders to spot indications of possible abuse, and their reluctance to believe that men held in great respect in the church could be guilty of such corruption, contributed significantly to the pain of the children.

While a genuinely abused child must not be hurt even further by being disbelieved, there is an explicit biblical duty not to entertain false accusations, especially against church leaders (1 Tim. 5:19).

Child abuse

Defining child abuse is no easy task. Differences of opinion exist as to what should be included. There is, however, general agreement regarding contact sexual abuse. Claire Draucker writes, 'All forms of sexual activity involving genital contact for either the offender or the victim, such as genital fondling and vaginal, anal, and oral intercourse, are usually included in definitions of sexual abuse. Also typically included are other forms of direct, physical sexual contact, such as fondling the breasts, buttocks, or thighs and sexual kissing.'[18]

Others, however, include non-contact sexual abuse, such as that which a child is forced to hear, see and do with others. It is the use of a minor to meet the sexual or sexual/emotional needs of another person. However, including non-contact sexual activities in the definition of sexual abuse is controversial.[19]

Abuse may be understood in a broader context still as an adult's failure to prevent harm. This may be as damaging to a child's emotional/psychological state as the actual harm itself. Moving wider still in the definition of abuse, general neglect is included, since it is the persistent failure to provide for the child's emotional, psychological or physical needs. According to the National Society for the Prevention of Cruelty to Children, one in ten young people in Britain have suffered serious abuse or neglect in this way during childhood. Each week at least one child will die as the result of an adult's abuse. A quarter of all rape victims are children.[20]

Some definitions of abuse go so far as to include corporal punishment.

How would the Lord Jesus Christ react if he were here in the flesh? His attitude towards children is well documented. When his disciples wanted to turn children away from his presence, 'He was greatly displeased and said to them, "Let the little children come to me, and do not forbid them; for of such is the kingdom of God... And he took them up in his arms, laid his hands on them, and blessed them' (Mark 10:14,16). On another occasion Jesus, in clear unambiguous terms, condemns any and every form of child abuse: 'But whoever causes one of these little ones who believe in me to stumble, it would be better for him if a millstone were hung around his neck, and he were thrown into the sea' (Mark 9:42).

There is, however, one area where the Lord Jesus would take exception — namely, to the inclusion in the classification of abuse of physical punishment used as part of child discipline. From a biblical perspective it is difficult to draw a clear line between legitimate child discipline and the physical abuse of the child. The application of physical punishment by a parent or guardian is permitted (some would argue that it is required) by God, yet it would be all too easy for 'untaught and unstable people' (2 Peter 3:16) to misunderstand such scriptures as Proverbs 13:24; 22:15; 23:13-14; 29:15 as a mandate for the most severe form of chastisement. Wisdom is required by all who would engage in the training of children. The justice of God would bring caution to bear upon all forms of discipline; punishment must be appropriate to the wrongdoing, to the time and place, and the age and understanding of the child. Where parents or guardians achieve a consistent approach to child-raising, they are able to establish a regime in which punishment becomes a rare occurrence. Those who outlaw smacking usually resort to other means of punishment. Shutting a child up in a room, screaming at him/her in public or private, totally ignoring the child or the withdrawal of privileges might just as easily be designated as 'abuse'. It may also be argued that psychological and emotional punishment is far more damaging than a smack.

Damage caused by child sexual abuse

Children who are subjected to abuse are described as 'victims', since they are powerless to stop the attacks. Adults who have been subjected to abuse are re-ferred to as 'survivors', since they have found ways of surviving the trauma of sexual abuse. With Christian love and care, and the grace of God in their lives, there is the prospect of going beyond simply *surviving*, to live, as any other Christian, 'in newness of life' (Rom. 6:4), full and free (John 10:10).

The long-term effects of childhood sexual abuse are many and varied: shame, guilt, fear, anxiety, sadness, grief, depression, isolation, inclination to suicide, sexual dysfunction, failure in personal relationships, substance abuse and other self-destructive behaviour. Finkelhor and Browne[21] have proposed a conceptual framework classifying four ways in which sexual abuse causes problems:

1. Traumatic sexualization

Traumatic sexualization results when characteristics in the abuse situation affect the development of the child's sexuality. A childhood experience of abuse 'often leads to disruptions in sexual functioning manifest in disorders of sexual arousal, response, and satisfaction'.[22]

'Feelings of shame, being unclean, even revulsion make touch and intimacy difficult. Sex may be associated with pain, degradation, fear or forced obedience and may trigger flashbacks and nightmares.'[23]

Survivors of childhood sexual abuse experience more marital and family conflict, more physical and sexual problems, more sexual guilt, anxiety and dissatisfaction.

2. Stigmatization

Stigmatization occurs when children are told they are bad, shameful, or worthless. As one survivor recorded, 'The feelings of guilt and fear increased in me. I felt very confused, helpless, dirty and disgusted. There was no one to talk to. I was very much alone and very lonely. I was desperately unhappy and cried silently for help but no one could hear me... My personal hygiene became an obsession in order to cleanse my mind and body of the dirty feelings from the abuse which was forced upon me. I hated him for abusing me and gaining pleasure from it and causing me pain and misery.'[24]

Perpetrators seek to manipulate their victims by flattery, threats or blame. The child is made to feel responsible for the violation by being seductive, 'sexy', wicked or evil. Punishment is often inflicted following the sexual activity, thus compounding the abuse.

3. Betrayal

Betrayal results when children realize that an adult whom they trusted and depended on has caused them harm. This betrayal of trust causes a profound reaction. The closer the relationship and the deeper the trust, the worse the sense of betrayal. But when the perpetrator is a highly respected, trusted member of church and community, victims often conclude that the fault lies within themselves: 'Something is wrong with me.'

4. Powerlessness

Powerlessness 'results when children's attempts to meet their needs are persistently frustrated or when they are threatened with injury or harm. Powerlessness results from invasion of the body, violence accompanying the sexual activity, or from children's inability to halt or alter the course of the abuse.'[25] Abuse is in essence about a powerless state, and the inability to express anger towards the real culprit is enough to plunge anyone into the depths of despair. For any child in these circumstances who has cried out to God, depression is more than sadness, it is the bleak isolation of Psalm 13:

How long, O LORD?
Will you forget me for ever?
How long will you hide your face from me?
How long shall I take counsel in my soul,
Having sorrow in my heart daily?
How long will my enemy be exalted over me?

(Ps. 13:1-2).

The grim aftermath of childhood sexual abuse is seen in traumatic sexualization, stigmatization, betrayal and powerlessness. Nevertheless, each survivor has unique experiences, and the impact of their violation will depend upon a wide range of factors:

The degree of damage depends on the degree of traumatic sexualization, stigmatization, betrayal and powerlessness, the child has experienced. This in turn depends on a number of factors such as:

• who the abuser was
• what took place
• what was said
• how long the abuse went on for
• how the child felt and how she interpreted what was happening
• if the child was otherwise happy and supported
• how other people reacted to disclosure or discovery of the abuse
• how old the child was.[26]

Counselling survivors

All counselling of minors must be conducted in the presence of a parent or guardian. When issues of sexual abuse involve trusted members of the family, then a mature Christian woman should be constantly in attendance. A church leader *must never be alone* with a child, whether in a house, in a church building, in a car or in the open air.

The extent of childhood sexual abuse is such that it may well be assumed that a large proportion of those female adults who seek help from their pastors have experienced this trauma. At the same time elders engaged in counselling must beware of jumping to conclusions on slight evidence. The normal components of good Christian counselling are to be applied: self-awareness, listening, reflection, checking of one's perceptions, empowering and loving gracious responses. Survivors will not generally find it easy to open up and share painful, shameful experiences. If the disclosure of abuse is met with expressions of horror – 'Oh no! How dreadful!' – or doubt – 'Are you sure?' – or excessive questioning, based on voyeuristic curiosity rather than concern, healing will be halted from the outset. Pastors should never pressurize or manipulate a survivor to disclose painful experiences.

An assurance of confidentiality is essential. The counsellor must be comfortable with periods of silence and guide the session at an unrushed pace. He should carefully resist the temptation to introduce his own experiences or issues. According to Kim Etherington, 'Researchers have found that the presence of someone in whom to confide and who is supportive appears to be important in helping individuals overcome the effects of abuse...'[27]

The 'nature, the circumstances, and the impact of sexual abuse can differ greatly'.[28] Each case must be studied individually and the approach and response of the counsellor adapted accordingly. The adult survivor's own perception of the experience and its impact is the focal point, not the counsellor's judgement and assessment. Unwise reactions from pastors may worsen already painful memories. Since powerlessness is one of the devastating effects of violation, it is important that counsellors do not behave in a paternalistic fashion, nor act as rescuers. Rescuers take control, whereas the counsellor's task is one of enabling or empowering so that survivors sense they are regaining or maintaining control of their own lives. This is powerfully illustrated in the Holy Spirit's indwelling of the believer (1 Cor. 6:19-20) and enabling *self*-control (Gal. 5:23). 'Guidance, experience, new perspectives from another can all be helpful if offered, not imposed.'[29]

Since the perpetrators of childhood sexual abuse are more often male and the victims more often female, it may be extremely difficult, if not impossible, for a survivor to talk with a (male) elder or elders. Sensitivity on the part of church leaders may result in the introduction of competent 'mothers in Israel' who, by virtue of their spiritual maturity and wisdom, may work alongside the eldership, and under their overall supervision, in these difficult cases. When sisters in Christ exercise a counselling role in such cases, it is important that an elder is introduced into the scene as soon as the survivor is comfortable for that to occur. True healing comes when a survivor is able to relate with a man in a relaxed and secure setting.

Great skill is required of male counsellors when faced with survivors of childhood sexual abuse. Early violation as a child may result in the adult's not knowing the proprieties of normal relationship. Speech and conduct may be misconstrued by a male counsellor, resulting either in a reprimand for inappropriate behaviour, or falling into an unprofessional relationship where emotional and physical boundaries are transgressed.

Christians often tell survivors they should forgive their abuser. 'This may be well meaning, but is dangerously simplistic, ill-informed and frequently re-abusive.'[30] Forgiveness 'is not a prerequisite to their healing, but is a personal choice some survivors may make as they begin to move toward a resolution of their abuse experience'.[31]

As survivors open the door to painful memories they may experience intense shame, guilt, fear, anxiety, sadness, grief, depression, isolation and inclination to suicide. Godly counsellors will hear the expressions of pain and distress and reassure the sufferer of the love of God and the comfort and empowering of the Holy Spirit.

The healing process

The healing process necessitates at least three steps:

1. Disclosure of the abuse

This will include the frequency and nature of the abuse, the age of the child and that of the abuser; the relationship between the two; identifying others involved who were unwilling or unable to help; the reasons for termination of the abuse and the involvement of social services or police.

Sometimes memories of horrific experiences in childhood may be suppressed. This dissociation, or disconnection, begins as a mechanism for escaping the trauma — 'blanking out or blacking out, or living in a fantasy world'.[32] In later life this can prove a great hindrance. 'Bad feelings and memories "escape" as nightmares, panic attacks, fears, depression, sexual difficulties, flashbacks and many other problems. These problems are the symptoms; the underlying cause is the sexual abuse and this needs to be dealt with' first.[33]

Great care is required in exploring memories. Pastors must avoid implanting ideas, thoughts, or suggestions into the mind of the person being counselled. Immense damage inevitably results from 'false' memories. Asking the survivor to bring family photographs and talk about family members and their own experiences at the time the picture was taken may enable the awareness and subsequent disclosure of abuse.

Discernment is required not only to know *whom to trust* with the disclosure, but also *whom to burden* with the disclosure. Some relatives or close friends may not be able to cope and this may result in the survivor's regretting the disclosure. One male survivor disclosed his childhood suffering to his wife: 'All that I remember of her reaction was that it was very angry, and that she was insistent about knowing who had done this to me, and what precisely. The cork seemed to be slipping faster; I could see that now I had shared this knowledge with another, I had lost control of it. This is a truly terrifying experience.'[34]

2. Reinterpreting the abuse from an adult perspective

Survivors generally believe that they were somehow responsible for the attacks. Looking back as an adult, they agonize over why they did not stop the attacks, resist them, or disclose them to others. Photographs serve to reinforce the age (and obvious powerlessness) of the child at the time. Viewing the events from a child's perspective removes self-blame. They begin to understand that what occurred was the responsibility of the adult, or the older, or more powerful other person, irrespective of the child's behaviour. The offender, not the child, is always to blame for the abusive sexual behaviour.

Sexual abuse may awaken self-blame based on the survivor's guilt: the child may have appreciated the attention, the concern and the affection, while hating the abuse. An abused girl may feel culpability at deriving some pleasure and satisfaction from the events. An abused boy may further misinterpret any experience of pleasure or sexual arousal as latent homosexual feelings that may lead to gender anxiety and confusion in later life. Since men and boys are culturally conditioned to be strong, male survivors of childhood sexual abuse often blame themselves for failing to protect themselves. The task of the counsellor is to assist the survivor to distinguish the horror of abuse from the pleasures of care and attention and also the physiological responses to sexual stimulation that may occur.

3. Making desired changes to one's way of life

'Dealing with sexual abuse is not about wiping out the past. You can never do that. Neither is it about blocking off the past by burying your feelings or building a wall to keep the memories away. It is about dealing with the way the abuse has affected your life and the way you feel about yourself. You will never be able to forget about the abuse but you will be able to release your feelings of guilt and reclaim your self-respect.'[35]

'I may develop (often unconscious) behaviours that increase my vulnerability and can even feed the abusive behaviour of authority figures. Learning to identify and change these, to protect myself at a reasonable level, is one of the transforming steps of healing.'[36]

A skilled male counsellor is invaluable in working through these issues to understand how to establish wholesome and God-honouring relationships between the genders.

The church and child abuse

Writing in the context of Amy Carmichael's Dohnavur fellowship in South India, Christian psychiatrist Gaius Davies is convinced that 'Only a tight-knit caring community like Dohnavur can deal with the feelings and pressures that child abuse can generate.'[37] This raises a question about the quality of loving support and care provided by our churches. The New Testament pictures Christians sharing life well beyond the weekly routine of Lord's Day worship and midweek prayer and Bible study. Those who have been deprived of a stable and loving home environment benefit greatly from the loving, generous support of fellow believers. The converted alcoholic needs new friends to take the place of his/her drinking partners; the converted criminal needs new friends to take the place of his criminal fraternity; so the survivor of childhood sexual abuse needs the loving support of sisters *and brothers* who will provide the friendship and fellowship of normal godly relationships.

This level of caring places great demands upon the church of Jesus Christ. Yet how else are we to fulfil the injunction: 'Bear one another's burdens, and so fulfil the law of Christ'? (Gal. 6:2). How else are we to 'weep with those who weep'? (Rom. 12:15). The local church resembles a body feeling the pain and discomfort of each member: 'If one member suffers, all the members suffer with it' (1 Cor. 12:26). While we may not be able to replicate the tight-knit fellowship of Dohnavur, we can at least provide a God-honouring, caring community where the broken can be restored and the sick strengthened (Ezek. 34:16). Is not this the ministry of Christ that we are to emulate? (Luke 4:18; cf. Isa. 61:1-2).

In Christ we have amazing resources not known by the world. The gospel is not only 'the power of God to salvation for everyone who believes' (Rom. 1:16); it is also wonderfully able to transform lives. There is complete cleansing, healing and restoration and a new inner capacity by the indwelling Spirit of God.

In the Bible there is beautiful and profound imagery of the people of God who have 'washed their robes and made them white in the blood of the Lamb' (Rev. 7:14). The prophet Isaiah provides a graphic presentation of human sinfulness when he says, '... we are all like an unclean thing, and all our righteousnesses are like filthy rags' (Isa. 64:6). While this refers to our own personal sin and the feeling of filthiness associated with it, there is also an application to those who feel unclean because of the treatment of others. In Christ there is total cleansing of the inner self — however that self has been despoiled! All Christians, irrespective of their background and experiences, may delight in the new clothing freely given by God:

> I will greatly rejoice in the LORD,
> My soul shall be joyful in my God;
> For he has clothed me with the garments of salvation,
> He has covered me with the robe of righteousness,
> As a bridegroom decks himself with ornaments,
> And as a bride adorns herself with her jewels
>
> (Isa. 61:10).

In the death of the Saviour at Calvary 'a fountain' was 'opened ... for sin and for uncleanness' (Zech. 13:1). The paralysed man at Bethesda was challenged by Jesus: 'Do you want to be made well?' (John 5:6). It is evident from the succeeding context that the Lord was offering the man more than physical healing, but also a wholeness of heart, mind and soul. Survivors of childhood abuse should be gently challenged in this way. When we become Christians our past is no longer able to dominate us — unless we allow it to, by dwelling upon it in our minds and hearts: 'Therefore, if anyone is in Christ, he is a new creation; old things have passed away; behold, all things have become new' (2 Cor. 5:17).

Survivors need to disclose the abuse, reinterpret it from an adult perspective and make desired life-changes. They need also to file the horrid experience away as a life experience — and then move on. This may take time and may only be achieved by continued reference to the positive injunctions of the Scriptures.

Renewal of the mind is crucial. Paul urges Christians with a bad history to 'put off, concerning your former conduct [and thinking] ... and be renewed in the spirit of your mind, and ... put on the new man which was created according to God, in true righteousness and holiness' (Eph. 4:22-24). This is to be achieved by replacing the old ways of thinking with new ways of thinking. He urges that 'all bitterness, wrath, anger, clamour and evil speaking be put away ... with all malice' (Eph. 4:31). Here in this context bitterness, wrath and anger indicate 'violent inward resentment and displeasure against others', says

Matthew Henry, 'and, by *clamour* [is meant], big words, loud threatenings, and other intemperate speeches, by which bitterness, wrath and anger, vent themselves'. Thought processes must be brought under control:

> Beloved, do not avenge yourselves, but rather give place to wrath; for it is written, 'Vengeance is mine, I will repay,' says the Lord. Therefore

> 'If your enemy hungers, feed him,
> if he thirsts, give him a drink;
> for in so doing you will heap coals of fire on his head.'

> Do not be overcome by evil, but overcome evil with good
> (Rom. 12:19-21).

The past can cripple any of God's children, either by the remembrance of our personal sins, or the remembrance of others in their sins against us. In Christ there is the power to leave the past behind and to 'walk in newness of life' (Rom. 6:4). Once the past has been faced, evaluated and understood as far as is possible, survivors should be 'forgetting those things which are behind and reaching forward to those things which are ahead' as they 'press toward the goal for the prize of the upward call of God in Christ Jesus' (Phil. 3:13-14).

All God's children are precious to him. Our personal worth is so great that God has given his Son for each believer. Christian survivors of abuse need to embrace the fact that they are loved by God, clothed in Christ's righteousness and are sons or daughters of the King of heaven. Each Christian can say with Paul, 'I have been crucified with Christ; it is no longer I who live, but Christ lives in me; and the life which I now live in the flesh I live by faith in the Son of God, *who loved me and gave himself for me*' (Gal. 2:20, emphasis added).

> Yes, *I have loved you with an everlasting love;*
> Therefore with loving-kindness I have drawn you
> (Jer. 31:3 emphasis added).

Conclusion

Each church should not only establish a child-protection policy, but be prepared to take seriously any disclosures or suspicions of abuse within the leadership. Careful investigation must ensue. The church's responsibility, however, is not only to care for the vulnerable church member, but also to care for the vulnerable church leader. Many churches have unrealistic expectations of their paid employees. Love for the church must also include love for the church leader. Realistic goals should be established for hours of work, duties and responsibilities.

The church is like the inn where the Good Samaritan lodged the wounded traveller (Luke 10:35). We are commissioned to take care of those whom Christ entrusts to us. Everything must be done to ensure that the broken are not further damaged within our charge. Our task is a healing ministry. Church leaders will be called to account: 'We shall receive a stricter judgement' (James 3:1). May we discharge our responsibilities to the people of God in our charge, and within the sphere of our ministries, in such a manner that one day we shall hear him say, 'Well done, good and faithful servant... Enter into the joy of your lord' (Matt. 25:21).

Appendix III
Counselling and homosexuality

Counselling and homosexuality

There has been a phenomenal increase in homosexual interest and activity. A number of factors may be identified in the present-day promotion of homosexuality as a natural and valid alternative to heterosexuality.

Social factors

Firstly, *the media* has been won over to an almost exclusively supportive and positive stance, eager to promote the cause of 'gay liberation'. The impact of television and radio, especially through 'soap operas', is widespread and pervasive. Claiming to be *following* public opinion, they are in reality *forming* public opinion. As with the media, so it is with the government, in the UK at least. Law and Bowden comment: 'With the massive barrage of pro-homosexual propaganda in the media and the numerous homosexuals in the Government and Civil Service passing laws that promote their cause, it is little wonder that many young boys consider it quite a normal and socially acceptable lifestyle.'[1]

Secondly, the impact of *feminism* needs to be taken into account. According to Piper and Grudem, '... the feminist minimization of sexual role differentiation contributes to the confusion of sexual identity that, especially in second and third generations, gives rise to more homosexuality in society'.[2] Dorothy Patterson writes that 'The efforts of contemporary society to eradicate the differences between the sexes have spawned an increase in strident lesbianism and open homosexuality...'[3]

A third factor may be the drastic increase in *the number of children who are being reared solely by women*, or being smothered by mother-love. Boys, and indeed girls, do not have sufficient natural and wholesome contact with men.

The church's response

Nevertheless, whatever the cause, our concern here is for the pastoral care of those who have fallen victim to the propaganda, the hype or the corrupting influence of others.

Those who are struggling with the problem of homosexuality will not generally find it easy to broach the subject with the pastor of an evangelical church unless there has been periodic teaching on family life. Regular ministry should include careful teaching on singleness, courting, marriage, parenting, widowhood, death and bereavement. Within this series there is scope for a careful, balanced handling of the subject of homosexuality, lesbianism, pre-marital sex and adultery, with an emphasis upon the grace of God in forgiveness and healing. Prejudice is not easily dispelled and all Christians need regular reminders that we were all sinners until washed in that fountain especially opened 'for sin and for uncleanness' (Zech. 13:1).

Same-sex friendships

A preference for same-sex company has been redefined as homosexual orientation. This is a travesty and does great damage to normal and wholesome friendships. The grave menace of such a view is that any deep friendship or Christian affection between persons of the same gender becomes suspect as sexually based. Other Christian friends may form wrong conclusions about such relationships; the persons themselves may be so fearful of being misjudged that they break off their friendship, or if they continue it, be burdened with unjustified guilt.

The fact that God's children may enjoy deep personal relationships with members of their own gender without any issue of homosexuality is abundantly clear from the Scriptures. King David enjoyed a deep friendship with Jonathan. At the death of Jonathan David expressed his devastating grief:

I am distressed for you, my brother Jonathan;
You have been very pleasant to me;
Your love to me was wonderful,
Surpassing the love of women

(2 Sam. 1:26).

Where Christians are fearful of being misjudged about same-gender relationships, let them reflect upon the relationship of Jesus with Peter, James and John, who seem to have been particularly close to the Saviour (Matt. 17:1-13; 26:37-46), especially John, who is generally believed to be referring to himself as 'the disciple whom Jesus loved' (John 19:26; 20:2; 21:7,20).

The correct definition of homosexual orientation is where there is sexual attraction to persons of one's own sex. Neither Paul nor any other biblical writer speaks of a 'homosexual orientation' or of a sexual attraction for members of one's own sex.[4] Nor do they confuse the issue in any way that would make same-sex deep friendships or Christian affection suspect.

To quote Welch, 'Homosexuality can be defined as thoughts or actions, in adult life, motivated by a definite erotic (sexual-genital-orgiastic) attraction to members of the same sex, usually but not necessarily leading to sexual relations with them.'[5] For a relationship to be sinful there must be an erotic element, such as sexual desire, sexual excitement or sexual stimulation. These ingredients may just as easily be present in relationships with persons of the other gender. Christ condemns sexual fantasies as severely as sinful sexual acts (Matt. 5:28). The Word of God is to guide our relationships and our behaviour.

The teaching of Scripture

The Word of God declares homosexual acts to be sinful: 'But we know that the law is good if one uses it lawfully, knowing this: that the law is not made for a righteous person, but for the lawless and insubordinate, for the ungodly and for sinners, for the unholy and profane, for murderers of fathers and murderers of mothers, for manslayers, for fornicators, *for sodomites*, for kidnappers, for liars, for perjurers, and if there is any other thing that is contrary to sound doctrine, according to the glorious gospel of the blessed God...' (1 Tim. 1:8-11, emphasis added).

Furthermore, 'The wrath of God is revealed from heaven against all ungodliness and unrighteousness of men', with the result being that the Lord gives sinners 'up to vile passions. For even their women exchanged the natural use for what is against nature. Likewise also the men, leaving the natural use of the woman, burned in their lust for one another, men with men committing what is shameful, and receiving in themselves the penalty of their error which was due' (Rom. 1:18,26-27).

Though God condemns homosexuality, along with many other expressions of sinfulness, he nevertheless extends wonderful hope as he administers a fearful warning. After declaring in no uncertain way that homosexuality excludes a sinner from heaven, he assures all believers of a complete cleansing through the sacrifice of Christ on the cross: 'Do you not know that the unrighteous will not inherit the kingdom of God? Do not be deceived. Neither fornicators, nor idolaters, nor adulterers, *nor homosexuals, nor sodomites,* nor thieves, nor covetous, nor drunkards, nor revilers, nor extortioners will inherit the kingdom of God. And such were some of you. *But you were washed,* but *you were sanctified,* but *you were justified* in the name of the Lord Jesus and by the Spirit of our God' (1 Cor. 6:9-10, emphasis added). So while, on the one hand, God condemns homosexuality as sin, he makes it clear that it is by no means an unforgivable sin.

The media presents the view that homosexuals are born with a natural tendency of sexual attraction for the same sex over which they have no control. Some Christian leaders show sympathy with this outlook. John Stott writes, '... we have grown accustomed to distinguish between a homosexual orientation or "inversion" (for which people are not responsible) and homosexual physical practices (for which they are)... We may not blame people for what they are, though we may for what they do.'[6]

No genetic link to homosexuality has yet been established but, as Welch says, 'Even if practising homosexuals were consistently genetically distinct from heterosexuals, this would not make homosexuality a biologically based behaviour for which people bear no moral responsibility. Biology is not the sufficient, determinative cause of biblically prohibited behaviour. Our desire to practise it is.'[7]

Nature or nurture may predispose sinners to express sin in a multitude of ways. Our sinful hearts express themselves in behaviour via hundreds of factors (biology being one). To quote Welch again, 'A person whose sinful heart acts out in murder may have been influenced by unjust treatment, by parents who allowed him to vent his rage on siblings, and by Satan's incessant suggestions to kill. But none of these influences remove his personal responsibility for his intentions or actions. The ultimate cause of sin is always the sinful heart.'[8] Jay Adams comments: 'In every biblical reference, homosexuality is considered an irresponsible way of life, not an irresistible state that results from genetic factors or social conditioning.'[9]

Pastoral care

The 'counsel of the ungodly' (Ps. 1:1) is likely to be in sharp contrast to the guidance given by the Christian pastor.

This is the kind of advice given by secular counsellors: 'Exploring past history, events, thoughts, and feelings about them, can help. But most of all, making encouraging statements such as: "It is OK to be gay; many good people are homosexual; many lesbians lead their lives without a great deal of worry; for many, homosexuality is just an ordinary part of their lives." In this way, the counsellor will quite quickly detect whether there is an underlying problem to be the subject of further counselling intervention. Where there is no underlying problem, straightforward information about where to meet others (perhaps through a local Lesbian and Gay Switchboard) and where to buy the gay press is all that is needed, with the offer of further support if needed.'[10] Or again: '... in our society homosexuality has been condemned variously by the Church as sinful, by doctors as sick, by the law as criminal, and by education as unmentionable. The counsellor will therefore need to enable clients to see how this very negative image of homosexuality has induced them to have a negative image of themselves.'[11] Since the book from which these quotations are taken is edited by three members of the British Association for Counselling, it may be concluded that this represents the general attitude of that association.

God's people are warned against being cheated through worldly wisdom that is 'not according to Christ' (Col. 2:8).

The Christian pastor takes quite a different stance, though he will be careful to gain a clear understanding of the problem. Welch advises that 'Listening is a good place to start. After all, how can we bring truth to a person unless we know him? So you might begin with questions. What is it like to struggle with homosexuality? What are some of the events that shaped the present expression of homosexuality? Salient past events may need to be addressed. Was the person homosexually raped? Was he or she manipulated into sexual activity by an older person? This victimization doesn't explain homosexuality, and it doesn't mean that people are not responsible for their future thoughts and actions. But God certainly speaks with compassion to those who have been sinned against, and homosexuals must hear this. How has the person been hurt in relationships? How has it been painful to pursue a homosexual lifestyle? What is it like to be confronted suddenly with having to leave close friends, long-term partners, or a supportive community? "I ached physically from all the emotional turmoil," said a man who was leaving his partner. "But several Christian heterosexual men made themselves available any time of day or night. I'm alive today because those guys loved me."'[12] Godly male friendship enabled this man to break free from his sinful past and begin to 'walk in newness of life' (Rom. 6:4).

Where there is an openness to see human life from God's perspective through God's Word, there is real hope. When homosexuality is recognized as sin, there is hope. God has the answer to this problem. Christ died for sins and the Holy Spirit empowers us to overcome sinful practices.

Three steps to healing

Step 1: Recognition

Homosexual activity in mind or body is sinful and condemned by God:[13] 'Do you not know that the unrighteous will not inherit the kingdom of God? Do not be deceived. Neither fornicators, nor idolaters, nor adulterers, nor homosexuals, nor sodomites, nor thieves, nor covetous, nor drunkards, nor revilers, nor extortioners will inherit the kingdom of God. *And such were some of you.* But you were washed, but you were sanctified, but you were justified in the name of the Lord Jesus and by the Spirit of our God' (1 Cor. 6:9-11, emphasis added).

Step 2: Repentance

'For godly sorrow produces repentance leading to salvation, not to be regretted; but the sorrow of the world produces death' (2 Cor. 7:10).

> When I kept silent, my bones grew old
> Through my groaning all the day long.
> For day and night your hand was heavy upon me;
> My vitality was turned into the drought of summer.
> I acknowledged my sin to you,
> And my iniquity I have not hidden.
> I said, 'I will confess my transgressions to the LORD,'
> And you forgave the iniquity of my sin
>
> (Ps. 32:3-5).

Step 3: Reformation

All Christians battle with sin, and though 'those who are Christ's have crucified the flesh with its passions and desires' (Gal. 5:24), it is a daily exercise to reckon ourselves 'to be dead indeed to sin, but alive to God in Christ Jesus our Lord' (Rom. 6:11).

Therefore do not let sin reign in your mortal body, that you should obey it in its lusts (Rom. 6:12).

Therefore I run thus: not with uncertainty. Thus I fight: not as one who beats the air. But I discipline my body and bring it into subjection, lest, when I have preached to others, I myself should become disqualified (1 Cor. 9:26-27).

For the grace of God that brings salvation has appeared to all men, teaching us that, denying ungodliness and worldly lusts, we should live soberly, righteously, and godly... (Titus 2:11-12).

Therefore ... let us lay aside every weight, and the sin which so easily ensnares us, and let us run with endurance the race that is set before us, looking unto Jesus, the author and finisher of our faith, who for the joy that was set before him endured the cross, despising the shame, and has sat down at the right hand of the throne of God (Heb. 12:1-2).

An individual's life can be radically transformed by replacing an old sinful pattern of life with a new God-honouring pattern of life: '... put off, concerning your former conduct, the old man which grows corrupt according to the deceitful lusts, and be renewed in the spirit of your mind, and ... put on the new man which was created according to God, in righteousness and true holiness' (Eph. 4:22-24).

Homosexuality may be eliminated by putting off past sinful patterns and learning to live by God's patterns of life instead. Jay Adams gives the following guidelines:

1. All past associations or friendships that exist with homosexuals must be terminated...

2. The course of his/her life must be restructured so as to avoid places in which homosexual contacts frequently have been or may be made...

3. Homosexuality must be recognized as 'a life-dominating sin which permeates every phase and activity of... life'.[14]

'Total Structuring means looking at the problem in relationship to all areas of life. The problem affects all areas, and whenever all areas are in proper relationship to God, the dotted lines become solid lines and the problem dissolves. The ... diagram [on the following page] is not intended to be comprehensive, but suggestive.'[15]

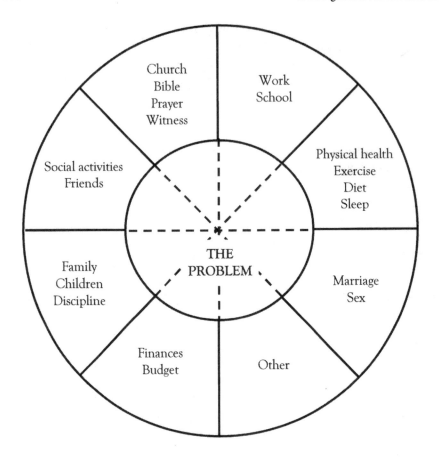

Conclusion

Law and Bowden conclude: 'That men and women will be held responsible for their aberrant sexual behaviour proves to the Christian that a normal human choice of lifestyles is involved, and they are *not* driven by any genetic factors within their metabolism over which they have no control ... there is no such thing as a homosexual, but only sinners with perverted sexual desires. Sinners are commanded to repent of such sinful desires or else they will never see the kingdom of heaven.'[16]

The church of Jesus Christ has a golden opportunity to extend hope and healing to those whose lives are gripped and controlled by sinful behaviour. Those whose sinful hearts have involved them in imagined or actual homosexual activity, who have now truly repented and come to faith in Christ, need the loving support of a community of God's people. They, like all sinners, need the passionate proclamation of the gospel of God's grace, faithful teaching about life lived in Christ and a Christian community prayerfully engaged in mutual support and encouragement. They also need the special friendship of heterosexual men who are comfortable and secure in their own sexuality and who are ready and willing to spend time with them.

Postscript

The following points are adapted from the Christian Institute Briefing Paper, *Homosexual age of consent*, published in 2004 in the light of proposed changes in legislation in the United Kingdom:[17]

Christian viewpoints

Although liberalism has made many inroads into the church, most Christian denominations throughout the world still uphold biblical teaching on homosexuality. In the UK, Roman Catholic leaders have been particularly firm.

Gay rights campaigners have urged churches to change their stance. They have succeeded within sections of the Methodist and United Reformed denominations and among some liberal bishops in the Church of England.

However, for Anglicans, the Lambeth Conference in 1998 firmly restated that homosexual practice is incompatible with the Bible. While some liberal bishops from the UK and USA opposed Lambeth Resolution 1.10, the vast majority agreed with its statement that:

- Homosexual practice is incompatible with the Bible.
- Christians can experience same-sex attraction and that the church should seek sensitively to minister to such people.
- For those not called to marriage, sexual abstinence is the right course.
- Same-sex unions are to be rejected. [18]

Risks associated with a homosexual lifestyle

A homosexual lifestyle carries great health risks. The largest and most detailed study at the time of writing, *Sexual Attitudes and Lifestyles*, showed that the proportion of men reporting large numbers of partners was much higher for homosexuals than for heterosexuals. Of those men who had had sexual partners within the previous five years, 24% of homosexuals had had ten or more partners compared with 5% of heterosexuals.[19]

In the UK 72% of all male HIV infections are through homosexual intercourse. Heterosexuals (other than those already in a high-risk category) make up only 4% of infections.[20]

Men who have ever engaged in any homosexual sex are banned for life from giving blood in the UK, even if it was 'safe sex' with a condom.[21]

The risk of HIV infection from anal intercourse is extremely high; for men it is at least 2,700 times the risk from vaginal intercourse.[22]

The condom company Durex said in October 2000, 'Anal intercourse is a high-risk activity because of the potential for infection from STDs including HIV transmission. Currently there are no specific standards for the manufacture of condoms for anal sex. Current medical advice is therefore to avoid anal sex.'[23]

Most parents want their children to grow up to get married and have children. Legitimizing homosexual acts involving teenage boys threatens that by increasing the likelihood that they will be drawn into homosexuality, denying them the opportunity of marriage and having children.

Notes

Introduction
1. J. D. MacMillan, 'Eldership Today', *Monthly Record*, February 1988, p.29.
2. J. D. MacMillan. 'Eldership Today', *Monthly Record*, March 1988, p.53.
3. *Ibid.*, p.54.
4. Frank Shuffelton, *Thomas Hooker (1586-1647)*, (Princeton, New Jersey: Princeton University Press, 1977), p.8.
5. Charles Whitworth, 'Theological Training Today', *Reformation Today*, 1978, no. 42, p.7.
6. G. Berghoef and L. De Koster, *The Elder's Handbook: a practical guide for church leaders* (Grand Rapids, Michigan: Christian's Library Press, 1979), p.23.
7. *Ibid.*

Chapter 1 — The training method
1. Richard Coekin, 'Perfecting Tomorrow's Pastors: apprenticeship schemes are a vital component in training for full-time Word ministry', *Briefing*, 8 May 1999, pp.6-9.
2. John Foskett and David Lyall, *Helping the Helpers: supervision and pastoral care* (London: SPCK, 1988), p.44.
3. *Ibid.*
4. Charles F. Boyd, 'Sharing the Preaching Load', *Leadership*, January / February 2000.
5. Steve Timmis, 'Mentoring: the perils, pitfalls, pleasure and pain', *Briefing*, 8 May 1999, pp.10-11.
6. Jay E. Adams, *More than Redemption: a theology of Christian counseling* (Grand Rapids, Michigan: Baker, 1979), p.88.
7. *Ibid.*, pp.88-9.
8. Ray Evans, 'Is this training for ministry?' *Evangelicals Now*, May 2000, p.10.
9. Walter Wright, *Relational Leadership* (London: Paternoster Press), p.44.
10. *Ibid.*, p.45.
11. Foskett and Lyall, *Helping the Helpers*, p.6.
12. *Ibid.*, p.8.
13. Thomas C. Oden, *Pastoral Theology: essentials of ministry* (London: Harper and Row, 1983), p.60.
14. Robert Alliott, 'Facilitatory mentoring in general practice', *British Medical Journal*, vol. 313, 1996, p.1 (of seven available at bmj.com).
15. Oden, *Pastoral Theology*, pp.157-8.
16. Adams, *More than Redemption*, p.90.
17. Alliott, 'Facilitatory mentoring in general practice', p.4 (of seven available).
18. *Ibid.*
19. Fred Smith, 'Mentoring that Matters: reviving an ancient teaching method that adds life to ministry', *Leadership*, Winter 1999, p.94.

20. Timmis, 'Mentoring', p.11.
21. Nancy Henry, 'Mentoring Myths and Tips', Internet.
22. Timmis, 'Mentoring', p.10.
23. *Ibid.*, p.11

Chapter 2 — Pastoral oversight

1. J. Oswald Sanders, *Spiritual Leadership* (Basingstoke, Marshall Morgan and Scott, 1967), p.39.
2. R. C. H. Lenski. *The Interpretation of the Acts of the Apostles* (Minneapolis, Minnesota: Augsburg Publishing House, 1934), p.847.
3. John Shakespeare, *Pastors, Elders and Bishops: a study in N.T. church order* (Walsall: Midland Road Strict and Particular Baptist Church, 1983), p.6.
4. Neil Summerton, *A Noble Task: eldership and ministry in the local church* (Carlisle: Paternoster Press, 1987), pp.127-8.

Chapter 3 — Team spirit

1. Charles D. Alexander, *The Great Eldership Fallacy* (Liverpool: Bible Exposition Fellowship, no date), p.1.
2. William Arnot, *Studies in Acts: the church in the house* (Grand Rapids, Michigan: Kregel Publications,1978), pp.379-80.
3. Alexander, *The Great Eldership Fallacy*, p.4.
4. Shakespeare, *Pastors, Elders and Bishops*, pp.8-9.
5. Malcolm Watts, 'The Gospel Ministry', *Evangelical Times*, November 1993, p.15.
6. Erroll Hulse, 'The Eldership and Protocol', R. O. Beardmore (ed.), *Shepherding God's Flock: essays on leadership in the local church* (Harrisonburg, Virginia: Sprinkle, 1988), p.39.
7. Clifford C. Pond, *Only Servants: a view of the place, responsibilities and ministries of elders in local churches* (London: Grace Publications Trust, 1991), p.52.
8. MacMillan, 'Eldership Today', March 1988, p.54.
9. Pond, *Only Servants*, p.60.
10. Shakespeare, *Pastors, Elders and Bishops*, p.9.
11. John Zens. ' "Paul Summoned the Elders of the Assembly": problems with the "pastor" separate doctrine,' *Searching Together*, no date, p.3 (emphasis his).
12. J. D. MacMillan, 'Eldership Today', *Monthly Record*, April 1988, p.79.
13. Hulse, 'The Eldership and Protocol', p.43.
14. Summerton, *A Noble Task*, p.83.
15. MacMillan, 'Eldership Today,' *Monthly Record*, March 1988, p.54.
16. Summerton, *A Noble Task*, pp.85-6.
17. Pond, *Only Servants*, pp.92-8.
18. Adapted from Philip D. Jensen and Tony Payne, *Fellow Workers: Discussion Papers for the church committee* (London: St Matthias Press, 1989, pp.17-20.
19. Summerton, *A Noble Task*, pp.87-8.

Chapter 4 — Pastoral leadership

1. Rick Warren, *The Purpose Driven Church: growth without compromising your message and mission* (Grand Rapids, Michigan: Zondervan, 1995), p.48.
2. Philip D. Jensen and Tony Payne, *Fellow Workers: Discussion Papers for the church committee* (London: St Matthias Press, 1989), p.51.
3. *Ibid.*, p.52.
4. Warren, *The Purpose Driven Church*, p.80.

5. *Ibid.*, p.218.

6. Peter Drucker, cited by Warren, *ibid.*, p.90.

7. Berghoef and De Koster, *The Elder's Handbook*, pp.70-72.

8. J. Angell James, 'Democracy Comes to Church,' *Sword and Trowel*, July / August 1982, p.30.

9. *Ibid.*

10. James A. Spurgeon. 'The System of Church Government at the Metropolitan Tabernacle', *Sword and Trowel*, July / August 1982, p.31.

11. Warren, *The Purpose Driven Church*, p.105.

12. Peter Masters, 'Church Membership in the New Testament', a supplement to *Sword and Trowel*, March 1981, p.4.

13. Wayne A. Mack and David Swavely, *Life in the Father's House: a member's guide to the local church* (Phillipsburg, New Jersey: Presbyterian and Reformed, 1996), p.20.

14. *Ibid.*, p.21.

15. Erroll Hulse, *Baptism and Church Membership* (Leeds: Carey Publications, 1972), p.15.

16. Mack and Swavely, *Life in the Father's House*, p.27.

17. Peter Masters, 'Church Membership in the New Testament', p.2.

18. *Ibid.*, p.3.

19. Grace Baptist Assembly, *We Believe: The Baptist affirmation of faith 1966 and a Guide for Church fellowship* (London: Grace Baptist Assembly, 1983), p.61.

20. John Eadie, *Commentary on the Epistle of Paul to the Galatians* (Minneapolis, Minnesota: James and Klock, 1977), p.434.

Chapter 5 — Pastoral visiting

1. Thomas C. Oden, *Pastoral Counsel* (New York: Crossroad, 1989), p.169.

2. *Ibid.*, p.171.

3. Jay E. Adams, *Shepherding God's Flock: a preacher's handbook on pastoral ministry, counseling, and leadership* (Phillipsburg, New Jersey: Presbyterian and Reformed, 1980), p.76.

4. John Calvin, *The Acts of the Apostles, 14-28* (Edinburgh: Saint Andrew Press, 1966), p.175.

5. Adams, *Shepherding God's Flock*, p.76.

6. Richard Baxter, *The Reformed Pastor* (Edinburgh: Banner of Truth Trust, 1974 [first published 1656]), pp.122-3.

7. William G. T. Shedd, *Homiletics and Pastoral Theology* (London: Banner of Truth Trust, 1965 [first published 1867]), p.347.

8. Oden, *Pastoral Counsel*, p.171.

9. Baxter, *The Reformed Pastor*, p.112.

10. Shedd, *Homiletics and Pastoral Theology*, p.349.

11. *Ibid.*, p.347.

12. Baxter, *The Reformed Pastor*, p.119.

13. Adams, *Shepherding God's Flock*, p.89.

14. Baxter, *The Reformed Pastor*, p.121.

Chapter 6 — Leadership qualifications

1. A. Billings, 'Pastors or Counsellors?' *Contact*, 1992, no. 108 (2) p.4.

2. J. Oswald Sanders, *Spiritual Leadership* (Basingstoke, Marshall Morgan and Scott, 1967), p.10.

3. R. C. H. Lenski, *The Interpretation of St Paul's Epistles to the Colossians, to the Thessalonians, to Timothy, to Titus and to Philemon* (Minneapolis, Minnesota: Augsburg Publishing House, 1964 [first published 1937]), pp.580-81.

4. Summerton, *A Noble Task* (Carlisle: Paternoster Press, 1987), p.24.

5. Pond, *Only Servants*, p.69.

6. J. K. Davies, 'A Man whose Children "Believe"?' *Reformation Today*, no. 63, 1981, p.31.

7. John MacArthur Jr., *Rediscovering Pastoral Ministry: shaping contemporary ministry with biblical mandates* (London: Word, 1995), pp.92-4.

8. Pond, *Only Servants*, p.72.

9. Jay E. Adams, 'The Pastor and his Family,' *Reformation Today*, no. 81, 1984, p.29.

10. Summerton, *A Noble Task*, p.25.

11. Berghoef and De Koster, *The Elder's Handbook*, p.25.

12. Peter Masters, *Sword and Trowel*, 1985, no. 2, p.24.

13. Charles Whitworth. 'Elders', *Reformation Today*, no. 72, 1983, p.14.

14. Sanders, *Spiritual Leadership*, pp.55, 56, 45.

Chapter 7 — The leader's personal life

1. Cited by C. H. Spurgeon, *Lectures to my Students*, First Series (London: Passmore and Alabaster, 1883), p.2.

2. *Ibid.*, p.1.

3. Samuel Chadwick, *The Path of Prayer* (London: Hodder and Stoughton, 1931), p.16.

4. Sanders, *Spiritual Leadership*, p.78.

5. D. Martyn Lloyd-Jones, *Preaching and Preachers* (London: Hodder and Stoughton, 1971), p.172.

6. Charles Bridges, *The Christian Ministry: with an inquiry into the causes of its inefficiency* (London: Banner of Truth Trust, 1967 [first published 1830]), p.51.

7. Berghoef and De Koster, *The Elder's Handbook*, p.68.

8. Shedd, *Homiletics and Pastoral Theology*, pp.344-5.

9. Pond, *Only Servants*, p.85.

10. Summerton, *A Noble Task*, p.27.

11. Andrew Cornes, *Divorce and Remarriage: biblical principles and pastoral practice* (London: Hodder and Stoughton, 1993), p.74.

12. R. Whitfield. 'The Prevention of Marital Distress', W. Dryden, (ed.), *Marital Therapy in Britain*, vol. 2, 'Special Areas' (Milton Keynes: Open University Press, 1985), p.144.

13. Jack Dominian, *Passionate and Compassionate Love: a vision for Christian marriage* (London: Darton, Longman & Todd, 1991), p.51.

14. C. Clulow and J. Mattinson, *Marriage Inside Out: understanding problems of intimacy* (London: Penguin Books, 1989), p.23.

15. R. Beech, *Staying Together: a practical way to make your relationship succeed and grow* (Chichester: John Wiley & Sons, 1985), p.64.

16. Adams, *Shepherding God's Flock*, p.51.

17. R. Smith, 'Making Decisions about Gospel Work', *Briefing*, no. 186, p.11.

Chapter 8 — Preaching and teaching

1. Spurgeon, *Lectures to my Students*, First series, p.53.

2. James I. Packer, 'Why Preach?', S. T. Logan (ed.), *Preaching: the preacher and preaching in the Twentieth Century* (Welwyn: Evangelical Press, 1986), p.3.

3. Jay E. Adams, *Preaching with Purpose* (Phillipsburg, New Jersey: Presbyterian and Reformed, 1982), p.43.

4. J. M. Boice, 'The Preacher and Scholarship', Logan, ed., *Preaching*, pp.91-2.

5. Andrew W. Blackwood, *Expository Preaching for Today* (New York: Abingdon Press, 1953), pp.34-5.

6. A. L. Halvorson, *Authentic Preaching: the creative encounter between the person of the preacher, the biblical text, and contemporary life and literature in gospel proclamation* (Minneapolis: Augsburg Publishing House, 1982), p.48.

7. *Ibid.*, p.49.

8. Robert L. Dabney, *Discussions: Evangelical and Theological*, vol. 1 (Edinburgh: Banner of Truth Trust, 1967 [first published 1890]), p.596.

9. Bridges, *The Christian Ministry*, p.343.

10. Peter Lewis, *The Genius of Puritanism* (Haywards Heath: Carey, 1975), p.20.

11. William E. Sangster, *The Craft of the Sermon* (London: Epworth Press, 1954), p.8.

12. H. Mackenzie, *Preaching the Eternities* (Edinburgh: Saint Andrew Press, 1963), p.93.

13. Warren, *The Purpose Driven Church*, p.226.

14. William E. Sangster, *Power in Preaching* (London: Epworth Press, 1958), p.57.

15. Halvorson, *Authentic Preaching*, p.74.

16. Peter Adam, *Speaking God's Words: a practical theology of preaching* (Leicester: IVP, 1996, p.20).

17. Packer, 'Why Preach?', p.26.

18. Oden. *Pastoral Theology*, p.129.

19. Adapted from Carol A. Stinton, *Professional Achievements through Communication Expertise* (P.A.C.E. Consultants Handouts, no date, no page numbers).

20. Charles H. Spurgeon, *Lectures to my Students*, Second series (London: Passmore and Alabaster, 1882), pp.96-136.

21. D. Martyn Lloyd-Jones, *Preaching and Preachers* (London: Hodder and Stoughton, 1971), pp.118-19.

22. Stinton, *Professional Achievements through Communication Expertise*.

23. Lloyd-Jones, *Preaching and Preachers*, p.120.

24. Halvorson, *Authentic Preaching*, pp.13, 21.

25. James H. Thornwell, *The Collected Writings of James Henley Thornwell*, vol. 4, 'Ecclesiastical' (Edinburgh: Banner of Truth Trust, 1974 [first published 1875]), p.569.

Chapter 9 — Pastoral counselling

1. Lewis Carroll, *Through the Looking-Glass*, quoted in *The Oxford Library of Words and Phrases*, vol. 1, 'Quotations', p.64, no. 8.

2. Tony Bolger, 'Research and Evaluation in Counselling', Windy Dryden et al. (eds.), *Handbook of Counselling in Britain* (London: Routledge, 1989), p.385.

3. Richard Nelson-Jones, 'Eclecticism, Integration and Comprehensiveness in Counselling Therapy and Practice', *British Journal of Guidance and Counselling*, 1985, no. 13 (2), p.129.

4. Jay E. Adams, *The Christian Counselor's Manual* (Phillipsburg, New Jersey: Presbyterian and Reformed, 1973), p.33.

5. Carl R. Rogers, *On Becoming a Person: a therapist's view of psychotherapy* (London: Constable, 1967), pp.282-4.

6. Thomas C. Oden, *Kerygma and Counseling: toward a covenant ontology for secular psychotherapy* (Philadelphia: Westminster, 1966), pp.83ff.

7. Rogers, *On Becoming a Person*, p.26.

8. David Mearns and Brian Thorne, *Person-Centred Counselling in Action* (London: Sage, 1988), p.13.

9. Albert Ellis and R. A. Harper, *A New Guide to Rational Living* (California: Wilshire Book Co., 1975); R. Di Giuseppe, 'Thinking what to feel', Windy Dryden and P. Trower (eds.), *Developments in Rational-Emotive Therapy* (Milton Keynes: Open University Press, 1988), pp.22-9.

10. Albert Ellis, *Reason and Emotion in Psychotherapy* (New York: Lyle Stuart, 1962), p.133.

11. R. R. Carkhuff, *Helping and Human Relations: a primer for lay and professional helpers*, vol. 1, 'Selection and training' (New York: Holt, Rinehart and Winston, 1969), p.35.

12. Martin and Deidre Bobgans, *How to Counsel from Scripture* (Chicago: Moody Press, 1985), p.22.

13. Lawrence J. Crabb, *Effective Biblical Counselling: how to become a capable counsellor* (Basingstoke: Marshall Morgan Scott, 1977), p.29.

14. Adams, *The Christian Counselor's Manual*, p.24, note 12.

15. Bobgans, *How to Counsel from Scripture*, p.46.

16. David Atkinson. 'Covenant and Counselling: some counselling implications of a covenant theology', *Anvil*, 1984, no. 1 (2), p.132.

17. Bobgans, *How to Counsel from Scripture*, p.xv.

18. A. E. Munro, *Counselling: a skills approach* (London: Methuen, 1979), p.32.

19. Richard Nelson-Jones, *Practical Counselling Skills* (New York: Holt, Rinehart and Winston, 1983), p.19.

20. Gerard Egan, *The Skilled Helper: a systematic approach to effective helping* (Pacific Grove, California: Brooks/Cole, 1986), p.79.

21. Lawrence J. Crabb, *Understanding People: deep longings for relationship* (Basingstoke, Hants: Marshall Morgan and Scott, 1987), p.21.

22. Thomas C. Oden, *Care of Souls in the Classic Tradition* (Philadelphia: Fortress Press, 1984), p.12.

23. Oden, *Pastoral Theology*, pp.11-12.

24. Oden, *Care of Souls*, p.12.

25. Adapted from Jay E. Adams, *The Christian Counselor's Casebook* (Phillipsburg, New Jersey: P & R, 1974), case no.24, pp.48-9.

26. Adapted from *ibid.*, case no.28, pp.178-9.

27. Adapted from *ibid.*, case no.11, pp.22-3.

28. David Atkinson, *Pastoral Ethics in Practice* (Eastbourne: Monarch, 1989), p.25.

Chapter 10 – Local church evangelism

1. John R. W. Stott, *Christian Mission in the Modern World: what the church should be doing now!* (Downers Grove, Illinois: IVP, 1975), p.39.

2. J. I. Packer, *Evangelism and the Sovereignty of God* (Leicester: IVP, 1961), p.41.

3. Stott, *Christian Mission in the Modern World*, pp.37-8.

4. Stuart Olyott, 'What is Evangelism?', *Banner of Truth* magazine, July-August 1969.

5. James Henley Thornwell, 'The Sacrifice of Christ the Type and Model of Missionary Effort', *The Collected Writings of James Henley Thornwell*, vol. 2: 'Theological and Ethical' (Edinburgh: Banner of Truth Trust, 1974 [first published 1875]), p.442-3.

6. Based on ideas in Michael Green, *Evangelism through the Local Church* (London: Hodder and Stoughton, 1990), pp.11-16.

7. Roy Joslin, *Urban Harvest* (Darlington: Evangelical Press, 1982), p.29.

8. See R. B. Kuiper, *God-Centred Evangelism: a presentation of the Scriptural theology of evangelism* (Edinburgh: Banner of Truth Trust, 1961), pp.85-94.

9. Thornwell, 'The Sacrifice of Christ ...', p.434.

10. Warren, *The Purpose Driven Church*, p.200.

11. Steve Timmis and Tim Chester, 'The Principles of Gospel Ministry', *The Briefing*, vols. 234-47, 2000-2001.

12. Tom Wells, *A Vision for Missions* (Edinburgh: Banner of Truth Trust, 1985), p.116.

13. Thornwell, 'The Sacrifice of Christ ...', p.446.

14. Wells, *A Vision for Missions*, p.15.

15. Robert Dabney, 'The World White to Harvest: reap, or it perishes', *Discussions: Evangelical and Theological*, vol. 1, p.579.

Chapter 11 — Missionary endeavour

1. Robert Haldane, *An Exposition of the Epistle to the Romans* (McLean, Virginia: MacDonald Publishing Co., 1958), p.444.
2. Don Fortner, 'Why should we Support Missionaries?', *The Church of God* (Darlington: Evangelical Press, 1991), p.152.
3. Malcolm H. Watts, 'Missionary work and the local church', *Evangelical Times*, October 1991, p.12.
4. Bill James, 'A Missionary Policy', *Reformation Today*, no.163, May/June 1998, p.24.
5. Watts, 'Missionary work and the local church', p.12.
6. Donald Macleod, 'God's vision for the church', *Foundations*, no. 47, Autumn 2001, p.4.
7. Peter Milsom, 'The Local Church and World Mission', *Foundations*, no. 44, Spring 2000, p.32.
8. Five sub-headings based on the suggestions of Peter Milsom, *ibid.*, pp.32-3.
9. Ray Porter, 'Preaching Mission in the Regular Life of the Church', *Foundations*, no. 44, Spring 2000, p.7.
10. Peter Back, *Workers for the Harvest: raising in our churches future evangelists and missionaries*, Church and Mission Monographs (Stoke on Trent: Tentmaker Publications, 2000), p.5.
11. James, 'A Missionary Policy', p.26.
12. Ian Tait, 'The Local Church and Missionary work', *Local Church Practice* (Leeds: Carey Publications, 1978), pp.146-7.
13. Milsom, 'The Local Church and World Mission', p.34.
14. (Anon.) 'Teaching English — a doorway to mission', *Evangelicals Now*, February 2001, p.12.
15. Milsom, 'The Local Church and World Mission', p.31.
16. Tait, 'The Local Church and Missionary work', p.143.
17. James, 'A Missionary Policy', p.23.
18. Macleod, 'God's vision for the church,' p.5.
19. Porter, 'Preaching Mission in the Regular Life of the Church', p.7.
20. Tait, 'The Local Church and Missionary work', p.147.
21. James, 'A Missionary Policy', p.23.
22. Peter Barnes, *Knowing Where We Stand: the message of John's epistles* (Darlington: Evangelical Press, 1998), pp.145-8.

Chapter 12 — Church-planting

1. Alex. R. Hay, *New Testament Order for Church and Missionary* (Wirral, Cheshire: New Testament Missionary Union, 1947), p.226.
2. The use of the term 'Pastoral Epistles' dates from 1753. See R. C. H. Lenski, *The Interpretation of St Paul's Epistles to the Colossians, to the Thessalonians, to Timothy, to Titus and to Philemon* (Minneapolis, Minnesota, Augsburg Publishing House, 1964), p.481.
3. Hay, *New Testament Order*, p.227.
4. Lenski, *The Interpretation of St Paul's Epistles...*, p.481.
5. John Bannerman, *The Church of Christ* (Edinburgh: Banner of Truth Trust, 1960 [first published 1869], pp.235-6.
6. Shakespeare, *Pastors, Elders and Bishops*, p.4.
7. Shakespeare, *Studies in New Testament Evangelism*, p.17.
8. *Ibid.*, p.11.

9. For analysis see Shakespeare, *Studies in New Testament Evangelism*, pp.17-20; Joslin, *Urban Harvest*, pp.156-62.

10. Jim Petersen, *Evangelism as a lifestyle: reaching into your world with the gospel* (New Malden, Surrey: NavPress, 1985), p.50.

11. Shakespeare. *Studies in New Testament Evangelism*, p.17.

12. Susanne Heine, *Women and Early Christianity: are the feminist scholars right?* (London: SCM, 1987), p.86.

13. Elizabeth Catherwood, 'Women in the Home', Shirley Lees (ed.), *The Role of Women* (Leicester: InterVarsity Press, 1984), p.29.

14. *Ibid.*

Chapter 13 — Elders and deacons

1. R. P. Kuiper, 'The office of the deacon', *The Glorious Body of Christ* (Edinburgh: Banner of Truth Trust, 1967), p.155.

2. *Ibid.*

3. H. Carson, 'The role of the deacon', *Reformation Today*, no. 50, 1980, p.2.

4. Kuiper, 'The office of the deacon', p.154.

5. J. Murray, 'Office in the Church', *Collected Writings of John Murray*, vol. 2, 'Systematic Theology', (Edinburgh: Banner of Truth Trust, 1977), p.364.

6. Kuiper, 'The office of the deacon', p.156.

7. Carson, 'The role of the deacon', p.4.

8. Fortner, *The Church of God*, p.75.

9. *Ibid.*, p.76.

10. J. K. Davies, 'Reformation for elders and deacons', *Reformation Today*, p.3.

11. J. Benton, *Grace Magazine*, no. 60, 1981, pp.8-9.

12. *Ibid.*, p.9.

13. Lenski, *The Interpretation of St Paul's Epistles ...*, p.592.

14. A. Morrison,. 'Rulership and service: a biblical understanding of Christian ministry for men and women', *Diakrisis*, Spring/Summer 1998, issue 5, p.72.

15. *Ibid.*

16. C. Hamer, *Being a Christian Husband: a biblical perspective* (Darlington: Evangelical Press, 2005), p.72.

17. D. Prime, *A Christian's Guide to Leadership – for the whole church* (Darlington: Evangelical Press, 2005), pp. 41-2.

18. Adams, 'The Pastor and his Family', p.29.

19. Davies, 'Reformation for elders and deacons', p.5

20. Carson, 'The role of the deacon', p.6.

21. H. Carson, 'Deaconesses,' *Reformation Today*, no. 51, 1980, p.20.

22. P. Fairbairn, *Pastoral Epistles* (Minneapolis, Minnesota: Klock and Klock, reprint 1980), pp.150-51.

23. Morrison, 'Rulership and service', p.74.

24. A. Sargent, 'Elders and Deacons', unpublished paper, 2002, pp.6-7.

Appendix I — Counselling and depression

1. D. Martyn Lloyd-Jones, *Spiritual Depression: its causes and cure* (London: Pickering and Inglis, 1965), p.11.

2. Herbert Carson, *Depression in the Christian family* (Darlington: Evangelical Press, 1994), pp.59-60.

3. Robert Buckman, *What you really need to know about depression*, Videos for Patients, no. CNS02 (London: Royal Pharmaceutical Society, 1993).

4. *Ibid.*, p.117.

5. Jim Winter, *Depression: a rescue plan* (Epsom, Surrey: Day One Publications, 2000), p.66.

6. Edward T. Welch, *Blame it on the Brain? Distinguishing chemical imbalances, brain disorders and disobedience* (Phillipsburg, New Jersey: Presbyterian and Reformed, 1998), p.127.

7. Robert J. K. Law and Malcolm Bowden, *Breakdowns are good for you! A unique manual for true Biblical counselling* (Bromley, Kent: Sovereign, 1999), p.58.

8. Jay E. Adams, *Competent to Counsel* (Phillipsburg, New Jersey: Presbyterian and Reformed, 1974), p.119.

9. Lloyd-Jones, *Spiritual Depression*, pp.13-14.

10. See Richard Gilpin, *Daemonologia Sacra; or A Treatise of Satan's Temptations* (Edinburgh: James Nichol, 1867).

11. Carson, *Depression in the Christian family*, p.88.

12. Welch, *Blame it on the Brain?* p.121.

13. William Bridge, *A lifting up for the downcast* (Edinburgh: Banner of Truth, 1961 [first published 1649]); Lloyd-Jones, *Spiritual Depression*. See also Richard Sibbes, 'The soul's conflict with itself', *Complete Works*, vol. 1 (Edinburgh: James Nichol, 1862), pp.130-294.

14. Lloyd-Jones, *Spiritual Depression*, p.20.

15. John White, *The Masks of Melancholy* (Leicester: Inter-Varsity Press, 1982), p.185.

16. Law and Bowden, *Breakdowns are good for you!*, p.46.

17. Dorothy Rowe, *The Depression handbook: the way of understanding depression which leads to wisdom and freedom* (London: Collins, 1991), p.109.

18. Welch, *Blame it on the Brain?*, p.117.

19. Law and Bowden, *Breakdowns are good for you!*, p.117.

20. *Ibid.*, p.60.

21. *Ibid.*, p.120.

22. *Ibid.*, pp.74-84.

23. *Ibid.*, p.58.

24. Winter, *Depression*, p.24.

25. White, *The Masks of Melancholy*, p.18.

26. Adams, *The Christian Counselor's Manual*, p.375.

27. *Ibid.*, p.377.

28. *Ibid.*, p.378.

29. Winter, *Depression*, p.115.

30. Welch, *Blame it on the Brain?*, pp.115-16.

31. Carson, *Depression in the Christian family*, p.7.

32. Peter Lewis, 'Luther, librium and laughter', *Evangelical Times*, November 1980, p.9.

33. *Ibid.*, p.9.

34. Richard Baxter, 'The right method for a settled peace of conscience and spiritual comfort', *Practical Works*, vol. 9 (London: James Duncan, 1830), p.22.

35. *Ibid.*, pp.22-5.

36. Dorothy Rowe, cited by Law and Bowden, *Breakdowns are good for you!*, p.60.

Appendix II — Counselling and abuse

1. Claire Burke Draucker, *Counselling Survivors of Childhood Sexual Abuse* (London: Sage, 1992), p.1.

2. Jane Chevous, *From Silence to Sanctuary: a guide to understanding, preventing and responding to abuse* (London: SPCK, 2004), p.14.

3. *Ibid.*, p.100.

4. *Ibid.*, p.114.

5. Carson, *Depression in the Christian family*, p.123.

6. Adams, *The Christian Counselor's Manual*, p.398.

7. Adams, *Competent to Counsel*, p.205.

8. Chevous, *From Silence to Sanctuary*, p.139.

9. *Ibid.*, p.122.

10. Annie Imbens and Ineke Jonker, *Christianity and Incest* (Tunbridge Wells: Burns and Oates, 1992), p.5.

11. H. C. Leupold, *Exposition of Genesis*, vol. 1 (Grand Rapids, Michigan: Baker, 1942), pp.559-60.

12. John Calvin, *A Commentary on Genesis* (London: Banner of Truth Trust, 1965), pp.499-500.

13. John Murray, *Principles of conduct: aspects of biblical ethics* (London: Tyndale Press, 1957), p.47.

14. *Matthew Henry's Commentary on the Whole Bible*, New Modern Edition (Electronic Database. Copyright © 1991 by Hendrickson Publishers, Inc.).

15. Imbens and Jonker, *Christianity and Incest*, p.viii.

16. *Ibid.*, p.5.

17. Chevous, *From Silence to Sanctuary*, p.17.

18. Draucker, *Counselling Survivors of Childhood Sexual Abuse*, p.1.

19. *Ibid.*, p.2.

20. Chevous, *From Silence to Sanctuary*, p.12.

21. Cited by Draucker, *Counselling Survivors of Childhood Sexual Abuse*, p.42.

22. *Ibid.*, p.100.

23. Chevous, *From Silence to Sanctuary*, p.36.

24. Cited by Carolyn Ainscough and Kay Toon, *Breaking Free: help for survivors of child sexual abuse* (London: SPCK, 1993), p.12.

25. Draucker, *Counselling Survivors of Childhood Sexual Abuse*, pp.42-3.

26. Ainscough and Toon, *Breaking Free*, p.32.

27. Kim Etherington. *Narrative Approaches to Working with Adult Male Survivors of Child Sexual Abuse: the clients', the counsellor's and the researcher's story* (London: Jessica Kingsley Publishers, 2000), p.230.

28. Imbens and Jonker, *Christianity and Incest*, p.25.

29. Chevous, *From Silence to Sanctuary*, p.85.

30. *Ibid.*, p.79.

31. Draucker, *Counselling Survivors of Childhood Sexual Abuse*, p.109.

32. Ainscough and Toon, *Breaking Free*, p.29.

33. *Ibid.*, p.7.

34. Cited by Etherington, *Narrative Approaches to Working with Adult Male Survivors of Child Sexual Abuse*, p.79.

35. Ainscough and Toon, *Breaking Free*, p.7.

36. Chevous, *From Silence to Sanctuary*, p.22.

37. Gaius Davies, *Genius and grace: sketches from a psychiatrist's notebook* (London: Hodder and Stoughton, 1992), p.196.

Appendix III — Counselling and homosexuality

1. Law and Bowden, *Breakdowns are good for you!*, p.153.

2. John Piper and Wayne Grudem (eds.), *Recovering Biblical Manhood and Womanhood: a response to Evangelical Feminism* (Wheaton, Illinois: Crossway, 1991), p.82.

3. Dorothy Patterson, 'The high calling of wife and mother in Biblical perspective', Piper and Grudem (eds.), *Recovering Biblical Manhood and Womanhood*, p.376.

4. David J. Atkinson and David H. Field, *New Dictionary of Christian Ethics and Pastoral Theology* (Nottingham: IVP, 1995), p.451.

5. Welch, *Blame it on the Brain?*, p.151.

6. John Stott, *Issues Facing Christians Today: a moral appraisal of contemporary social and moral questions* (Basingstoke: Marshall Morgan and Scott, 1984) p.303.

7. Welch, *Blame it on the Brain?*, p.171.

8. *Ibid.*, p.169.

9. Adams, *The Christian Counselor's Manual*, p.407.

10. John Sketchley, 'Counselling and sexual orientation', W. Dryden *et al.* (eds.), *Handbook of Counselling in Britain*, p.239.

11. *Ibid.*, p.241.

12. Welch, *Blame it on the Brain?*, p.174.

13. For continuing study see: Robert A. J. Gagnon, Associate Professor of New Testament, Pittsburgh Theological Seminary, www.robgagnon.net (accessed on 7 November 2007).

14. Adams, *The Christian Counselor's Manual*, p.408.

15. *Ibid.*, p.410.

16. Law and Bowden, *Breakdowns are good for you!*, p.153.

17. The Christian Institute Briefing Paper, *Homosexual age of consent*, as at 28 August 2004.

18. www.anglicancommunion.org/acns/lambeth/lc093.html as at 1 March 2001.

19. A. M. Johnson, K. Wellings, *et al.*, *Sexual Attitudes and Lifestyles*, Blackwell, 1994, p.213. Calculations are based on eliminating those who have had no partners in the last five years.

20. Public Health Laboratories, Communicable Disease Report, 2 July 1997, vol. 7, no.30, p.272, table 2. The 4% figure given in the text assumes that all 'unknown' categories are heterosexual.

21. *Do not give blood without reading this leaflet*, The UK Blood Transfusion Services, Department of Health, December 1995.

22. G. Stewart, *Health Care Analysis*, 1994, 2, pp.279-86.

23. http://www.durex.com/scientific/faqs/faq_4.ntml, as at 26 April 2001.

Index

A wide range of Christian books is available from Evangelical Press. If you would like a free catalogue please write to us or contact us by e-mail. Alternatively, you can view the whole catalogue online at our website:

www.evangelicalpress.org.

Evangelical Press
Faverdale North, Darlington, Co. Durham, DL3 0PH, England

e-mail: sales@evangelicalpress.org

Evangelical Press USA
P. O. Box 825, Webster, New York 14580, USA

e-mail: usa.sales@evangelicalpress.org